D1234015

RIVERS AND STREAMS

THE LIVING EARTH

RIVERS AND STREAMS

EDITED BY JOHN P. RAFFERTY, ASSOCIATE EDITOR, EARTH AND LIFE SCIENCES

Britannica
Educational Publishing

IN ASSOCIATION WITH

ROSEN
EDUCATIONAL SERVICES

Published in 2011 by Britannica Educational Publishing
(a trademark of Encyclopædia Britannica, Inc.)
in association with Rosen Educational Services, LLC
29 East 21st Street, New York, NY 10010.

Distributed exclusively by Rosen Educational Services.
For a listing of additional Britannica Educational Publishing titles, call toll free (800) 237-9932.

First Edition

Britannica Educational Publishing
Michael I. Levy: Executive Editor
J.E. Luebering: Senior Manager
Marilyn L. Barton: Senior Coordinator, Production Control
Steven Bosco: Director, Editorial Technologies
Lisa S. Braucher: Senior Producer and Data Editor
Yvette Charboneau: Senior Copy Editor
Kathy Nakamura: Manager, Media Acquisition
John P. Rafferty: Associate Editor, Earth Sciences

Rosen Educational Services
Heather M. Moore Niver: Editor
Nelson Sá: Art Director
Cindy Reiman: Photography Manager
Matthew Cauli: Designer, Cover Design
Introduction by Greg Roza

Library of Congress Cataloging-in-Publication Data

Rivers and streams / edited by John P. Rafferty.
    p. cm. — (Living earth)
"In association with Britannica Educational Publishing, Rosen Educational Services."
Includes bibliographical references and index.
ISBN 978-1-61530-326-7 (library binding)
1. Rivers. 2. Stream ecology. I. Rafferty, John P.
GB1203.7.R58 2011
551.48'3—dc22

2010025157

Manufactured in the United States of America

On the cover: Rivers, streams, and even waterfalls such as Brooks Falls in Alaska's Katmai
National Park play a major role in commerce, culture, habitat, and diet. *Shutterstock.com*

On page x: The longest river on Earth, the Nile, is formed from three main streams: the
Blue Nile, the Atbara, and the White Nile. *AFP/Getty Images*

On pages v, 1, 34, 66, 89, 111, 139, 172, 201, 242 262, 263, 264, 268, 270, 278: Iguaçu Falls
on the Iguaçu River at the Argentina-Brazil border. © *R. Manley/Superstock*

CONTENTS

INTRODUCTION

Rivers have long played an important role in the cultures and economies of the world's greatest civilizations—from the Mesopotamian societies that took root between the Tigris and Euphrates rivers, to the dramatic rise of New York City at the mouth of the Hudson River. Pioneers searching for viable land on which to settle have typically chosen areas close to major rivers. Rivers offer a convenient source of food, fresh water for agriculture, and a means of transportation. For well-established settlements, rivers are vital for the development of economic and industrial endeavours. This thorough overview of rivers and streams will remove any doubt in the mind of the reader why so many of the world's largest cities are strategically situated on the banks of major rivers.

Yet, the same civilizations that depend on rivers also risk harming them. Modern societies have altered the way rivers flow using dams to create hydroelectric power and canals to aid transportation and agriculture. Others have created fisheries and factories to aid their economies. These developments benefit the local economies, but they also damage natural habitats and the wildlife that depend on the environmental services of rivers for their survival. Scientists have spent many years studying rivers to help reduce the risks posed by human activity.

Several criteria are used to compare the world's greatest rivers, including the length of the main stem, the size of the drainage area, and the mean discharge of the river's flow. However, it is difficult to say exactly which river is the "greatest." For example, most people know that the Nile River in Africa is the longest river in the world, but many don't realize that the Amazon River in Brazil has the greatest drainage area and accounts for one-fifth of all the ocean runoff from world rivers.

Many factors affect the distribution and flow of Earth's rivers, including terrain, climate, precipitation, glacier melt, water tables, and drainage basins. The manner in which these factors shape a river's seasonal cycle defines the river's regime. For example, a river may be slow and shallow during the winter, but swift and deep during spring snowmelt.

The drainage patterns of rivers vary greatly based on the geological makeup of the land. The shape and direction of a river depends on the type of land over which it flows. River formation occurs fastest on weak rocks. Tributaries form along faults. Streams that form fastest often become the main rivers in a network. Movement in Earth's crust can create raises or folds that change a river's course.

American hydraulic engineer Robert E. Horton developed the concept of stream order to better analyze and understand river networks. A river that forms the source of other rivers is known as a first-order river. When two first-order rivers join, the result is a second-order river. Two second-order rivers come together to form a third-order river, and so on. This concept forms the basis for the morphometry—or measurement—of drainage systems. Morphometry is, in turn, used to study the evolution and the hydraulic geometry of drainage systems.

Hydraulic geometry is the study of variations in river channel characteristics, which include water-surface width, depth, velocity, sediment load, downstream slope, and channel friction. Data regarding these characteristics are collected and analyzed in relation to the river discharge, or the volume rate of water flow at any given location. River channels patterns are sorted into several categories. The most common types include straight, meandering, and braided channels.

A sudden change in elevation of a river channel, which causes the water flow to drop vertically, or nearly so, generates waterfalls. Waterfalls that are less steep are called cascades. The taller a waterfall is and the swifter its current, the stronger its erosive power. In many cases the site of the waterfall moves gradually upstream as the current erodes the ground beneath it. Erosion may also cause a tall waterfall to flatten out over time. The power of falling water can also erode the riverbed at the bottom of the waterfall, creating deep bowls called plunge pools.

Although large, well-known waterfalls—such as Niagara Falls on the border of New York State and Canada, and Angel Falls in Venezuela—may seem eternal, they are ephemeral features when compared to the length of geologic time. Niagara Falls, for example, formed as recently as 11,700 years ago as the last glaciers retreated north. In time, the falls will weaken into mere rapids.

Waterfalls primarily form in three types of terrain: along the margins of high plateaus; along fall lines (a geological boundary between erosion resistant rocks and rocks that erode more easily); and in mountains, particularly those shaped by glaciers in the recent past. Some waterfalls are created by the discordance of their river profile. This means that they are the result of Earth's plates shifting and creating new landforms, or from glaciation. Others are formed by differential erosion, which occurs where weak and strong rocks are positioned next to each other. Still other waterfalls form as a result of human-constructed barriers and dams.

Perhaps the most important aspect of river study in correlation to human civilizations is the rapid variation in water-surface level of river channels over time. This includes an understanding of peak discharge or peak flow, better known as flooding. Peak flow is primarily influenced by precipitation and snowmelt. For small rivers and streams, peak flow lasts for a relatively short time. For larger rivers, peak flow can last for days, causing flooding and the related problems for communities and businesses situated on the floodplain.

Forecasting floods can be difficult for many reasons. The chance of a flood occurring depends on the amount of precipitation, the rate of evaporation, the makeup of the terrain, and storm characteristics such as length and severity. Nonetheless, a long-term study of peak discharge for a given area can increase the chances of predicting a flood. Such predictions help determine how to protect communities from future floods and whether an area is a safe place to develop new communities.

Sediments are created from rock in a process called weathering. Over many years, solid rock cracks under geological pressures and forces. Water and roots work their way into these cracks, loosening them. The freezing and thawing of water in the cracks creates blocks of rock, which are further broken down by physical and chemical processes. Smaller pieces of rock tumble into streams and are slowly eroded by the stream's current. Soils and sediments are washed out of the ground by runoff, flow into streams, and are carried away.

The river's sediment yield, which is measured by weight or volume, is the amount of sediment carried away from a drainage basin, that is, the area that feeds water into a given stream or river. The eroded deposits carried by a river are called its sediment load, and sediment load is classified into three categories. Bed load is made up of rocks and sand that rest on the bottom of the river. These materials are drawn along slowly by the current. The suspended load of a river—the largest sediment load component—is made up of clays and silts floating in the water. Last, the dissolved load is comprised of chemicals and minerals mixed in with the water.

Eventually, sediments are deposited downriver. Some are carried all the way to an ocean or lake where they settle and form clay. Sediments may form fanlike landforms called deltas at the end of a river. Deltas are areas rich in minerals. Historically, these landforms—such as the Nile River delta in Egypt—have served as productive farmland. The deposition of sediments can be affected by human activities such as dam building and irrigation. Dams create reservoirs that become mammoth receptacles for sediments, and irrigation systems can move sediments out of the rivers and back onto land.

Rivers are more than just conduits for water and sediments. Over many years, they transform the geological landscape around them. Rivers cut through soil and rock, eroding and sculpting the land. They carry sediment to new areas where it collects and forms new geological structures. As such, rivers contribute greatly to landscape evolution.

Several present-day gorges and canyons were formed by recent tectonic activity. The Grand Canyon, for example, was formed by the uplift of the Colorado Plateau. The uplift of the Allegheny Plateau in the eastern United States has resulted in smaller but similar gorges and canyons that occur from New York to West Virginia. These landforms often become conduits for streams and rivers, upon which they enter the early stages of valley development.

A river running through a valley may be the one that originally formed the valley many years ago, or the initial river may have been diverted into another valley. The running water of a stream or river continually washes sediment downstream, carving out a bed. Early in a river's existence, waterfalls are common. But as time passes, rivers gradually smooth out the valley floor. Most valleys begin as narrow landforms that grow wider until they reach their baselevel, or the lowest point at which its water can flow.

Rivers that flow through valleys are surrounded by relatively flat land called a floodplain. A valley bottom is often one large floodplain, and the surface of a floodplain is built on layers of alluvium—sediments deposited by the river during floods. Flooding delivers a rich supply of sediment-born nutrients to the soil, and thus the areas around rivers with wide floodplains are often used for farming.

A river that becomes narrower over time can create multiple floodplains at different elevations. These landforms are called terraces. A terrace has two distinct parts—a flat surface (the old floodplain), and a scarp, or steep slope connecting the new floodplain to the former floodplain. Terraces are formed when a river abruptly becomes narrower. The new river and its narrower floodplain cut a channel into the valley floor, creating "steps."

Valleys, canyons and floodplains often occur in the upper and middle courses of rivers and streams. However, different features—such as alluvial fans, deltas, and estuaries—tend to form at the ends of rivers and streams, where rivers and streams empty into larger water bodies.

An alluvial fan is a cone-shaped sediment deposit in a wide area not contained by a river valley, or at the mouth of a river. Alluvial fans are especially common in mountainous areas where snowmelt creates temporary streams. These streams erode the soil and rock and carry the sediment down to a valley basin. When the narrow stream reaches an open slope or plain, the sediments spread out in a fan share, giving the landform its name. There are two types of alluvial fans. Dry fans form as a result of ephemeral flow, such as in the mountain streams already mentioned. Wet fans are created by continually flowing streams.

As previously mentioned, deltas are fanlike plains of deposited sediment that forms at a river's mouth. These landforms create new shoreline over time as the sediment accumulates. Many deltas are cone-shaped and thus resemble alluvial fans. A cone-shaped delta is created when many smaller streams break off of the main river trunk as the river approaches the sea. Deltas can be found all over the world, particularly at the ends of major rivers with a substantial sediment yield. Deltas have three parts. The upper delta plain begins where the river leaves the area where its water is confined by valley walls. Here the river breaks into numerous channels that radiate away from the river mouth. Marshes, swamps, and freshwater lakes may exist between these channels. The lower delta plain begins at the highest tidal level. This zone features both marine and fluvial (river) activity. The subaqueous delta plain is the part of the delta that remains completely below sea level.

An estuary is a coastal body of water that is partially surrounded by land. Estuaries form where freshwater from rivers and streams mixes with seawater. The size and extent of an estuary depends on several factors, particularly the distance to which tidal waters reach inland. Modern estuaries, such as the prominent embayments of Chesapeake Bay in North America, were formed at the end of the last ice age as sea levels rose. Estuaries have always been important locations for developing societies. Many cultures used them as centres for shipping, trade, and commerce. Today, because such unique species reside in estuaries, many are protected by law.

In the pages that follow, the reader will travel across the globe in search of the world's greatest rivers. From the mighty Mississippi River of North America to the Yangtze of China, Earth's rivers are both natural treasures and important tools for the industries and economies of modern societies. They also serve as valuable geological laboratories for scientists, teachers, and students.

CHAPTER 1

RIVERS

A river is any natural stream of water that flows in a channel with defined banks (ultimately from Latin *ripa*, "bank"). Modern usage includes rivers that are multichanneled, intermittent, or ephemeral in flow and channels that are practically bankless. The concept of channeled surface flow, however, remains central to the definition. The word stream (derived ultimately from the Indo-European root *srou-*) emphasizes the fact of flow; as a noun it is synonymous with river and is often preferred in technical writing. Small natural watercourses are sometimes called rivulets, but a variety of names—including branch, brook, burn, and creek—are more common, occurring regionally to nationally in place-names. Arroyo

Water cycles back to rivers and oceans by way of precipitation such as snow.
Robert Atanasovski/AFP/Getty Images

and (dry) wash connote ephemeral streams or their resultant channels. Tiny streams or channels are referred to as rills or runnels.

Rivers are nourished by precipitation, by direct overland runoff, through springs and seepages, or from meltwater at the edges of snowfields and glaciers. The contribution of direct precipitation on the water surface is usually minute, except where much of a catchment area is occupied by lakes. River water losses result from seepage and percolation into shallow or deep aquifers (permeable rock layers that readily transmit water) and particularly from evaporation. The difference between the water input and loss sustains surface discharge or streamflow. The amount of water in river systems at any time is but a tiny fraction of the Earth's total water; 97 percent of all water is contained in the oceans and about three-quarters of fresh water is stored as land ice; nearly all the remainder occurs as groundwater. Lakes hold less than 0.5 percent of all fresh water, soil moisture accounts for about 0.05 percent, and water in river channels for roughly half as much, 0.025 percent, which represents only about one four-thousandth of the Earth's total fresh water.

Water is constantly cycled through the systems of land ice, soil, lakes, groundwater (in part), and river channels, however. The discharge of rivers to the oceans delivers to these systems the equivalent of the water vapour that is blown overland and then consequently precipitated as rain or snow (i.e., some 7 percent of mean annual precipitation on the globe and 30 percent of precipitation on land areas).

Rivers are one hundred times more effective than coastal erosion in delivering rock debris to the sea. Their rate of sediment delivery is equivalent to an average lowering of the lands by 30 cm (12 inches) in nine thousand years, a rate that is sufficient to remove all the existing continental relief in 25 million years.

Rock debris enters fluvial systems either as fragments eroded from rocky channels or in dissolved form. During transit downstream, the solid particles undergo systematic changes in size and shape, traveling as bed load or suspension load. Generally speaking, except in high latitudes and on steep coasts, little or no coarse bed load ever reaches the sea. Movement of the solid load down a river valley is irregular, both because the streamflow is irregular and because the transported material is liable to enter temporary storage, forming distinctive river-built features that range through riffles, midstream bars, point bars, floodplains, levees, alluvial fans, and river terraces. In one sense, such geomorphic features belong to the same series as deltas, estuary fills, and the terrestrial sediments of many inland basins.

Rates of erosion and transportation, and comparative amounts of solid and dissolved load, vary widely from river to river. Least is known about dissolved load, which at coastal outlets is added to oceanic salt. Its concentration in tropical rivers is not necessarily high, although very high discharges can move large amounts; the dissolved load of the lowermost Amazon averages about 40 parts per million, whereas the Elbe and the Rio Grande, by contrast, average more than eight hundred parts per million. Suspended load for the world in general perhaps equals two and one-half times dissolved load. Well over half of suspended load is deposited at river mouths as deltaic and estuarine sediment. About one-quarter of all suspended load is estimated to come down the Ganges–Brahmaputra and the Huang He (Yellow River), which together deliver some 4.5 trillion tons a year; the Yangtze, Indus, Amazon, and Mississippi deliver quantities ranging from about

500 million to approximately 350 million tons a year. Suspended sediment transport on the Huang He equals a denudation rate of about 3,090 tons per square km (8,000 tons per square mile) per year; the corresponding rate for the Ganges–Brahmaputra is almost half as great. Extraordinarily high rates have been recorded for some lesser rivers: for instance, 1,060 tons per square km per year (2,750 tons per square mile per year) on the Ching and 1,080 tons per square km per year (2,800 tons per square mile per year) on the Lo, both of which are loess-plateau tributaries of the Huang He.

THE IMPORTANCE OF RIVERS

Since prehistoric times, humans have valued the economic and environmental services provided by rivers. Water, as well as the rich soil deposited by the movement of water, allowed for the development of croplands, animal domestication, and the rise of towns and cities. Rivers continue to serve as aquatic highways that facilitate trade, and since the late 19th century, many rivers have been harnessed to provide hydroelectric power. These ribbons of water, however, are also sites of environmental degradation that results from bottom channelization and pollution.

SIGNIFICANCE IN EARLY HUMAN SETTLEMENTS

The inner valleys of some great alluvial rivers contain the sites of ancestral permanent settlements, including pioneer cities. Sedentary settlement in Hither Asia began about 10,000 years ago at the site of Arīḥā (ancient Jericho). Similar settlement in the Tigris–Euphrates and Nile valleys dates back to at least 6000 BP (years before present). The first settlers are thought to have practiced a hunting economy, supplemented by harvesting of wild grain. Conversion to the management of domesticated animals and the cultivation of food crops provided the surpluses that made possible the rise of towns, with parts of their populations freed from direct dependence on food getting. Civilization in the Indus Valley, prominently represented at Mohenjo-daro, dates from about 4500 BP, while civilization in the Ganges Valley can be traced to approximately 3000 BP. Permanent settlement in the valley of the Huang He has a history some four thousand years long, and the first large irrigation system in the Yangtze catchment dates to roughly the same time. Greek invaders of the SyrDarya, Amu Darya, and other valleys draining to the Aral Sea, east of the Caspian, encountered irrigating communities that had developed from about 2300 BP onward.

The influence of climatic shifts on these prehistoric communities has yet to be worked out satisfactorily. In wide areas, these shifts included episodic desiccation from 12,000 or 10,000 BP onward. In what are now desert environments, increased dependence on the rivers may have proved as much a matter of necessity as of choice. All of the rivers in question have broad floodplains subject to annual inundation by rivers carrying heavy sediment loads. Prehistoric works of flood defense and irrigation demanded firm community structures and required the development of engineering practice. Highly elaborate irrigation works are known from Mohenjo-daro. The ziggurats (temple mounds) of the Euphrates Valley may well have originated in ancient Egypt in response to the complete annual inundation of the Nile floodplain, where holdings had to be redefined after each flood subsided. It is not surprising that the communities named have been styled hydraulic civilizations. Yet, it would be oversimplistic to claim that riparian sites held the monopoly of the developments described. Elaborate urban systems arising in Mexico, Peru, and the eastern Mediterranean from about 4000 BP onward were not immediately dependent on the resources of rivers.

Where riverine cities did develop, they commanded ready means of communication. The two lands of Upper and Lower Egypt, for instance, were unified by the Nile. At the same time, it can be argued that early riverine and river-dependent civilizations bore the seeds of their own destruction, independent of major climatic variations and natural evolutionary changes in the river systems. High-consuming cities downstream inevitably exploited the upstream catchments, especially for timber. Deforestation there may possibly have led to ruinous silting in downstream reaches, although the contribution of this process to the eventual decline of civilization on the Euphrates and the Indus remains largely a matter of guesswork. An alternative or conjoint possibility is that continued irrigation promoted progressive salinization of the soils of irrigated lands, eventually preventing effective cropping. Salinization is known to have damaged the irrigated lands of Ur, progressively from about 4400 to 4000 BP, and may have ruined the Sumerian Empire of the time. The relative importance of environmental and social deterioration in prehistoric hydraulic civilizations, however, remains a matter of debate. Furthermore, defective design and maintenance of irrigation works promote the spread of malarial mosquitoes, which certainly afflicted the prehistoric hydraulic communities of the lower Tigris–Euphrates Valley. These same communities also may have been affected by bilharziasis, or schistosomiasis (blood fluke disease), which requires a species of freshwater snail for propagation and which even today follows many extensions of irrigation into arid lands.

At various intervals of history, rivers have provided the easiest, and in many areas the only, means of entry and circulation for explorers, traders, conquerors, and settlers. They assumed considerable importance in Europe after the fall of the Roman Empire and the dismemberment of its roads. Regardless of political structures, control of crossing points was expressed in strongholds and the rise of bridge-towns. Rivers in medieval Europe supplied the water that sustained cities and the sewers that carried away city waste and were widely used, either directly or with off-takes, as power sources. Western European history records the rise of 13 national capitals on sizable rivers, exclusive of seawater inlets; three of them, Vienna, Budapest, and Belgrade, lie on the Danube, with two others, Sofia and Bucharest, on feeder streams above stem floodplain level. The location of provincial and corresponding capitals is even more strongly tied to riparian sites, as can be readily seen from the situation in the United Kingdom, France, and Germany. In modern history, in both North America and northern Asia, natural waterways directed the lines of exploration, conquest, and settlement. In these areas, passage from river system to river system was facilitated by portage along lines defined by temporary ice-marginal or ice-diverted channels. Many pioneer settlers of the North American interior entered by means of natural waterways, especially in Ohio.

Significance to Trade, Agriculture, and Industry

The historical record includes marked shifts in the appreciation of rivers, numerous conflicts in use demand, and an intensification of use that has rapidly accelerated during the 20th century. External freight trade became concentrated in estuarine ports rather than in inland ports when oceangoing vessels increased in size. Even the port of London, though constrained by high capital investment, has displaced itself toward its estuary. The Amazon remains naturally navigable by ocean ships for 3,700 km (2,300 miles), the Yangtze for 1,000 km (about 600 miles), and the partly artificial St. Lawrence Seaway for 2,100 km (1,300 miles). Internal freight traffic on the Rhine system and its associated canals amounts to one-quarter or more of the total traffic in the basin and to more than half in some parts. After a period of decline from the later 1800s to about the mid-1900s, water transport of freight has steadily increased. This trend can in large part be attributed to advances in river engineering. Large-scale channel improvement and stabilization projects have been undertaken on many of the major rivers of the world, notably in the northern plain lands of Russia and in the interior of the United States (e.g., various large tributaries of the Mississippi River).

Demand on open-channel water increases as population and per capita water use increase and as underground water supplies fall short. Irrigation use constitutes a comparatively large percentage of the total supply. With a history of at least five thousand years, controlled irrigation now affects roughly 2 million square km (770,000 square miles) of land, three-quarters of it in East and South Asia and two-fifths in mainland China alone. Most of this activity involves the use of natural floodwater, although reliance on artificially impounded storage has increased rapidly. Irrigation in the 1,300-km (800-mile) length of the Indus Valley, for instance, depends almost exclusively on barrages (i.e., distributor canals) running down alluvial fans and along floodplains.

HYDROELECTRIC POWER

Hydroelectric power is electricity produced from generators driven by water turbines that convert the potential energy in falling or fast-flowing water to mechanical energy. In the generation of hydroelectric power, water is collected or stored at a higher elevation and led downward through large pipes or tunnels (penstocks) to a lower elevation. The difference between these two elevations is known as the head. At the end of its passage down the pipes, the falling water causes turbines to rotate. The turbines in turn drive generators, which convert the turbines' mechanical energy into electricity. Transformers are then used to convert the alternating voltage suitable for the generators to a higher voltage suitable for long-distance transmission. The structure that houses the turbines and generators, and into which the pipes or penstocks feed, is called the powerhouse.

Hydroelectric power plants are usually located in dams that impound rivers, thereby raising the level of the water behind the dam and creating as high a head as is feasible. The potential power that can be derived from a volume of water is directly proportional to the working head, so that a high-head installation requires a smaller volume of water than a low-head installation to produce an equal amount of power. In some dams, the powerhouse is constructed on one flank of the dam, part of the dam being used as a spillway over which excess water is discharged in times of flood. Where the river flows in a narrow steep gorge, the powerhouse may be located within the dam itself.

In most communities, electric-power demand varies considerably at different times of the day. To even the load on the generators, pumped-storage hydroelectric stations are occasionally built. During off-peak periods, some of the extra power available is supplied to the generator operating as a motor, driving the turbine to pump water into an elevated reservoir. Then, during periods of peak demand, the water is allowed to flow down again through the turbine to generate electrical energy. Pumped-storage systems are efficient and provide an economical way to meet peak loads.

In certain coastal areas, such as the Rance River estuary in Brittany, France, hydroelectric power plants have been constructed to take advantage of the rise and fall of tides. When the tide comes in, water is impounded in one or more reservoirs. At low tide, the water in these reservoirs is released to drive hydraulic turbines and their coupled electric generators.

Falling water is one of the three principal sources of energy used to generate electric power, the other two being fossil fuels and nuclear fuels. Hydroelectric power has certain advantages over these other sources: it is continually renewable owing to the recurring nature of the hydrologic cycle and produces neither atmospheric nor thermal pollution. Hydroelectric power is a preferred energy source in areas with heavy rainfall and with hilly or mountainous regions that are in reasonably close proximity to the main load centres. Some large hydro sites that are remote from load centres may be sufficiently attractive to justify the long high-voltage transmission lines. Small local hydro sites may also be economical, particularly if they combine storage of water during light loads with electricity production during peaks.

Present-day demands on rivers as power sources range from the floating of timber, through the use of water for cooling, to hydroelectric generation. Logging in forests relies primarily on flotation during the season of melt-water high flow. Large power plants and other industrial facilities are often located along rivers, which supply the enormous quantities of water needed for cooling purposes. Manufacturers of petrochemicals, steel, and woolen cloth also make large demands. Hydroelectric power generation was introduced more than one hundred years ago, but the majority of the existing installations have been built since 1950. Many of the world's major industrial nations have developed their hydropower potential to the fullest, though a few like the United States still have some untapped resources. It has been estimated that 75 percent of the potential hydropower in the contiguous United States has been developed, and about 13 percent of the total annual electrical energy demands of the country are met by hydroelectric power plants. By contrast, there are some countries, such as Norway and Switzerland, that depend almost entirely on hydropower for their various electrical energy needs. There is great potential for supplies of hydropower in Central

Asia and in many of the developing countries in the region of the Himalayas, Africa, and South America.

Use demand of more immediate kinds are related to freshwater fisheries (including fish-farming), to dwelling in houseboats, and to recreational activities. Reliable data for these kinds of dependence on rivers do not exist. Published estimates that freshwater and migratory fish provide up to about 15 percent of world catch may be too low. Certainly, millions of people are concerned with freshwater fishery and houseboat living, principally in the deltaic areas of East Asia, where dwelling, marketing, and travel can be located almost exclusively on the water. Furthermore, recreational use of rivers has increased over the years. In North America many waterways, particularly those with relatively light commercial traffic, support large numbers of recreational craft. In Europe pleasure cruisers transport multitudes of sightseers up and down the Rhine and Seine each year, while various derelict canals of such systems as the Thames have been restored for boating.

DRAINAGE BASINS

Drainage basins, which are also known as catchment areas or watersheds, are areas from which all precipitation flows to a single stream or set of streams. For example, the total area drained by the Mississippi River constitutes its drainage basin, whereas that part of the Mississippi River drained by the Ohio River is the Ohio's drainage basin. The boundary between drainage basins is a drainage divide: all the precipitation on opposite sides of a drainage divide will flow into different drainage basins.

A drainage basin provides a limited surface area within which physical processes pertinent to the general hydrology may be considered. The climatic variables and the water and sediment discharge, water storage, and evapotranspiration may be measured; from these measurements, denudation rates and moisture and energy balances may be derived, each of which is useful in the consideration and understanding of landscape formation.

ENVIRONMENTAL PROBLEMS ATTENDANT ON RIVER USE

The ever-increasing exploitation of rivers has given rise to a variety of problems. Extensive commercial navigation of rivers has resulted in much artificial improvement of natural channels, including increasing the depth of the channels to permit passage of larger vessels. In some cases, this lowering of the river bottom has caused the water table of the surrounding area to drop, which has adversely affected agriculture. Also, canalization, with its extensive system of locks and navigation dams, often seriously disrupts riverine ecosystems.

An even more far-reaching problem is that of water pollution. Pesticides and herbicides are now employed in large quantities throughout much of the world. The widespread use of such biocides and the universal nature of water makes it inevitable that the toxic chemicals would appear as stream pollutants. Biocides can contaminate water, especially of slow-flowing rivers, and are responsible for a number of fish kills each year.

In agricultural areas the extensive use of phosphates and nitrates as fertilizers may result in other problems. Entering rivers via rainwater runoff and groundwater seepage, these chemicals can cause eutrophication. This process involves a sharp increase in the concentration of phosphorus, nitrogen, and other plant nutrients that promotes the rapid growth of algae (so-called algal blooms) in sluggish rivers and a consequent depletion of oxygen in the water. Under normal conditions, algae contribute to the oxygen balance in rivers and also serve as food for fish, but in excessive amounts they crowd out populations of other organisms, overgrow, and finally die owing to the exhaustion of available nutrients and autointoxication. Various species of bacteria then begin to decay and putrefy the dead algal bodies, the oxidation of which sharply reduces the amount of oxygen in the river water. The water may develop a bad taste and is unfit for human consumption unless filtered and specially treated.

Urban centres located along rivers contribute significantly to the pollution problem as well. In spite of the availability of advanced waste-purification technology, a surprisingly large percentage of the sewage from cities and towns is released into waterways untreated. In effect, rivers are used as open sewers for municipal wastes, which results not only in the direct degradation of water quality but also in eutrophication.

Still another major source of pollutants is industry. Untreated industrial chemical wastes can alter the normal biological activity of rivers, and many of the chemicals react with water to raise the acidity of rivers to a point where the water becomes corrosive enough to destroy living organisms. An example of this is the formation of sulfuric acid from the sulfur-laden residue of coal-mining operations. Although upper limits for concentrations of unquestionably toxic chemicals such as arsenic, barium, cyanide, lead, and phenols have been established for drinking water, no general rules exist for the treatment of industrial wastes because of the wide variety of organic and inorganic compounds involved. Moreover, even in cases where a government-imposed ban checks the further discharge of certain dangerous substances into waterways, the chemicals may persist in the environment for years. Such is the case with polychlorinated biphenyls (PCBs), the chlorinated hydrocarbon by-products of various industrial processes that were routinely discharged into U.S.

waterways until the late 1970s when the federal government not only prohibited the continued discharge of the chemicals into the environment but their production as well. Because PCBs cannot be broken down by conventional waste-treatment methods and are degraded by natural processes very slowly, scientists fear that these compounds will continue to pose a serious hazard for decades to come. PCBs have been found in high concentrations in the fatty tissues of fish, which can be passed up the food chain to humans. An accumulation of PCBs in the human body is known to induce cancer and other severe disorders.

As previously noted, many industrial facilities, including nuclear power plants, steel mills, chemical-processing facilities, and oil refineries, use large quantities of water for cooling and return it at elevated temperatures. Such heated water can alter the existing ecology, sometimes sufficiently to drive out or kill desirable species of fish. It also may cause rapid depletion of the oxygen supply by promoting algal blooms.

THE DISTRIBUTION OF RIVERS IN NATURE

Rivers require a supply of moisture to maintain the flow of water at the surface. The moisture supply may be higher during one season than in another, and other factors may influence the speed and quantity of water that moves downstream. Small streams join with each other to form larger ones to drain individual plots of land, landscapes, regions, and, ultimately, large portions of continents. The largest of Earth's rivers are significant features that move tremendous volumes of water from terrestrial environments to the oceans.

THE WORLD'S PRINCIPAL RIVERS, RANKED ACCORDING TO DRAINAGE AREA

RIVER	DRAINAGE AREA		LENGTH (KM)*	MEAN DISCHARGE			
	EXTENT (000 SQ KM)	PERCENT OF THE WORLD'S LAND AREA		(000 CU M/SEC)	RANK ORDER	PERCENT OF WORLD TOTAL	CU M/ SEC/SQ KM
mazon	7,050	4.8	6,400	180	1	19.2	0.0255
raná	4,144	2.8	4,880	22	5	2.3	0.0052
ngo	3,457	2.3	4,700	41	2	4.4	0.0121
le	3,349	2.3	6,650	3	—	0.3	0.0009
ississippi- issouri	3,221	2.2	5,971	18	8	2.0	0.0057
-Irtysh	2,975	2.0	5,410	15	10	1.7	0.0053
nisey	2,580	1.7	5,540	19	6	2.0	0.0073
na	2,490	1.7	4,400	16	9	1.7	0.0065
ngtze	1,959	1.3	6,300	34	4	3.6	0.0174
ger	1,890	1.3	4,200	6	—	0.7	0.0032
nur	1,855	1.3	2,824	12	10	1.3	0.0066
ackenzie	1,841	1.2	4,241	11	—	1.2	0.0061
nges- ahmaputra	1,621	1.1	2,897	38	3	4.1	0.0237
wrence- eat Lakes	1,463	1.0	4,000	10	—	1.1	0.0069
lga	1,360	0.9	3,530	8	—	0.9	0.0058
mbezi	1,330	0.9	3,500	7	—	0.8	0.0053
dus	1,166	0.8	2,900	5	—	0.6	0.0047
att 'Arab igris- phrates)	1,114	0.8	2,800	1	—	0.1	0.0012

me figures are rounded to the nearest ten or hundred kilometres.

RIVER	DRAINAGE AREA		LENGTH (KM)*	MEAN DISCHARGE			
	EXTENT (000 SQ KM)	PERCENT OF THE WORLD'S LAND AREA		(000 CU M/SEC)	RANK ORDER	PERCENT OF WORLD TOTAL	CU M. SEC/S· KM
Nelson	1,072	0.7	2,575	2	—	0.2	0.002
Murray-Darling	1,057	0.7	3,780	0.4	—	0.04	0.000
Tocantins	906	0.6	2,699	10	—	1.1	0.011
Danube	816	0.6	2,850	7	—	0.8	0.008
Columbia	668	0.5	2,000	7	—	0.7	0.010
Rio Grande	445	0.4	3,060	0.08	—	0.01	0.000
Rhine	160	0.1	1,320	2	—	0.2	0.013·
Rhône	96	—	800	2	—	0.2	0.017·
Thames	10	—	340	0.08	—	0.01	0.008

* Some figures are rounded to the nearest ten or hundred kilometres.

Obvious bases by which to compare the world's great rivers include the size of the drainage area, the length of the main stem, and the mean discharge. However, reliable comparative data, even for the world's greatest rivers, do not exist. Some approximate values, however, do exist. The Nile, the world's longest river, is about 250 km (about 150 miles) longer than the Amazon. It is possible that well over one hundred of the greatest rivers may exceed a 1,600-km (1,000-mile) length on their main stems.

Area–length–discharge combinations vary considerably, although length tends to increase with area and area and discharge to increase through their individual ranking series. On all counts except length, the Amazon is the world's principal river. The Congo and the Paraná are among the first five by area and discharge. The Mississippi, however, fourth in length and fifth in area, is only seventh in discharge. The Ganges–Brahmaputra, third in discharge, is 13th (or lower) in area and well down the list of length for its two main stems taken separately.

The 20 greatest of these rivers, draining about 30 percent of the world's land area, discharge nearly 40 percent of total runoff, reckoned from a mean equivalent of 29.2 cm (11.5 inches) of precipitation. They deliver to the sea about 92 cubic km (22 cubic miles) of water per day, or roughly 33,325 cubic km (about 8,000 cubic miles) annually. Specifically, the Amazon, the Paraná, the Congo, and the Ganges–Brahmaputra, combined, discharge more than 54 cubic km (13 cubic miles) a day and nearly 20,800 cubic km (about 5,000 cubic miles) a year, one-third of the world's total runoff to the oceans, with the Amazon alone accounting for almost one-fifth.

World average external runoff is about 0.01 cubic metre per second per square km (0.6 cubic foot per second per square mile). Great rivers with notably higher discharges are fed either by the convectional rains of equatorial regions or by monsoonal rains that are usually increased by altitudinal effects. The Huang He averages 0.046 cubic metre per second per square km (0.28 cubic foot per second per square mile), the Irrawaddy 0.032 cubic metre per second per square km (0.19 cubic foot per second per square mile), the Magdalena and the Amazon 0.026 cubic metre per second per square km (0.16 cubic foot per second per square mile), the Orinoco 0.021 cubic metre per second per square km (0.13 cubic foot per second per square mile), and the Ganges–Brahmaputra above 0.024 cubic metre per second per square km (0.14 cubic foot per second per square mile).

Bridge over the Alto Paraná River between Ciudad del Este, Paraguay, and Foz do Iguaçu, Brazil. © Tony Morrison/South American Pictures

Very high mean discharges per unit area are also recorded for lesser basins in mountainous coastlands exposed to the zonal westerlies of mid-latitudes. Among great rivers with mean discharges near or not far below world averages per unit area are those of Siberia, the Mackenzie, and the Yukon (828,000 square km [320,000 square miles], 5,900 cubic metres [208,000 cubic feet] per second), all affected by low precipitation for which low evaporation rates barely compensate. The basins of the Mississippi, Niger, and Zambezi include some areas of dry climate. The Nelson illustrates the extreme effects of low precipitation in a cool climate, while the Nile, Murray–Darling, and Shaṭṭ al-ʿArab (Tigris–Euphrates) experience low precipitation combined with high evaporation losses.

In addition, the Rhine, Rhône, and Danube record regimes that vary along the length of their courses in response to glacier melt in the headwaters and the entry of contrasting tributaries downstream. The Rio Grande, like the Orange and the Colorado, suffers progressive downstream losses, both natural and irrigational. The Thames is special, because it experiences particularly high tidal range in its estuary, which makes flood control especially difficult.

PRINCIPLES GOVERNING DISTRIBUTION AND FLOW

Moisture supply sufficient to sustain channeled surface flow is governed primarily by climate, which regulates precipitation, temperature, and evapotranspiration water loss caused by vegetation. In rainy tropical and exposed mid-latitude areas, runoff commonly equals 38 cm (15 inches) or more of rain a year, rising to more than 102 cm (40 inches). Negligible external runoff occurs in subtropical and rain-shadow deserts. Perennial, intermittent, and ephemeral lakes, expanding in response to local runoff, prevent the drainage of desert basins from finding escape routes.

RUNOFF

In hydrology, runoff is described as a quantity of water discharged in surface streams. Runoff includes not only the waters that travel over the land surface and through channels to reach a stream but also interflow, the water that infiltrates the soil surface and travels by means of gravity toward a stream channel (always above the main groundwater level) and eventually empties into the channel. Runoff also includes groundwater that is discharged into a stream. Streamflow that is composed entirely of groundwater is termed base flow, or fair-weather runoff, and it occurs where a stream channel intersects the water table. The total runoff is equal to the total precipitation less the losses caused by evapotranspiration (loss to the atmosphere from soil surfaces and plant leaves), storage (as in temporary ponds), and other such abstractions.

VARIATION OF STREAM REGIME

Seasonal variation in discharge defines river regime. Three broad classes of regime can be distinguished for perennial streams. In the megathermal class, related to hot equatorial and tropical climates, two main variants occur: discharge is powerfully sustained throughout the year, usually with a double maximum (two peak values), but in some areas with a strong single maximum. In the mesothermal class some regimes resemble those of tropical and equatorial areas, with single or double summer maxima corresponding to heavy seasonal rainfall, while others include sustained flow with slight warm-season minima. Where mid-latitude climates include dry summers, streamflow decreases markedly and may cease altogether in the warm half of the year. In areas affected by release of meltwater, winter minima and spring maxima of discharge are characteristic. Microthermal regimes, which are influenced by snow cover, include winter minima and summer maxima resulting from snowmelt and convectional rain. Alternatively, spring meltwater maxima are accompanied by secondary fall maxima that are associated with late-season thunder rain, or spring snowmelt maxima can be followed by a summer glacier-melt maximum, as on the Amu Darya. Megathermal regimes, which are controlled by systematic fluctuations in seasonal rain, and microthermal regimes, which are controlled by seasonal release of meltwater, may be more reliable than mesothermal regimes.

The regime can vary considerably along the length of a single river in timing and in seasonal characteristics. Spring maxima in the Volga headwaters are not followed by peak flows in the delta until two months later. The October seasonal peak on the upper Niger becomes a December peak on the middle river; the swing from tropical-rainy through steppe climate reduces volume by 25 percent through a 500-km (300-mile) stretch. The seasonal head-water flood wave travels at 9 cm (3.5 inches) per second, taking some four months over 2,000 km (1,250 miles), but earlier seasonal peaks are reestablished on the lower river by tributaries fed by hot-season rains. The great Siberian rivers, flowing northward into regions of increasingly deferred thaw, habitually cause extensive flooding in their lower reaches, which remain ice-covered when upstream reaches have already thawed and are receiving the melt-waters of late spring and summer.

Extremes of regime characteristics come into question when streams are classified as perennial, intermittent, or ephemeral. These terms are in common use but lack rigid definition. Whereas the middle and lower reaches of streams in humid regions rarely or never cease flowing and can properly be called perennial, almost every year many of their upstream feeders run dry where they are not fed by springs. In basins cut in impermeable bedrock, prolonged droughts can halt flow in most channel reaches. Karst (limestone country) that has some surface drainage often includes streams that are spatially intermittent. Frequently, it also contains temporally intermittent streams that flow only when heavy rain raises the groundwater table and reactivates outlets above the usual level. Temporally intermittent streams also occur in dry areas where, at low stage, only some channel reaches contain flowing water.

There is a continuous progression from perennial streams through intermittent streams to ephemeral streams: the latter command much attention, especially because their effects in erosion, transportation, and deposition can be inordinately great and also because they relate closely to periods and cycles of gullying. Their channels generally have higher width–depth ratios than those of unbraided channels in humid areas (e.g., 150:1 or more on small streams). In extreme cases, ephemeral streamflow merges into sheetflood. Streambeds, usually sandy, are nearly flat in cross section but contain low bars where gravel is available. These behave in many ways like riffles or braid bars elsewhere. Although beds and banks are erodible, the fine-material fraction is usually enough to sustain very steep channel banks and gully walls. Rapid downcutting produces flat-floored trenches, called arroyos, in distinction from the often V-shaped gullies of humid areas.

Discontinuous vegetation cover, well-packed surface soil, and occasionally intense rainfall promote rapid surface runoff, conversion of overland to channeled flow, and the multiplication of channels. Although reliable comparative data are scarce, it seems likely that ephemeral channel systems develop higher order ranking, area for area, than do perennial streams: channels as high as 11th order are recorded for basins of about 1,300 square km (about 500 square miles), whereas the Mississippi is usually placed only in the 10th order. This apart, geometry of ephemeral nets obeys the laws of drainage composition that apply to perennial streams: stream length, stream number, channel width, and water discharge can be expressed as exponential functions of stream order, and drainage area and channel slope as power functions, whereas slope and discharge can be expressed as power functions of width and drainage area.

At-a-station (a particular cross section) variations in width, depth, and velocity with variation in discharge in ephemeral streams resemble the corresponding variations in perennial streams. Differences appear, however, when downstream variations are considered. For a given frequency of discharge, the rate of increase in width differs little between the two groups, but ephemeral streams increase the more slowly in depth, becoming increasingly shallow in proportion in the downstream direction. This effect is compensated by a more rapid downstream increase in velocity, which reflects high concentrations of suspended sediment and a resultant reduction of friction. Ultimately, however, the ephemeral flood may lose so much water by evaporation and percolation that the stream is dissipated in a terminal mudflow.

Trenching, the extension of gullies, and their conversion into arroyo systems, implies valley fills of erodible surficial material. Like streams of humid regions, ephemeral stream systems record complex histories of cut and fill: it is reasonable to expect comparable timing for climatically controlled events. Whatever the effect upon stream erosion of historical settlement in the western United States, inland eastern Australia, and New Zealand, the present episode of gullying seems merely to have been intensified by man's use of the land. Accelerated channeling frequently involves three processes not characteristic of humid regions: piping, headcutting, and the formation of channel profiles that are discontinuous over short distances.

In piping, water that has penetrated the topsoil washes out the subsoil where this is exposed in section, forming small tunnels that may attain lengths of many metres. Collapse of tunnel roofs initiates lateral gullying and lengthens existing cuts headward. Headcutting is commonly associated with piping, because headcuts frequently expose the subsoil. A headcut is an abrupt step in the channel profile, some centimetres to some metres high, and may originate merely as a bare or trampled patch in a vegetated channel bed but will increase in height (like some very large waterfalls) as it works upstream. At the foot of the headcut is a plunge pool, downstream of which occurs a depositional slope of low downstream gradient.

Formation of successive headcuts, say at an average spacing of 150 metres (about 500 feet), and the construction of depositional slopes below each, causes the profile to become stepped. Ephemeral streams with stepped profiles are called discontinuous gullies. Speed of headcut recession varies widely with the incidence and intensity of rainfall. Ultimately, when the whole profile has been worked along and the bed widened, the original even slope is restored, though at a lower level than before.

DETERMINING FACTORS

Long-term effects expressed in mean seasonal regimes and short-term effects expressed in individual peak flows are alike affected by soil-moisture conditions, groundwater balance, and channel storage. Channeled surface flow begins when overland flow becomes deep enough to be erosive, and depth of overland flow represents a balance between short-term precipitation and soil infiltration. Rate and capacity of infiltration depend partly on antecedent conditions and partly on permeability. Seasonal assessments are possible, however, and numbers of commercial crops can take up and transpire the equivalent of 38 cm (15 inches) of precipitation during the growing season. In many mid-latitude climates the rising curves of insolation and plant growth during spring and early summer cause soil moisture depletion, leading eventually to a deficit that is often strong enough to reduce runoff and streamflow. Soil-moisture recharge during colder months promotes high values of runoff frequently in the spring quite independently of the influence of precipitation regime or snowmelt.

Storage of water in groundwater tables, stream channels, on floodplains, and in lakes damps out variations in flow, whereas snow and ice storage exaggerate peaks. For the world as a whole, groundwater contributes perhaps 30 percent of total runoff, although the proportion varies widely from basin to basin, within basins, and through time. Shallow groundwater tables in contact with river channels absorb and release water, respectively at high and low stage. Percolation to greater depths and eventual discharge through springs delays the entry of water into channels. Many groundwater reservoirs carry over some storage from one year to another. Similar carryover occurs with glaciers and to some extent also with permanent snowfields. Water abstracted by the ice caps of high latitudes and by large mountain glaciers can be retained for many years, up to about 250,000 years in the central Antarctic cap. Temperate glaciers, however, with temperatures beneath the immediate subsurface constantly near the freezing (or the melting) point, can, like their associated snowfields, release large quantities of water during a given warm season. Their losses through evaporation are small.

Meltwater contributions to streamflow, however, can range from well above half the total discharge to well below the level of the snow line. They are vital to irrigation on alluvial fans rimming many dry basins, as in the Central Valley of California and the Tarim Basin of the Takla Makan Desert of China: meltwater is released during the planting or growing seasons. Within the limiting constraints of precipitation or meltwater input or both, and the outputs of evapotranspiration and percolation, the actual distribution of rivers in nature is affected by available drainage area, lithology, and vegetation. Vegetation is obviously climate dependent to a large extent but might well be capable of reaching thresholds of detention ability that do not match recognized climatic boundaries. It is, moreover, liable to the influence of climatically independent factors where it has been disturbed by human activity. Runoff on the plain lands of northern Asia, expressed as a percentage of mean annual precipitation, ranges from about 75 in the tundra, through about 70 in the boreal forest and 50 through boreal forest with perennially frozen ground, down through less than 40 in mixed forest, to five in semi-desert. Clear felling of forest increases runoff in the short and medium term because it reduces surface detention and transpiration. In areas of seasonal snow cover, forest influences seasonal regime considerably. However, though there may be a jump in short-term runoff characteristics between areas of continuous vegetation (forest and grass sward) on the one hand and discontinuous vegetation (bunchgrass and scrub) on the other, comprehensive general studies of precipitation–temperature runoff characteristics suggest that mean annual runoff decreases, at a decreasing rate through the range that is involved, as temperature increases and as precipitation (weighted in respect of seasonal incidence) decreases.

Lithology is significant mainly in connection with permeability. The capacity of karst to swallow and to reissue water is well known, as is the role of permeable strata generally in absorbing water into groundwater tables. An extreme case of a special kind is represented by an artesian aquifer, which in favourable structural conditions can take water for a considerably long time from the surface and immediately connected circulations, returning it only if the artesian pressure becomes strong enough to promote the opening of flowing springs. Less directly, but with considerable effect on infiltration and short-term runoff, the mechanical grade of bedrock or of surficial deposits can considerably affect the response to individual storms.

Both the ultimate possible extent of drainage basins and the opening of individual headwater channels are influenced by available drainage area. A hypothetical

Meltwater irrigation is critical to areas on alluvial fans adjoining dry basins, such as in Central Valley in California. David McNew/Getty Images

limit for especially large basins could probably be constructed from considerations of stem length, basin shape, computed area, and continental extent. The Amazon probably approaches the hypothetical maximum. At the other extreme, basin morphometry (geometric aspects of basins and their measurement) can be made to indicate the limiting average area necessary to sustain a given length of channel. In large areas of the mid-latitudes, the ratio is close to 2.25 square km (0.87 square miles) of drainage area for a channel 1.6 km (1 mile) in length. Estimates for the conterminous United States, an area of about 7.7 million square km (3 million square miles), give some 5.23 million km (3,250,000 miles) of channel length. These estimates include 1.5 million unbranched fingertip tributaries—each having an average length of 1.6 to 2.4 km (1 to 1.5 miles).

THE RIVER SYSTEM THROUGH TIME

Natural river systems can be assumed to have operated throughout the period of geologic record, ever since continental masses first received sufficient precipitation to sustain external surface runoff. The Precambrian portion of the record, prior to 570 million years ago, is complicated by the widely metamorphosed character of the surviving rocks, although even here the typical cross-bedding of shallow-water sands can be recognized in many places. The Cambrian and post-Cambrian succession of the last 570 million years contains multiple instances of deposition of deltaic sandstones, which record intermittent deposition by rivers in many areas at many intervals of past time. The span since the Precambrian is long enough, at present rates of erosion, for rivers to have shifted the equivalent of 25 to 30 times the bulk of the existing continental masses, but the rate of erosion and sedimentation is estimated to have increased with time. Of necessity, river systems now in existence date from times not earlier than the latest emergence of their basins above sea level, but this limitation allows numbers of them to have histories of one hundred million years or more in length.

DRAINAGE DIVERSION BY STREAM CAPTURE

A river system of appreciable size is likely to have undergone considerable changes in drainage area, network pattern, and profile and channel geometry. Adjoining streams compete with one another for territory. Although competition is effectively nil where divides consist of expanses of plateau or where opposing low-order streams of similar slope flow down the sides of ridges, it frequently happens that fluvial erosion is shifting a divide away from some more powerful trunk stream and toward a weaker competing trunk. In extreme cases, the height difference is so marked that a tributary head from one system can invade, and divert, a channel in the adjoining system: such diversion, termed stream capture, has already been noted as a principal mechanism in the adjustment of network patterns to structural patterns. Close general adjustment to structure implies multiple individual adjustments, unless the stream network has developed solely by the headward extension of tributaries along lines of structural and lithologic weakness: the network predicated on a single regional slope is dendritic in pattern. By encroachment and capture a successfully competing stream becomes yet more powerful, the headward extension of its basin increasing the discharge of the trunk channel and permitting reduction of slope (i.e., additional downcutting). Seaward extensions of basins occur where deltas lead the outbuilding of alluvial plains and where crustal uplift (and also at times strandline movements) result in emergence. Conversely, basin area is reduced along the seaward edge by submergence, in response to crustal depression or rise in sea level. The potential limits to basin size are fixed by available areas of continent with surface moisture surplus, in combination with theoretical optimum shape of basin. However, actual basin shapes, for all large rivers, are to some extent affected by crustal deformation.

Non-Fluvial Invasion and Deposition

Derangements other than the captures effected in stream competition include those due to non-fluvial invasion and deposition. Regional flooding by basalts, as during the Paleogene and Neogene periods (from 65.5 million to 2.6 million years ago) in the Deccan of India and the northwestern part of the United States, obliterates the former landscape and provides a new surface on which new drainage networks form. Major invasions by continental ice displaces fluvial systems for the time being. Glacial deposits, especially till sheets, can conceal the preglacial topography and provide initial slope systems for post-glacial streams. Individual diversions occur at and near ice fronts, also where preglacial divides in mountain country are breached by the ice of caps or impounded mountain glaciers. The full history of drainage derangement by con-tinental ice is often complex, depending on the particular combinations of preglacial outlet directions, extent of glacial invasion, relationship of regional slope to direc-tion of ice advance, thickness of glacial sedimentation, amount and speed of postglacial isostatic rebound, and self-selection of postglacial outlet directions and drain-age lines. The North American Great Lakes and Midwest areas, the Thames Basin in England, and the Eurasiatic plain all record intricate histories of damming during glacial maxima, with postglacial networks and outlets dif-fering markedly from those of preglacial times. Glacial breaching of divides requires the passage of thick ice through a preglacial notch or gap, with erosion severe enough to provide a new drainage line when the ice melts. The spinal divide of Scandinavia was breached by the ice cap centred over the Gulf of Bothnia, just as the highland rim of Greenland is being breached by effluent glaciers today. After deglaciation, areas of divide breaching display streams with anomalous courses through gaps in major relief barriers. Morphologically related to glacial breach-ing, especially with respect to indeterminate present-day divides, are the disordered drainage nets of formerly glaci-ated terrains where bedrock is widely exposed and where relief is subdued.

Changes through time in channel slope have already been partly treated in connection with terraces. In the long view, streams must tend to reduce their slopes as the basin relief is lowered, although isostatic (balancing) compensation for erosional reduction of load largely offsets the reduction of slope. The effects involved here are independent of, although necessarily associated with, glacial–deglacial changes in the strandline level, crustal warping, and isostatic rebound from glacial reduction of load. It can be argued that large river systems, removing large quantities of sediment and dumping them offshore, should promote intermittent isostatic uplift when yield thresholds are passed and, in consequence, promote the generation of new waves of erosion that, working upstream, are recorded in sequences of cyclic knickpoints. The implications of this conceptual view have been applied especially to the unglaciated shield areas (central and oldest part of continents, generally) of tropical latitudes and extratropical parts of the Southern Hemisphere, in all of which rivers descend in high falls or lengthy cascades across the edges of major erosional platforms. In the shorter term, severe and rapid erosion of a trunk channel can leave a tributary valley stranded at height. Channel geometry demands that tributary glacier troughs should hang above the floors of main troughs, while tributary stream valleys often hang above trunk valleys formerly occupied by long glacier tongues. Hanging valleys on shorelines are correspondingly due to the outpacing of channel erosion by cliffing.

THE EFFECTS OF CLIMATIC CHANGE

Climatic shifts are known to be capable of effecting fill or clearance of channels and valleys: they can also change channel habit. In addition to the alternation in some near-glacial areas between braiding during maximum cold and meandering during interglacial warmth, the record includes conversions of channel width and meander pattern. On numerous mid-latitude streams, existing channels have been much reduced from their earlier dimensions; and on many, but by no means all streams, existing floodplains are contained in the floors of meandering valleys where the wavelength is determined by the plan of the floodplain as opposed to the existing channel. Valley meanders were cut by streams 20 to one hundred times as voluminous as existing streams, at the bank-full stage. They illustrate only one variant, although a widespread one, of the underfit stream, which combines a former large with an existing reduced channel. Reduction to the underfit state is commonly, although not invariably, accompanied by the infilling of former large channels both laterally and from below, so that existing floodplains are contained in valley-bottom fills. Accidents of capture and glacial diversion apart, the underfit condition results generally from climatic shift. The last major shift responsible for channel shrinkage appears to have occurred in the interval 12,000–9,000 BP, or later in areas that were still ice-covered nine thousand years ago. Involving a reduction of bed width to as much as one-tenth of earlier values, and in meander wavelength by similar proportions, channel shrinkage is known to have been succeeded in well-studied areas by lesser fluctuations that are recorded in episodes of partial clearance followed by renewed fill. Significant alternations between cut and fill during the last 10,000 to 20,000 years have perhaps averaged a periodicity of one thousand to two thousand years. There is no a priori reason to suppose that the corresponding periodicity differed from this value during the whole Pleistocene, 2 million to 3 million years in duration so far. Inferences about pre-Pleistocene fluctuations await detailed analysis of rates of deposition of graded beds, coral growth, and the like.

On account of the temporal–dynamic qualities that have been discussed, river channels and networks are to be regarded as open systems (those open to additions or subtractions of materials or energy through time), whether in relation to short-term adjustments to individual peak discharges, in relation to accommodation to the constraints of climate, vegetal cover, characteristics of infiltration and overland flow, or in relation to the long-term influences of crustal movement, interbasin competition, and land wastage. Channels and networks experience inputs and outputs of matter and energy. Some of them, but probably a small minority at any one time and for a minor duration of total time in any one channel or network, act as open systems in disequilibrium. The general tendency seems to be for channel and river systems to attain steady-state conditions, wherein negative feedback tends to counter individual disequilibrium tendencies, and counteracting effects ensure variations about recurrent norms of form and behaviour.

CHAPTER 2
DRAINAGE PATTERNS AND GEOMETRY

Rivers follow the path of least resistance from their headwaters upstream to their terminal reaches downstream. The shape of river channels and the regions they drain are governed by the existing topography of a landscape and the geology that underlies it. Over their entire course, rivers widen, contract, straighten out, meander, and divide in response to changes in the landscape and as a result of the physical and chemical effects of flowing water on landscape features.

THE DRAINAGE PATTERNS OF RIVERS

Distinctive patterns are acquired by stream networks in consequence of adjustment to geologic structure. In the early history of a network, and also when erosion is reactivated by earth movement or a fall in sea level, downcutting by trunk streams and extension of tributaries are most rapid on weak rocks, especially if these are impermeable, and along master joints and faults. Tributaries from those streams that cut and grow the fastest encroach on adjacent basins, eventually capturing parts of the competing networks therein. In this way, the principal valleys with their main drainage lines come to reflect the structural pattern.

Flat-lying sedimentary rocks devoid of faults and strong joints and the flat glacial deposits of the Pleistocene Epoch (from approximately 2,600,000 to 11,700 years ago) exert no structural control at all: this is reflected in branching networks. A variant pattern, in which trunk streams run subparallel, can occur on tilted strata. Rectangular patterns form where drainage lines are adjusted to sets of faults and marked joints that intersect at about right angles, as in some parts of ancient crustal blocks. The pattern is varied where the regional angle of structural intersection changes. Radial drainage is typical of volcanic cones, so long as they remain more or less intact. Erosion to the skeletal state often leaves the plug standing in high relief, ringed by concentric valleys developed in thick layers of ash.

Similarly, on structural domes where the rocks of the core vary in strength, valleys and master streams locate on weak outcrops in annular patterns. Centripetal patterns are produced where drainage converges on a single outlet or sink, as in some craters, eroded structural domes with weak cores, parts of some limestone country, and enclosed desert depressions. Trellis (or espalier) drainage patterns result from adjustment to tight regional folding in which the folds plunge. Denudation produces a zigzag pattern of outcrops, and adjustment to this pattern produces a stream net in which the trunks are aligned on weak rocks exposed along fold axes and small feeder streams run down the sides of ridges cut on the stronger formations. Deranged patterns, in which channels are interrupted by lakes and swamps, characterize areas of modest relief from which continental ice has recently disappeared. These patterns may be developed either on the irregular surface of a till sheet (heterogeneous glacial deposit) or on the ice-scoured expanse of a planated crystalline block. Where a till sheet has been molded into drumlins (inverted-spoon-shaped forms that have been molded by moving ice), the postglacial drainage can approach a rectangular pattern. In glaciated highland, postglacial streams can pass anomalously through gaps if the divides have been breached by ice, and sheet glaciation of lowland country necessarily involves major derangement of river networks near the ice

Drumlins, inverted spoon-shaped forms, can shape postglacial drainage patterns. Shutterstock.com

front. At the other climatic extreme, organized networks in dry climates can be deranged by desiccation, which breaks down the existing continuity of a net. The largely linear systems of ephemeral lakes in inland Western Australia have been referred to this process.

Adjustment to bedrock structure can be lost if earth movement raises folds or moves faults across drainage lines without actually diverting them; streams that maintain their courses across the new structures are called antecedent. Adjustment is lost on a regional scale when the drainage cuts down through an unconformity into an under-mass with structures differing greatly from those of the cover: the drainage then becomes superimposed. Where the cover is simple in structure and provides a regional slope for trunk drainage, remnants of the original pattern may persist long after superimposition and the total destruction of the cover, providing the means to reconstruct the earlier network.

HORTON'S LAWS OF DRAINAGE COMPOSITION

Great advances in the analysis of drainage nets were made by Robert E. Horton, an American hydraulic engineer who developed the fundamental concept of stream order: An unbranched headstream is designated as a first-order stream. Two unbranched headstreams unite to form a second-order stream; two second-order streams unite to form a third-order stream, and so on. Regardless of the entry of first- and second-order tributaries, a third-order stream will not pass into the fourth order until it is joined by another third-order confluent. Stream number is the total number of streams of a given order for a given drainage basin. The bifurcation ratio is the ratio of the number of streams in a given order to the number in the next higher order. By definition, the value of this ratio cannot fall below 2.0, but it can rise higher, because streams greater than first order can receive low-order tributaries without being promoted up the hierarchy. Some estimates for large continental extents give bifurcation ratios of 4.0 or more.

Although the number system given here, and nowadays in common use, differs from Horton's original in the treatment of trunk streams, Horton's laws of drainage composition still hold, namely:

1. Law of stream numbers: the numbers of streams of different orders in a given drainage basin tend closely to approximate an inverse geometric series in which the first term is unity and the ratio is the bifurcation ratio.

2. Law of stream lengths: the average lengths of streams of each of the different orders in a drainage basin tend closely to approximate a direct geometric series in

which the first term is the average length of streams of the first order.

These laws are readily illustrated by plots of number and average length (on logarithmic scales) against order (on an arithmetic scale). The plotted points lie on, or close to, straight lines. The orderly relationships thus indicated are independent of network pattern. They demonstrate exponential relationships. Horton also concluded that stream slopes, expressed as tangents, decrease exponentially with increase in stream order. The systematic relationships identified by Horton are independent of network pattern: they greatly facilitate comparative studies, such as those of the influences of lithology and climate. Horton's successors have extended analysis through a wide range of basin geometry, showing that stream width, mean discharge, and length of main stem can also be expressed as exponential functions of order, and drainage area and channel slope as power functions. Slope and discharge can in turn be expressed as power functions of width and drainage area, respectively. The exponential relationships expressed by network morphometry are particular examples of the working of fundamental growth laws. In this respect, they relate drainage-net analysis to network analysis and topology in general.

MORPHOMETRY OF DRAINAGE NETWORKS

The functional relationships among various network characteristics, including the relationships between discharge on the one hand and drainage area, channel width, and length of main stem on the other, encourage the continued exploration of streamflow in relation to basin geometry. Attention has concentrated especially on peak flows, the forecasting of which is of practical importance.

And because many basins are gaged either poorly or not at all, it would be advantageous to devise means of prediction that, while independent of gaging records, are yet accurate enough to be useful.

A general equation for discharge maxima states that peak discharges are (or tend to be) power functions of drainage area. Such a relationship holds good for maximum discharges of record, but conflicting results have been obtained by empirical studies of stream order, stream length, drainage density, basin size, basin shape, stream and basin slope, aspect, and relative and absolute height in relation to individual peak discharges in the shorter term. One reason is that not all these parameters have always been dealt with. In any event, peak discharge is also affected by channel characteristics, vegetation, land use, and lags induced by interception, detention, evaporation, infiltration, and storage. Although frequency–intensity–duration characteristics (and, in consequence, magnitude characteristics) of single storms have been determined for considerable land areas, the distribution of a given storm is unlikely to fit the location of a given drainage basin. In addition, the peak flow produced by a particular storm is much affected by antecedent conditions, seasonal and shorter term wetting and drying of the soil considerably influencing infiltration and overland flow. Nevertheless, one large study attained considerable success by considering rainfall intensity for a given duration and frequency, plus basin area, and main-channel slope expressed as the height–distance relationship of points 85 and 10 percent of stem length above the station for which predictions were made. For practical purposes, the telemetering of rainfall in a catchment, combined with the empirical determination of its response characteristics, appears effective in forecasting individual peak flows.

STREAMBEDS

Streambeds, which are also called stream channels, appear as long, narrow, sloping depressions on land that have been shaped by flowing water. Streambeds can range in width from a few feet for a brook to several thousand for the largest rivers. The channel may or may not contain flowing water at any time; some carry water only occasionally. Streambeds may be cut in bedrock or through sand, clay, silt, or other unconsolidated materials commonly resulting from earlier stream deposition.

Stream channels cut in bedrock are generally more stable and usually have steeper slopes, less width, and greater local variations in gradient, with rapids and waterfalls being common. They most often occur in upstream areas and are somewhat straighter because they tend to follow faults, joints, or other weak structural elements. The downstream reaches of rivers or streams are commonly alluvial channels that have lower slopes and a general absence of rock ledges. These channels constantly shift vertically and laterally; and they are usually meandering, braided, or random, with few straight reaches. Narrow, more sinuous alluvial beds have a higher silt and clay composition than do straighter and wider beds. Sandy beds depend on vegetation to stabilize their banks.

The shape, or cross section, of a streambed is determined by a stream's discharge, the amount and size of sediment transported, and the resistance to erosion of the bedrock or alluvium of the banks and bottom. In its lower reaches, a larger stream (one with greater discharge) has a greater width-to-depth ratio. The side slopes are related to the silt-to-clay ratio of the sediments and to the erosive force of the flow. Steep banks generally occur in clay-rich materials. In many cases, the cross-section of a stream is almost trapezoidal and becomes asymmetrical along the curves of a stream's path, with the deepest part of the stream occurring at the outside of the curve.

To empirical analysis of the morphometry of drainage networks has been added theoretical inquiry. Network plan geometry is specifically a form of topological mathematics. Horton's two fundamental laws of drainage composition are instances of growth laws. They are witnessed in operation, especially when a new drainage network is developing; and, at the same time, probability statistics can be used to describe the array of events and forms produced.

Random-walk plotting, which involves the use of random numbers to lay out paths from a starting point, can produce networks that respond to analysis as do natural stream networks (i.e., length and number increase and decrease respectively, in exponential relationship to order, and length can be expressed as a power function of area). The exponential relationship between number and order signifies a constant bifurcation ratio throughout the network. A greater constancy in this respect would be expected from a randomly predicted network than from a natural network containing adventitious streams that join trunks of higher than one additional order. The exponential relationship between length and order in a random network follows from the assumption that the total area considered is drained to, and by, channels; the power relationship of length to area then also follows. The implication of the random-walk prediction of networks that obey the empirically derived laws of drainage composition is that natural networks correspond to, or closely approximate, the most probable states.

THE GEOMETRY OF RIVER SYSTEMS

The geometry of a river changes over its length. Such changes can be noted by observing differences in cross section between one point in the river or another, or they can be noted by viewing selected lengths of the river from above. In addition, some rivers contain waterfalls, which serve as major disruptions in river flow.

HYDRAULIC GEOMETRY

Hydraulic geometry deals with variation in channel characteristics in relation to variations in discharge. Two sets of variations take place: variations at a particular cross section (at-a-station) and variations along the length of the stream (downstream variations). Characteristics responsive to analysis by hydraulic geometry include width (water-surface width), depth (mean water depth), velocity (mean velocity through the cross section), sediment (usually concentration or transport, or both, of suspended sediment), downstream slope, and channel friction.

Graphs of the values of channel characteristics against values of discharge usually display some scatter or departure from lines of best fit. One main cause is that values on a rising flood often differ from those on a falling flood, partly because of the reduction of flow resistance, and hence the increase in velocity, as sediment-concentration increases on the rising flood. Bed scour and bed fill are also related. Nevertheless, the variations for a given cross section can be expressed as functions of discharge, Q. For instance, width, depth, and velocity are related to discharge by the expressions: $w \propto Q^b$, $d \propto Q^f$, and $v \propto Q^m$, where w, d, v and b, f, m are numerical constants. The sum of the exponents $b + f + m = 1$, because of the basic relation—namely that $Q = wdv$.

Similar functions can be derived for downstream variations, but, for downstream comparisons to be possible, the observed values of discharge and of channel characteristics must be referred to selected frequencies of discharge. When data are plotted on graphs with logarithmic scales for each of two discharge frequencies at an upstream and a downstream station, the four points for each channel characteristic define a parallelogram, whereby the hydraulic geometry of the stream is defined in respect of that characteristic. The values of exponents in the power equations differ considerably from one river to another: those shown here are theoretical optimum values. One common cause of difference is that many gaging stations are located where some channel characteristics are controlled, whether naturally as by rock outcrops or artificially as by bridge abutments. Constraints on variation in width, for instance, are mainly offset by increased variation in depth.

Analyses of downstream variation in channel slope with discharge commonly reveal contrasts between field results and the theoretical optima. The discrepancy is probably due in considerable part to the fact that the channel slope can vary in concert with channel efficiency, including channel habit, channel size, and channel form. Many past discussions of stream slope are invalidated by their restriction to the two dimensions of height and distance. In any event, the slopes of many natural channels are influenced by some combination of earth movement, change in baselevel, glacial erosion, glacial deposition, and change of discharge and load characteristics that result from change of climate. Consequently, although natural profiles from stream source to stream mouth suggest a tendency toward a smooth concave-upward form, many actually are irregular. Even without a change of baselevel, degradational tendency, or discharge, a change in channel sinuosity can produce a significant change of channel slope.

A marked downstream lessening of slope does not imply a decrease in velocity at a given frequency of discharge. Reduction of slope is accompanied, and offset, by an increase in channel efficiency mainly because of an increase in size. The lower Amazon, with a slope of less than 7.6 cm (3 inches) per 1.6 km (1 mile), flows faster at the bankfull stage than many mountain streams, at 2.4 metres (about 8 feet) per second. According to the assumptions made, an optimal velocity equation in hydraulic geometry can predict a slight increase, constancy, or a slight decrease in velocity downstream, for a given frequency of discharge. On the Mississippi, velocity at mean discharge (not a set frequency) increases downstream. Velocity at the overbank stages of the five-year and 50-year floods is constant downstream. Constant downstream velocity may well be first attained at the bank-full stage. The fact that relationships are highly disturbed at and near waterfalls and other major breaks of slope (the Paraná just below the site of the former Guaíra Falls, for instance, ran at 9 to 14 metres [30 to 46 feet] per second) has no bearing on the principles of hydraulic geometry, which apply essentially to streams in adjustable channels.

The interrelationships and adjustments among width, depth, width–depth ratio, suspended-sediment concentration, sediment transport, deposition, eddy viscosity, bed roughness, bank roughness, channel roughness, and channel slope in their relation to discharge, both at-a-station and in the downstream direction, plus the tendency at many sections on many streams for variation to occur about some modal value, all encourage the conception of rivers as equilibrium systems. The designation quasi-equilibrium systems is usually used, because not all variances can be simultaneously minimized, and minimization of some variances (e.g., of water-surface slope) can only be secured at the expense of maximizing others (e.g., channel depth).

RIVER CHANNEL PATTERNS

Distinctive patterns in the plan geometry of streams correspond to distinctive combinations of cross-sectional form, calibre of bed load, downstream slope, and in some cases cross-valley slope, tendency to cut or fill, or position within the system. The full range of pattern has not been identified: it includes straight, meandering, braided, reticulate, anabranching, distributary, and irregular patterns. Although individual patterns are given separate names, the total range constitutes a continuum.

STRAIGHT CHANNELS

Straight channels, mainly unstable, develop along the lines of faults and master joints, on steep slopes where rills closely follow the surface gradient, and in some delta outlets. Flume experiments show that straight channels of uniform cross section rapidly develop pool-and-riffle sequences. Pools are spaced at about five bed widths. Lateral shift of alternate pools toward alternate sides produces sinuous channels, and spacing of pools on each side of the channel is thus five to seven bed widths. This relation holds in natural meandering streams.

MEANDERING CHANNELS

Meandering channels are single channels that are sinuous in plan, but there is no criterion, except an arbitrary one, of the degree of sinuousity required before a channel is called meandering. The spacing of bends is controlled by flow resistance, which reaches a minimum when the radius of the bend is between two and three times the width of the bed. Accordingly, meander wavelength, the distance between two successive bends on the same side—or four-bend radii—tends to concentrate between eight and 12 bed widths, although variation both within and beyond this range seems to be related to variations in the cross-sectional form of the channel. Because bed width is related to discharge, meander wavelength also is related to discharge.

Meandering channels are equilibrium features that represent the most probable channel plan geometry, where single channels deviate from straightness. This deviation, and channel division in general, is related in part to the cohesiveness of channel banks and the abundance and bulk of midstream bars. When single channels are maintained, however, the meandering form is most efficient because it minimizes variance in water-surface slope, in angle of deflection of the current, and in the work done by the river in turning. This least-work property of meander bends is readily illustrated by the trace, identical with that of stream meanders, adopted by a bent band of spring steel. Meander plan geometry is simply describable by a sine function of the relative distance along the channel bend. The least-work and minimum-variance properties of the plan geometry, however, are secured only at the expense of maximizing the variance in depth. The longitudinal profile of the bed of a meandering stream includes pools at (or slightly downstream of) the extremities of bends and riffles at the inflections between bends. Increased tightness of bend, expressed by reduction in radius and increase in total angle of deflection, is accompanied by increased depth of pool. Where riffles are built of fragments larger than sand size, they behave as kinematic waves. In other words, the speed of transport of material through a given riffle decreases as the spacing of surface fragments decreases, and the total rate of transport attains a maximum where the spacing is about two particle lengths. Numerous sand-bed streams in dry regions, however, fail to develop pool-and-riffle sequences, maintaining approximately uniform cross sections even at channel bends.

Irregularities in meanders developed in alluvium relate primarily to uneven resistance, which is often a function of varying grain size. Variations in total sinuosity are probably in the main caused by adjustments of channel slope. The process of cutoff (short-circuiting of individual meanders) is favoured not only by the erosion of outer channel banks and by the tendency of meander trains to sweep down the valley but also by the stacking of meanders upstream of obstacles and by increases of sinuosity that accompany slope reduction.

Meandering streams that cut deeply into bedrock form entrenched meanders, the terminology of which is highly confused. It seems probable that, in actuality, the sole existing type of entrenched meanders is the ingrown type, where undercut slopes (river cliffs) on the outsides of bends oppose slip-off slopes (meander lobes) on the insides. For reasons not yet understood, lateral enlargement of ingrown meanders seems habitually to outpace downstream sweep, although the trimming of the upstream sides of lobes, and occasional cutoff, are well known. Many existing trains of ingrown meanders belong to valleys rather than to streams, relating to the traces of former rivers of greater discharge. Reconstruction of the original traces indicates approximate straightness at plateau level, as opposed to the inheritance of the ingrown loops from some former high-level floodplain.

In a broader context, meander phenomena cannot be understood as requiring cohesive banks of the kind usual in rivers. Meanders, with geometry comparable to that of rivers, have been recognized in the oceanic Gulf Stream and in the jet streams of the upper atmosphere. In this way, stream meanders are classed with wave phenomena in general.

BRAIDED CHANNELS

Braided channels are subdivided at low-water stages by multiple midstream bars of sand or gravel. At high water, many or all bars are submerged, although continuous downcutting or fixation by plants, or both, plus the trapping of sediment may enable some bars to remain above water. A single meandering channel may convert to braiding where one or more bars are constructed, as downstream of a tight bend where coarse material is brought up from the pool bottom. Each

New Zealand's Tasman Glacier terminus is a braided river. These form when there are weak banks, high width-to-depth ratio, strong shear on the streambed, and mobile bed material. Steve Casimiro/The Image Bank/Getty Images

of the subdivided channels is less efficient, being smaller than the original single channel. If its inefficiency is compensated by an increase in slope (i.e., by downcutting), the bar dries out and becomes vegetated and stabilized. However, many rivers that are largely or wholly braided along their length owe their condition to something more than local accidents. The braided condition involves weak banks, a very high width–depth ratio, powerful shear on the streambed (implied by the width–depth ratio), and mobile bed material. Thus, braided streams are typically encountered near the edges of land ice, where valleys are being filled with incoherent coarse sediment, and also on outwash plains, as the Canterbury Plains of South Island, New Zealand. Width–depth ratios can exceed 1,000:1. Studies on terraced outwash plains demonstrate that braided streams can readily excavate their valley floors—in other words, they are by no means solely an inevitable response to valley filling.

Distributary patterns, whether on alluvial fans or deltas, pose few problems. A delta pass that lengthens is liable to lateral breaching, whereas continued deposition, on deltas and on fans, raises the channel bed and promotes sideways spill down the least gradient. The branching rivers of inland eastern Australia, flowing across basin fills that range from thin sedimentary plains to thick fluvial accumulations, have affinities with deltaic distributaries even though their patterns are only radial in part. A branch may run for tens of kilometres before joining a trunk stream, whether its own or another.

WATERFALLS

Waterfalls, sometimes called cataracts, arise from an abrupt steepening of a river channel that causes the flow of water to drop vertically, or nearly so. Waterfalls of small height and lesser steepness are called cascades, a term often applied to a series of small falls along a river. Still gentler reaches of rivers that nonetheless exhibit turbulent flow and white water in response to a local increase in channel gradient are rapids.

Waterfalls are characterized by great erosive power. The rapidity of erosion depends on the height of a given waterfall, its volume of flow, the type and structure of the rocks involved, and other factors. In some cases the site of the waterfall migrates upstream by headward erosion of the cliff or scarp, whereas in others erosion tends to act downward to bevel the entire reach of river containing the falls. With the passage of time, by either or both of these means, the inescapable tendency of streams is to eliminate so gross a discordance of longitudinal profile as a waterfall. The energy of all rivers is directed toward the achievement of a relatively smooth, concave-upward, longitudinal profile; this is a common equilibrium, or adjusted condition, in nature.

Even in the absence of entrained rock debris that serves as an erosive tool of rivers, it is intuitively obvious that the energy available for erosion at the base of a waterfall is great. Indeed, one of the characteristic features associated with waterfalls of any great magnitude—with respect to volume of flow as well as to height—is the presence of a plunge pool, a basin that is scoured out of the river channel directly beneath the falling water. In some instances the depth of a plunge pool may nearly equal the height of the cliff causing the falls. Its depth depends not only on the erosive power of the falls, however, but also on the amount of time during which the falls remain at a particular place. The channel of the Niagara River below Horseshoe Falls, for example, contains a series of plunge pools, each of which represents a stillstand, or period of temporary stability, during the general upriver migration of the waterfall. The significance of this profile will be discussed in the following text, but in general it may be said that the fate of most waterfalls is their eventual transformation to rapids as a result of their own erosive energy.

The lack of permanence as a landscape feature is, in fact, the hallmark of all waterfalls. Many well-known occurrences such as the Niagara Falls came into existence as recently as 11,700 years ago, when the last of the great ice sheets retreated from middle latitudes. The oldest falls originated during the Neogene Period (23 million to 2.6 million years ago), when episodes of uplift raised the great plateaus and escarpments of Africa and South America. Examples of waterfalls attributable to such pre-Pleistocene uplift (which occurred more than 2.6 million years ago) include Kalambo Falls, near Lake Tanganyika; Tugela Falls, in South Africa; Tisisat Falls, at the headwaters of the Blue Nile on the Ethiopian Plateau; and Angel Falls, in Venezuela.

Paulo Afonso Falls on the São Francisco River, Alagoas, Brazil. Antonio Gusmao—TYBA/Agencia Fotografica Ltda.

Available data suggest that the falls of greatest height are seldom those of greatest water discharge. Many falls in excess of 300 metres (about 980 feet) exhibit but modest flow, and, in some cases, only a perpetual mist occurs near their bases. By way of contrast, the Khone Falls of the Mekong River in southern Laos, drop only 22 metres (72 feet), but the average discharge of this cataract is about 11,330 cubic metres (400,000 cubic feet) per second. In general, considering height and volume of flow jointly, it is understandable that Victoria, Niagara, and Paulo Afonso, among others, have each been proclaimed "the world's greatest falls" by various explorers and authorities.

THE WORLD DISTRIBUTION OF WATERFALLS

The distribution of waterfalls is not uniform, and large parts of the world are free of any notable occurrence. This is not surprising in view of the relatively large proportion of the Earth's land area that consists of deserts and semi-arid areas, which are understandably devoid of modern falls on climatic grounds. Ice-covered polar regions and relatively unbroken, low-lying plains and plateaus also are unfavourable sites of development.

Considered on a global basis, waterfalls tend to occur in three principal kinds of areas: (1) along the margins of high plateaus or the great fractures that dissect them; (2) along fall lines, which mark a zone between resistant crystalline rocks of continental interiors and weaker sedimentary formations of coastal regions; and (3) in high mountain areas, particularly those that were subjected to glaciation in the recent past.

High Plateaus

Notable falls along high plateaus include the world's highest, Angel Falls of the Churún River, Venezuela, with a drop of 979 metres (3,200 feet) and overall relief of more than 1,100 metres (3,600 feet); Tugela Falls, issuing from

Iguaçu Falls extend for 1.7 miles (2.7 km) and, during the rainy season, may rise as much as of 450,000 cubic feet (12,750 cubic metres) per second. Shutterstock.com

the Great Escarpment, South Africa, which is 948 metres (3,100 feet) in height; Victoria Falls (108 metres [350 feet]) on the Zimbabwe–Zambia border; and Kalambo Falls (427 metres [1,400 feet]) on the Tanzania–Zambia border. The volume of flow at Victoria Falls is relatively large, approximately 1,080 cubic metres (38,000 cubic feet) per second, but Guaíra Falls, a series of falls that until their submergence by the waters of Itaipú Dam in 1982 totaled 114 metres (375 feet) along the Paraná River, Brazil–Paraguay, had the largest known average discharge—13,300 cubic metres (about 470,000 cubic feet) per second. During flood stages, however, even this figure is exceeded at some falls along the Orange River and elsewhere. Angel Falls, Iguaçu Falls (82 metres [270 feet]), in Brazil, and several others occur along the margins of high plateaus, east of the Andes, between Venezuela and Argentina.

IGUAÇU FALLS

Iguaçu Falls (Spanish: Cataratas del Iguazú, Portuguese: Cataratas do Iguaçu or Saltos do Iguaçu) is a series of cataracts on the Iguaçu River, 23 km (14 miles) above its confluence with the Alto (Upper) Paraná River, at the Argentina-Brazil border. The falls resemble an elongated horseshoe that extends for 2.7 km (1.7 miles)—nearly three times wider than Niagara Falls in North America and significantly greater than the width of Victoria Falls in Africa. Numerous rocky and wooded islands on the edge of the escarpment over which the Iguaçu River plunges divide the falls into some 275 separate waterfalls or cataracts, varying between 60 and 82 metres (200 and 269 feet) in height. The name of the falls, like that of the river, is derived from a Guaraní word meaning "great water."

The rate of flow of the falls may rise to a maximum of 12,750 cubic metres (450,000 cubic feet) per second during the rainy season from November to March. Minimum flow occurs during the dry season from August to October. The mean annual rate of flow is about 1,756 cubic metres (62,000 cubic feet) per second.

The falls occur along a wide span where the Iguaçu River, flowing westward and then northward, tumbles over the edge of the Paraná Plateau before continuing its course in a canyon. Above the falls, islands and islets spread the river into numerous flows that feed the cataracts. A major portion of the river tumbles into a narrow, semi-circular chasm called the Garganta do Diabo (Spanish: Garganta del Diablo ["Devil's Throat"]), the effect of which has been described as "an ocean plunging into an abyss." Excellent views of this section (also called Union Falls) can be obtained from both the Brazilian and Argentine sides. With many of the individual falls broken midway by protruding ledges, the resultant deflection of the water, as well as the spray that arises, creates an array of rainbows. From the foot of the Garganta do Diabo, a curtain of mist rises some 150 metres (500 feet) into the air.

Among the many islands along the falls, the most notable is Isla Grande San Martín, which is situated downstream from the Garganta do Diabo (on the Argentine side). This island offers a fine view of many of the cataracts. Individual falls to be seen from the forest paths and trails on the Argentine side include those known as Dos Hermanas ("Two Sisters"), Bozzetti, San Martín, Escondido ("Hidden"), and Rivadavia. From the Brazilian shore, an impressive panorama of falls can also be seen. Among individual Brazilian falls are those known as Benjamin Constant, Deodoro, and Floriano.

The first Spanish explorer to visit the falls was Álvar Núñez Cabeza de Vaca in 1541. In 1897 Edmundo de Barros, a Brazilian army officer, envisaged the establishment of a national park at Iguaçu Falls. Following boundary rectifications between Brazil and Argentina, two separate national parks were established, one by each country — Iguaçu National Park (1939) in Brazil and Iguazú National Park (1934) in Argentina. Both parks were created to preserve the vegetation, wildlife, and scenic beauty associated with the falls. In 1984 the Argentine park was designated a UNESCO World Heritage site, and two years later the Brazilian park was also granted World Heritage status.

Fall Lines

Waterfalls that occur along fall lines are in some cases relatively indistinguishable from plateau examples — the Aughrabies Falls (146 metres [480 feet]), for instance, which occur where the Orange River leaves resistant crystalline rocks of the plateau in southern Africa. The typical fall-line example, however, occurs at the junction of the crystalline rocks of the Appalachian Mountains and the sedimentary coastal plain along the eastern United States. A number of major cities, including Philadelphia, Baltimore, and Washington, D.C., are a geographic consequence of the existence of falls along this line or zone because they present barriers to further inland navigation. In England there is an analogous example with respect to the line of towns including Cambridge that borders the Fens. The most spectacular fall-line waterfalls, however, include Churchill (formerly Grand) Falls, Labrador, Canada (75 metres [about 250 feet]); Jog Falls (Gersoppa Falls), Karnātaka, India (253 metres [830 feet]); and Paulo Afonso Falls, Brazil (84 metres [275 feet]).

Glaciated Mountains

The last category, mountainous and formerly glaciated regions, include such well-known waterfalls as Yosemite Falls, California (739 metres [about 2,400 feet]), with a three-section drop; Yellowstone Falls, Wyoming (94 metres [about 300 feet]), with a two-section drop; Sutherland Falls, South Island, New Zealand (580 metres [1,900 feet]); and Krimmler Waterfall, Austria (380 metres [about 1,250 feet]). Other falls of considerable height or volume of flow occur elsewhere in mountainous and formerly glaciated regions—namely, in the Alps, the Sierra Nevada and northern Rocky Mountains of North America, and South Island, New Zealand. The ice-free parts of Iceland and the fjord (drowned-valley) region of Norway also should be cited. Both areas contain numerous falls by reason of suitable topography and climate. Australia also has a few falls, notably the Wollomombi, in the Great Dividing Range, New South Wales (482 metres [about 1,600 feet]).

TYPES OF WATERFALLS

The several types of waterfalls that occur in nature may be classified according to a variety of schemes. One of the simplest of these is based on principal region of occurrence—high plateaus, fall lines, and formerly glaciated mountains, as discussed earlier. More meaningful, however, is an alternate, threefold classification system that places more emphasis on the specific ways in which geologic and physiographic conditions produce and affect waterfalls. Thus, falls can be categorized as: (1) those attributable to natural discordance of river profiles, whether caused by faulting (vertical movements of the Earth's crust), glaciation, or other processes; (2) those attributable to differential erosion, which occurs whenever weak and resistant rocks are juxtaposed in some way; and (3) those attributable to constructional processes that create barriers and dams, over which water must fall. These three basic types will be discussed in turn.

Falls Attributable to River Profile Discordance

In one sense, all falls must be attributable to a discordance of river profile by their very definition. This category is here arbitrarily restricted, however, to exclude profile breaks that are caused by differential erosion and constructional processes. Remaining are waterfalls along fault scarps, uplifted plateaus and cliffs, glacial features of several kinds, karst topography—the caves and cave systems produced by solution of carbonate rocks—and falls that result from the issuance of springs from canyon walls high above valley floors.

The enormous rigid plates that make up the outer shell of the Earth continually move relative to one another, resulting in seafloor spreading, continental drift, and mountain building. These large-scale motions cause a buildup of strain within the rocks of the crust at some depth below the surface. Ultimately, the rocks must yield or shift in order to release this strain, and, when they suddenly do so, an earthquake results. Commonly, there will be some visible evidence of this sudden release at the Earth's surface, perhaps manifested by the creation of a cliff or series of cliffs along a line or zone. The sloping surfaces that form the cliff fronts are called fault scarps. The vertical movements that produce fault scarps seldom amount to more than about 3 metres (about 10 feet) during an individual earthquake. Repeated faulting along the same line or zone, however, can produce scarps that are thousands of metres in height in relatively brief periods of geologic time. Waterfalls occur where the faults cross established drainage systems. The ultimate height of such falls depends not only on the total height of uplift but also on the rate of downcutting by the affected rivers. Rates of uplift tend to exceed rates of downcutting considerably in those parts of the world where uplift is ongoing today. Hence, it is normal for high waterfalls to exist due to uplift in many areas. In addition, some plateaus are produced by broader, regional uplifts that are relatively continuous and are not associated with earthquakes. The heights attained are nevertheless comparable after suitable time intervals. Major rift (fracture) systems of continental or subcontinental scale, some sea cliffs, and other features of this nature also are attributable to some form of faulting. All of them provide suitable sites for waterfall development.

The processes of glaciation have served this same end. Mountain ranges that formerly were glaciated contain falls at the outlets of cirques, bowl-shaped depressions in the headwaters of drainage areas that were formed by the accumulation of ice and its erosive action on the underlying bedrock. In addition, waterfalls are most common where hanging valleys occur. Such valleys generally form when glacier ice deeply erodes a main or trunk valley, leaving tributary valleys literally hanging far above the main valley floor. After the glaciers have melted and withdrawn, streams from such tributary valleys must fall in order to join the main valley drainage system below. Hanging valleys also can occur in response to faulting and in some other non-glacial situations: the chalk cliffs of England, for example, where small streams cannot cut downward with sufficient rapidity to keep pace with backwearing of the cliffs by marine erosion.

Other features that may result from glaciation include glacial potholes and glacial steps. The former are thought to originate principally as a result of the plastic flow of ice at the base of a glacier, which permits the gouging of semicylindrical holes in the bedrock beneath the path of flow. The holes or depressions are subsequently enlarged and

Waterfalls may occur at the outlets of cirques, which were formed in once-glaciated ranges such as Montana's Pioneer Mountains. Dr. Marli Miller/ Visuals Unlimited/Getty Images

deepened by meltwater runoff that is heavily laden with gravels, and they have become the sites of modern cascades in many instances.

The steps (or glacial stairway, as this feature is sometimes called) consist of treads and risers on a relatively giant scale that have been produced by the passage of ice over bedrock, particularly when alternating rock properties or joints offer differential resistance to the flow of ice. Again, the establishment of runoff after wastage of the ice has occurred will lead to a series of waterfalls or cascades at the site of each riser in the stairway.

Most spectacular among glacial features, however, are the overdeepened valleys along formerly glaciated coasts, as in Norway. These fjords are intimately associated with falls because the valley walls typically are both high and steep and because hanging valleys are ubiquitous.

Like the potholes previously mentioned, the solution of limestones and other carbonate rocks leads to the formation of pits, sinks, caves, and interconnected systems of caverns, which together are termed karst topography. Terrain of this kind commonly contains water in many of the included passages in the form of standing pools, streams, and, where discontinuities of cavern levels occur, waterfalls. There are a few parts of the world where karst topography and its associated drainage are prominent features of the landscape, but, on the whole, falls attributable to cave-forming processes are not numerous. Springs that issue from canyon walls high above main valley floors are in the same category. Most of these artesian (free-flowing) systems result from the same type of solution phenomenon along joints and fractures that produce caves in carbonate rocks.

Falls Attributable to Differential Erosion

Rocks differ markedly with regard to their resistance to erosion by running water. Although no quantitative scales to express this difference have been developed, widespread agreement exists on certain generalities. Metamorphic rocks (those that are formed from pre-existing rocks under the action of high temperatures and pressures), for example, are commonly more durable than are sedimentary rocks, and great differences can exist even among the latter because of a significant amount of variation in the degree of cementation and kinds of rock structure present in them. Thus, a quartz-rich sandstone whose constituent grains are cemented by silica tends to be much more resistant than a fissile shale, the clay-rich layers of which tend to split and separate. And the blocky character of some carbonate rocks (limestones and dolomites) and extrusive igneous rocks (formed by the cooling of lava flows) tends to enhance their resistance to fluvial erosion, notwithstanding their relatively low resistance to solution.

Regardless of the intrinsic toughness of any rock type, however, lengthy periods of weathering or the presence of intricate fracture patterns will render it easily erodible. There are, in fact, a veritable legion of factors that influence rock resistance to erosion, and it is for this reason that generalities must be invoked. Suffice it to say that some rocks are weak whereas others are strong and that waterfalls are promoted where these occur in certain geologic arrangements.

There are three such arrangements that are common in nature: (1) horizontal or nearly horizontal strata in which rocks of greater resistance overlie weaker rocks, forming a protective cap rock; (2) inclined strata involving beds or layers of alternating resistance; and (3) various kinds of non-sedimentary rock arrangements in which dikes or veins of hard crystalline rocks are juxtaposed with weaker rocks. In each of these cases the weaker rocks are eroded more readily and more rapidly by running water, and the harder, resistant rocks, as a consequence, stand higher and are "falls makers." In the special case of the cap-rock arrangement, waterfalls migrate upriver because the protective upper layers break off as the weaker supporting strata are eroded from beneath. Niagara Falls is the most notable example involving sedimentary rocks (a blocky dolomite cap overlies a series of less-resistant shales and sandstones). More commonly, a lava flow caps erodible strata.

Falls Attributable to Constructional Processes

There are four principal constructional processes that can lead to the creation of dams or barriers and, hence, to the formation of waterfalls. These processes are (1) precipitation of calcium carbonate from solution; (2) disruption of drainage by lava flows or the deposition of volcanic ash and other pyroclastic sediments; (3) ice damming and the construction of moraines, or ridgelike sedimentary deposits left at the sites of former glaciers; and (4) the deposition of landslide and avalanche debris.

The first of these, carbonate precipitation, can accumulate to considerable dimensions as spring deposits of travertine or calcareous tufa, often in a series of terraces. Where these ultimately block avenues of normal runoff, waterfalls result. The water in limestone caves also is rich in calcium carbonate, and where ponds occur in the path of small subterranean streams there is preferential precipitation at the spillage rims. The barriers that are raised are self-perpetuating, can attain heights of about 15 metres (about 50 feet) under certain circumstances, and have been called rimstone dams and falls.

Volcanic activity, principally in the form of basaltic lava flows, is related to waterfall development in many parts of the world. The flows compose the bulk of such great plateau areas as the Columbia River region of the United States and the Deccan Plateau in India and often serve as cap rock. The association of falls with plateaus in general and with cap-rock arrangements was noted previously, but, in addition, some falls result from drainage diversion and the ponding of streams and rivers by lava dams. This has occurred in some parts of New Zealand, Iceland, and Hawaii and, in general, in regions where volcanic activity is a prominent aspect of the landscape.

Ice dams can produce similar effects. One of the most interesting examples is Dry Falls, a "fossil waterfall" in the Columbia River Plateau, Washington, which formed in late Pleistocene time. A large ice sheet blocked and diverted the then-westward-flowing Columbia River and formed a vast glacial lake. The lake drained to the south when permitted to do so by periodically occurring ice dams, and torrents of water were released during these breakouts. The water flowed through the Grand Coulee channel and eroded a canyon nearly 300 metres (about 1,000 feet) deep. Dry Falls, about 120 metres (about 400 feet) high and 5 km wide (about 3 miles), occurs along this flow path. The Columbia River has reestablished its path to the sea since the disappearance of the ice sheet, so the falls are dry today.

The magnitudes of flow that must have occurred during the Pleistocene, however, can be appreciated from data on some of the great glacier outburst floods (*jøkulhlaups*) of modern history. The breaching of an ice dam at Grímsvötn, Ice., in 1922, for example, released about 7.1 cubic km (1.7 cubic miles) of water, and the discharge attained a value of 57,000 cubic metres (about 2 million cubic feet) per second.

There are other depositional features that may pond and dam streams, notably glacial moraines—which attain heights as great as 250 metres (about 800 feet) in the formerly glaciated valleys of the Alps—and landslides, avalanches, and other downslope movements of earth materials into valleys. The associated falls tend to be rather ephemeral, however, because all such unconsolidated material is cut through relatively swiftly, and smooth stream gradients are reestablished. The damming action of lava flows and glacier ice is far more important in nature. The lava flows consist of more durable material, and ice damming leads to outburst floods and great attendant erosion.

THE DEVELOPMENT OF WATERFALLS

With the passage of time a particular waterfall must either migrate upstream, as in the case of a cap-rock falls, or serve as the locus for general downcutting along the reach of river containing the falls. In either case, the process depends on the height of the falls, the volume of flow, and the nature and arrangement of the rocks involved. Any discussion of waterfall development requires knowledge of these three factors and, more importantly, knowledge of the former locations and configurations of any particular waterfall under consideration. If the changes of location through time are lacking, then rates of waterfall recession are basically indeterminate.

The available data on the recession of the Horseshoe Falls of the Niagara River are little short of astonishing in comparison to the general paucity of such information elsewhere. Instrumental surveys of the configuration and position of Horseshoe Falls were made in 1842, 1875, 1886, 1890, 1905, 1927, and 1950. Still earlier delineations of position were provided by visual observations as long ago as 1678. For this reason, general waterfall development must be considered in terms of the Horseshoe Falls example. It should be noted, however, that the recession rates pertaining to this cap-rock-type falls are not necessarily average rates for all falls of this kind. They certainly do not apply to non-cap-rock falls in crystalline rocks, for example, where much slower rates generally prevail.

The average rate of recession of any falls can be determined from knowledge of the total upstream distance of migration and the time period during which the migration occurred. In the case of Horseshoe Falls, the total distance involved is about 12 km (7.5 miles), and retreat of the falls has been accomplished in approximately 12,500 years, since the disappearance of the most recent ice sheet from the area. The average rate of recession is therefore about 1 metre (3 feet) per year. The several instrumental surveys, however, suggest that a rate of 1.2 metres (4 feet) per year occurred during the 1842–75 period and 2 metres (about 7 feet) per year during the 1875–1905 period.

By way of comparison, the average recession rate for the American Falls, which occur downstream and to one side of Horseshoe Falls because of branching by the Niagara River, is only 8 cm (3.1 inches) per year. And, in a comparable vein, upstream migration of the Gullfoss in Iceland during the last 10,000 years is estimated to have occurred at an average recession rate of 25 cm (10 inches) per year. This is, again, a far slower rate of falls recession than has occurred at Horseshoe Falls.

To some extent the various recession rates are related to differential resistance of the rocks to erosion. Indeed, the discrepancy between the 1842–75 and 1875–1905 rates for Horseshoe Falls have been attributed in the past not only to possible surveying errors but also to the relative abundance of joints (fractures) in different parts of the dolomite cap rock. One study of Horseshoe Falls suggests, however, that another factor is of still greater importance—namely, the configuration of the crest of the falls and the relative stability of differing kinds of configurations.

CHAPTER 3
STREAMFLOW AND SEDIMENT YIELD

Sediment is the name for bits of rock, soil, and other particulate material deposited by wind, water, or glaciers. Rivers are vehicles of sediment transport. However, the speed at which the water in the river travels and the volume of water delivered downstream by the river is not constant. Both factors govern the amount of sediment delivered downstream. However, the water's speed and volume are themselves governed by changes in precipitation, the melting rate of snow and ice, the topography of the landscape, and other factors.

PEAK DISCHARGE AND FLOODING

Rapid variations of water-surface level in river channels through time, in combination with the occurrence from time to time of overbank flow in flat-bottomed valleys, have promoted intensive study of the discharge relationships and the probability characteristics of peak flow. Stage (depth or height of flow) measurements treat water level: discharge measurements require determinations of velocity through the cross section. Although records of stage respond to frequency analysis, the analysis of magnitude and frequency is preferable wherever stage is affected by progressive scour or fill, and also where channels have been artificially embanked or enlarged or both. The velocity determinations needed to calculate discharge range from those obtained with portable Venturi flumes on very small streams, through observations with gaging staff or fixed Venturi flumes on streams of modest size, to soundings with current meters at intervals of width and depth at cross sections of large rivers. Frequent velocity observations on large rivers are impracticable. It is standard practice to establish a rating formula, expressed graphically by a rating curve. Such a curve relates height of water surface to the area of and velocity through the cross section and thus to discharge. Secular changes in rating occur where a stream tends progressively to raise or lower its bed elevation. Short-term changes are common where the bed is mobile and especially where the bed elevation–discharge relation, and thus the stage–discharge relation, differs between the rising and the falling limb of a single peak discharge curve. In such cases the rating curve describes a hysteresis loop. Rating curves for sand-bed streams can include discontinuities, chiefly during rising discharge, that relate to behavioral jumps on the part of the bed.

Floods in hydrology are any peak discharges, regardless of whether or not the valley floor (if present) is inundated. The time–discharge or time–stage characteristics of a given flood peak are graphed in the hydrograph, which tends to assume a set form for a given station in response to a given input of water. The peak flow produced by a single storm is superimposed on the base flow, the water already in the channel and being supplied from the groundwater reservoir. Rise to peak discharge is relatively swift and is absolutely swift in small basins and on torrents where the duration of the momentary peak is also short. On very large streams, by contrast, peak discharge can be sustained for lengths of days. Recession from peak discharge is usually exponential. The form of the hydrograph for any one station is affected by characteristics of the channel and the drainage net, as well as by basin geometry, all of which can be taken as permanent in this context.

As noted earlier, flood-flow prediction that is based on permanent characteristics has hitherto achieved but partial success. Transient influences, also highly and at times overwhelmingly important, include the storage capacity of bedrock and soil, the interrelationships of infiltration, evaporation, and interception and detention (especially by vegetation), plus storm characteristics, which vary widely with respect to amount, duration, intensity, and location of rainfall with respect to the catchment.

In the longer term, flood-frequency analysis based on recorded past events can nevertheless supply useful predictions of future probabilities and risks. Flood-frequency analysis deals with the incidence of peak discharges, whereas frequency analysis generally provides the statistical basis of hydraulic geometry. Percentage frequency analysis has been much used in engineering: here, the 1 percent and 90 percent discharges, for instance, are those that are equalled or exceeded 1 and 90 percent of time, respectively. General observations of the flashy character of floods in headwater streams, in contrast to the long durations of flood waves far downstream, combine with analytical studies to suggest, however, that percentage frequency is in some respects an unsuitable measure. Magnitude–frequency analysis, setting discharge against time, is directly applicable in studies of hydraulic geometry and flood-probability forecasting.

Regional graphs of magnitude–frequency can be developed, given adequate records, for floods of any desired frequency or magnitude. Predictions for great magnitudes and low frequencies, however, demand records longer than those usually available. Twelve years of record are needed to define the mean annual flood within 25 percent, with an expectation of correct results for 95 percent of time. And in general, a record should be at least twice as long as the greatest recurrence interval for which magnitude is desired.

Predictions of overbank flow, whether or not affected by artificial works, are relevant to floodplain risk and floodplain management. Notably in the conterminous United States, floodplain zoning is causing risks to be reduced by the withdrawal of installations from the most flood-liable portions of floodplains or risks to be totally accepted by occupiers.

In the long geomorphic term the transmission of sediment through floodplain storage systems and through stream channels seems to result mainly from the operation of processes of modest magnitude and high frequency. Specifically, analyses suggest that total sediment transport by rivers is normally affected by flows approximating bankfull over durations ranging down from 25 to 1 percent of total time. Infrequent discharges of great magnitude, which can be expected on grounds of the probabilities of precipitation, snowmelt, and streamflow, range widely in destructive effect. Severe flooding is normally accompanied by great loss of life and property damage, the mean annual floods along the Huang He themselves affecting some 29,800 square km (11,500 square miles) of floodplain, but geomorphic effects may be minimal, even with very large floods. The approximately one-hundred-year floods of eastern England in the spring of 1947, fed by unusually great and deferred snowmelt, scarcely affected either channels or floodplains. The 1955 floods in Connecticut, fed by rains amounting to 58 cm (23 inches) in places, produced only spotty effects of erosion and deposition, even where floodplains were inundated to a depth of 6 metres (20 feet). For a given valley, there could be a threshold of inundation, river velocity, and sediment load, beyond which drastic changes occur. This is suggested, for example, by the catastrophic alluviation of valleys in eastern Australia and New Zealand during the last four thousand or two thousand years.

Sudden catastrophes in historical and geomorphic records are related to special events, mainly nonrecurrent: the 1841 Indus flood, which destroyed an army; the Gohna

Lake flood of 1894 on the Ganges; and the 1925 Gros Ventre flood in Wyoming, accompanied the breaching of natural landslide barriers. The Lake Issyk-Kul (Kyrgyzstan) flood of 1963, which caused widespread erosion and deposition, followed the overtopping of a landslide barrier by waves produced by a mudflow. The Vaiont Dam (Italy), although itself holding, was overtopped in 1963 by 91-metre- (300-foot-) high waves raised by a landslide: the floods downstream took more than 2,500 lives in 15 minutes. On the Huang He the floods of 1887 took an estimated 900,000 lives. In late Pleistocene time the overtopping of an erodible natural dam by the then-existing Lake Bonneville eventually released nearly 1,666 cubic km (400 cubic miles) of water. The maximum discharge of about 280,000 cubic metres (9.9 million cubic feet) per second is comparable to the flow of the Amazon, but velocities were especially high, perhaps ranging to 7.6 metres (25 feet) per second. The greatest flood peak so far identified is that of the ice-dammed Lake Missoula in Montana, which, on release, discharged 2,085 cubic km (500 cubic miles) of water at an estimated peak flow of 8.5 million cubic metres (300 million cubic feet) per second. Iceland is notable for glacier bursts, which are nonrecurrent where they result from subglacial eruptions but recurrent where they involve the sudden failure of ice dams, as with Grímsvötn, which periodically releases 8.3 or more cubic km (2 cubic miles) of water in floods that peak at 57,000 cubic metres (about 2 million cubic feet) per second. Deposition by glacier-burst floods is illustrated by Iceland's Sandur plains.

Peak discharges that close the range between natural floods of great magnitude and low frequency on noncatastrophic streams and natural catastrophic floods of great magnitude and perceptible frequency include storm-water discharges from expanding urban areas. Because of the progressive spread of impermeable catchment and

In 1963 91-metre- (300-foot-) high waves raised by a catastrophic landslide crested Italy's Vaiont Dam, taking more than 2,500 lives within minutes. Popperfoto/Getty Images

efficient runoff systems, such floods tend to increase both in frequency and in magnitude.

SEDIMENT YIELD AND SEDIMENT LOAD

All the water that reaches a stream and its tributaries carries sediment eroded from the entire area drained by it. The total amount of erosional debris exported from such a drainage basin is its sediment yield. Sediment yield is generally expressed in two ways: either as a volume or as a weight, that is, as acre-feet (one-foot depth of material over one acre) or as tons. To adjust for the wildly differing sizes of drainage basins, the yield frequently is expressed as a volume or weight per unit area of drainage basin (e.g., as acre-feet per square mile or as tons per square mile or per square kilometre). The conversion between the two forms of expression is made by obtaining an average weight for the sediment and calculating the total weight from the measured volume of sediment. Further, sediment yield is usually measured during a period of years, and the results are thus expressed as an annual average.

The sediment delivered to and transported by a stream is its sediment load. This can be classified into three types, depending on sediment size and the competence of the river. The coarsest sediment, consisting of boulders and cobbles as well as sand, moves on or near the bed of the stream and is the bed load of the river. The finer particles, silts and clays, are carried in suspension by the turbulent action of flowing water. These fine particles, which are moved long distances at the velocity of the flowing water, constitute the suspended load of the river. The remaining component of the total sediment load is the dissolved load, which is composed of chemical compounds taken into solution by the water moving on or in the soils of the drainage basin. These three types of sediment constitute the total sediment load of the stream and, of course, the sediment yield of the drainage basin.

MEASUREMENT OF THE LOAD

The sediment load can be measured in different ways. Collection of water samples from a river and measurement of the sediment contained in each unit of water will, when sufficient samples have been taken and the water discharge from the system is known, permit calculation of annual sediment yield. Because sediment in a stream channel is transported in suspension, in solution, and as material rolling or moving very near the bed, the water samples will contain suspended and dissolved load and perhaps some bed load. Much of the bed load, however, cannot be sampled by existing techniques, as it moves too near the bed of a stream. It is fortunate, therefore, that the greatest part of the total sediment load is in the form of suspended load.

When a dam is constructed, the sediment transported by a stream is deposited in the still waters of the reservoir. In this case, both bed load and suspended load are deposited, but the dissolved load eventually moves out with the water released from the reservoir. Frequent, precise surveys of the configuration of the reservoir provide data on the volume of sediment that accumulates in the reservoir. Water samples can be taken to provide data on the dissolved load transported into the reservoir. When this quantity is added to the measurements of suspended and bed load, a reasonably accurate measure of sediment yield from the drainage basin above the reservoir can be obtained.

In areas where information on sediment yield is required but the necessary samples have not been taken (perhaps because of the infrequent occurrence of flow in ephemeral streams), estimates of sediment yields may be obtained from measurements of hillslope and channel erosion within the basin or by the evaluation of erosion conditions. Certain characteristics of the drainage basin, such as the average slope of the basin or the number and spacing of drainage channels, may be used to provide an estimate of sediment yield.

All of the techniques utilized to measure sediment yield are subject to considerable error, but data sufficiently accurate for the design of water-regulatory structures can be obtained by sampling or by reconnaissance surveys of the drainage systems.

Sediment Sources and the Nature of Deposition

The ultimate source of the sediment that is measured as sediment yield is the rock underlying the drainage basins.

Until the rock is broken or weathered into fragments of a size that can be transported from the basin, the sediment yield will be low. The diverse mechanisms, both chemical and physical, that produce sediment and soil from rock are termed weathering processes. Depending on type of rock and type of weathering process, the result may be readily transported silts, clays, and sands or less easily transported cobbles and boulders.

Most rocks have been fractured during the vicissitudes of geologic history, thereby permitting penetration of water and roots. Wedging by ice and growing roots produces blocks of rock that are then subject to further disintegration and decomposition by chemical and physical agencies. These rocks, if exposed on a hillslope, move slowly down the slope to the stream channel—the rate of movement depending on slope inclination; density of vegetation; frequency of freeze and thaw events; and the size, shape, and density of the materials involved. In addition, water moving through rocks and soil can dissolve soluble portions of rock or weathering products. This is especially important in limestone regions and in regions of warm, humid climate, where chemical decomposition of rocks is rapid and where the dissolved load of streams is at a maximum.

When sediment eroded from the hillslopes is not delivered directly to a channel, it may accumulate at the base of the slope to form a colluvial deposit. The sediment derived directly from the hillslope may be stored temporarily at the slope base; therefore, sediment once set in motion does not necessarily move directly through the stream system. It is more likely, in fact, that a given particle of sediment will be stored as colluvium before moving into the stream. Even then, it may be stored as alluvium in the floodplain, bed, or bank of the stream for some time before eventually moving out of the drainage system. Thus there is a steady export of sediment from a drainage basin, but an individual grain of sediment may be deposited and eroded many times before it leaves the system.

The preceding suggests that, over a period of time, the total erosion within a drainage basin is greater than the sediment yield of the system. Proof of this statement is the fact that the quantity of sediment per unit area that leaves a drainage system decreases as the size of the drainage basin increases. This is partly explained by the decrease in stream gradient and basin relief in a downstream direction. That is to say, much sediment is produced in the steeper areas near drainage divides, and sediment production decreases downstream. Moreover, the increasing width of valleys and floodplains downstream and the decreasing gradient of the streams provide an increasing number of opportunities for sediment to be deposited and temporarily stored within the system.

Each of the components of the drainage system—hill-slopes and channels—produces sediment. The quantity provided by each, however, will vary during the erosional development of the basin and during changes of the vegetational, climatic, and hydrologic character of the drainage system. Most rivers flow on the upper surface of an alluvial deposit, and considerable sediment is thus stored in most river valleys. During great floods or when floodplain vegetation does not stabilize this sediment, large quantities may be flushed from the system as the channel widens and deepens. At these times, the sediment produced by stream-channel erosion is far greater than that produced by the hillslopes, and sediment yields will be far in excess of rates of hillslope erosion. Such cycles of rapid channel erosion or gullying and subsequent healing and deposition are common in arid and semiarid regions.

ALLUVIUM

Alluvium is the material deposited by rivers. It is usually most extensively developed in the lower part of the course of a river, forming floodplains and deltas, but may be deposited at any point where the river overflows its banks or where the velocity of a river is checked—for example, where it runs into a lake.

Alluvium consists of silt, sand, clay, and gravel and often contains a good deal of organic matter. It therefore yields very fertile soils such as those of the deltas of the Mississippi, the Nile, the Ganges and Brahmaputra, and the Huang rivers. In some regions alluvial deposits contain gold, platinum, or gemstones and the greater part of the world's supply of tin ore (cassiterite).

It is clear that a great range of sediment sizes may be transported by a river. Sediment of small size (e.g., suspended load), when set in motion by erosive agents, may be transported through a river system to the sea, where it may be deposited as a deep-sea clay. Most sedimentary particles, however, have a more eventful journey to their final resting place. (In a geologic context, this may be a temporary resting place. Sediment, for example, when it reaches the coast, may be incorporated in a delta at the river mouth or be acted upon by tides, currents, and waves to become a beach deposit.)

If sediment is moved downstream into a progressively more arid environment, the probability of deposition is high. Thousands of metres of alluvial-fan deposits flank the mountains of the western United States, the basin-and-range terrain of Iran and Pakistan, and similar desert regions. In the arid climates of these areas the sediment cannot be moved far, because the transporting medium—water—diminishes in a downstream direction as it infiltrates into the dry alluvium. In extremely arid regions, wind action may be important: the transport of sand-size and smaller sediment by wind may be the only significant mechanism for the transport within and out of some drainage systems in deserts.

The effect of human activity on river flow has come to play a major role in determining the site of sediment deposition. The many dams that have been constructed for flood control, recreation, and power generation hold much of the sediment load of rivers in reservoirs. Furthermore, the contribution of sediment from the small upstream drainage systems has been decreased by the construction of stock-water reservoirs and various erosion-control techniques aimed at retaining both water and sediment in the headwater areas. Diversion of water for irrigation also decreases the supply of water available to transport sediment; and in many cases, the diversion actually moves sediment out of the streams into irrigation canals and back onto the land.

FACTORS THAT INFLUENCE SEDIMENT YIELD

Of greatest concern to the human community are the factors that cause rapid rates of erosion and high sediment yields. The quantity and type of sediment moving through a stream channel are intimately related to the geology, topographic character, climate, vegetational type and density, and land use within the drainage basin. The geologic and topographic variables are fixed, but short-term changes in climatic conditions, vegetation, and land use produce abrupt alterations in the intensity of erosion processes and in sediment yields.

The sediment yield from any drainage system is calculated by averaging the data collected over a period of years. It is, therefore, an average of the results of many different hydrologic events. The sediment yield for each storm or flood will vary, depending on the meteorologic character of the storm event and the resulting hydrologic character of the floods. High-intensity storms may produce sediment yields well above the norm, whereas an equal amount of precipitation occurring over a longer period of time may yield relatively little sediment. During short spans of time (days or years), sediment yields may fluctuate greatly because of natural or man-induced accidents (e.g., floods and fires), but over longer periods of time, the average sediment yield will be typical of the geologic and climatic character of a region.

Short-Term Variations

An example of a short-term change in sediment yield is provided by data on the sediment transported by the Colorado River in Arizona for the years 1926–54. It is evident that sediment yield varied widely from year to year. It is greatest for years of highest runoff, but for a given amount of runoff, the maximum sediment yield may be twice the minimum sediment yield. These variations reflect the frequency of storms and their duration and intensity during the years of record.

Another interesting aspect of the relation is that in each of the years after 1940 the annual sediment load at the Grand Canyon was 50 million to 100 million tons less than would be expected on the basis of the curve fitted to the data for the period 1926–40. This major decrease in sediment yield reflects some significant change in the hydrology of the Colorado River drainage basin. A study of the precipitation patterns for the years 1926–54 suggests that the change in the sediment yield–runoff relation beginning in 1941 is the result of a drought in the southwestern United States. The high-sediment-producing, weak-rock areas of the Colorado plateaus were affected

Ample sediment and areas of weak rock in the Colorado plateaus can be far more affected by drought than the hard rock and scant sediment of the Rocky Mountains. DEA/L. Romano/De Agostini/Getty Images

by the drought, but the low-sediment-producing, hard-rock areas of the Rocky Mountains were not. Thus, during the years 1941–50 the amount of water delivered from the main runoff-producing areas in Colorado, Wyoming, and northern Utah was normal. Runoff was much reduced from the high-sediment-producing areas in southern Utah and Arizona, however. The result was essentially normal runoff but greatly reduced sediment yield. From 1950 the drought encompassed the entire Colorado River Basin, and low runoff was recorded for the years 1950, 1951, 1953, and 1954; yet, the proportion of runoff produced by the high-sediment-producing areas remained low, as did the sediment yield.

It can be expected that sediment-yield rates will fluctuate with climatic variations. It is possible, therefore, that an average value of sediment yield obtained for a short period of record may not provide a valid measure of the characteristic sediment yield that would be expected over a longer period of years.

A further example of short-term variation of sediment yield, in this case the result of human activity on the landscape, is provided by data illustrating the change from natural conditions to conditions produced by upland farming and from farming conditions to urban conditions in the Piedmont region of the eastern United States. Sediment yields for forested regions normally are about 37 tons per square km (100 tons per square mile), and this was the case during the early part of the 19th century in this region. A significant increase in sediment yield occurred after 1820 as the land was occupied and farmed. During the period of intense farming, 1850–1930, the sediment yield reached almost 310 tons per square km (about 800 tons per square mile), but a decrease occurred between 1930 and 1960, as much land was permitted to revert to forest or grazing land. With the onset of construction and real estate development, however, vegetation was destroyed, and large quantities of sediment were eroded. The sediment yields for some small areas reached about 770 tons per square km (about 2,000 tons per square mile) during urbanization, but with the paving of streets, completion of sewage systems, and planting of lawns, the sediment yields decreased markedly. This example demonstrates very clearly both the long-term and short-term effects of human activity on sediment yield rates.

In any drainage basin, even one not affected unduly by human action, short periods of high sediment yield will alternate with periods of little export of sediment. Prime examples are small drainage basins in arid or semi-arid regions, where sediment yield occurs only during and following precipitation. Runoff and sediment yield can be zero between storms but high during and immediately following precipitation.

Even temperature variations have been demonstrated to influence sediment transport and sediment yields. Cooler water is more viscous, and this decreases the fall velocity of sediment particles and enables the stream to transport a larger amount of sediment. Thus, the sediment load of the Colorado River is greater during winter months.

The disastrous effect of fire on sediment yields may be seen in the example of the conditions that followed a major storm and flood in the steep drainage basins of the San Gabriel and San Bernardino mountains of California in 1938. Maximum vegetational cover on these drainage basins is only 65 percent at best, and they are notoriously high sediment producers under the most favourable conditions. Sediment-yield rates were established for several drainage basins that had been subjected to fires as recently as one year before the storm and as long as 15 years before the storm. The results shown further demonstrate the great effect of vegetational disturbance on sediment yields. For example, a drainage area with only 40 percent of the area burned had a 340 percent increase in sediment yield if the fire occurred one year before the storm. According to the information provided, the burned area one year after the fire had a 10 percent vegetational cover. Obviously, a storm immediately following the fire would have had even more disastrous consequences. Three years after the burn, a 35 percent vegetation cover had been established on the burned area, and sediment yields decreased markedly to only twice the yield preceding the fire. After seven years a 45 percent cover had been established on the burned area, and sediment yields were only 50 percent greater than pre-burn values. After 15 years a 55 percent vegetal cover had been established, and sediment yields were almost normal. The decrease in sediment yield with increased plant cover is apparent. It is also obvious that an average value of sediment yield from a burned drainage basin for a 15-year period would be meaningless; with progressive reestablishment of vegetation, sediment-yield rates progressively decrease with time.

LONG-TERM OR AVERAGE SEDIMENT YIELD

It has been estimated that modern sediment loads of the rivers draining to the Atlantic Ocean may be four to five times greater than the prehistoric rates because of the effects of human activity. Even where human impact is large, however, it is possible to recognize several other independent variables that exert a major influence on long-term sediment yield. These variables can be grouped into three main classes: geologic, geomorphic, and climatic-vegetational.

The major geologic influence on sediment yield is through lithology, or the composition and physical properties of rocks and their resistance to weathering and erosion. An easily weathered and eroded shale, siltstone, or poorly cemented sandstone will provide relatively large quantities of sediment, whereas a lava flow, a well-cemented sandstone, or metamorphic and igneous rocks produce negligible quantities of transportable sediment. The highest known sediment yields that have been recorded are produced by the erosion of unconsolidated silts (loess). Loess is readily eroded, especially when the protecting vegetational cover is disturbed, as has happened in the high-sediment-producing areas of western Iowa in the United States and the Huang He Basin in China.

The Great Sphinx at Giza, Egypt, was carved from limestone, which resists erosion in arid areas, allowing it to stand for centuries. Cris Bouroncle/ AFP/Getty Images

In general, sediment yield from drainage systems underlain by granitic rocks is from one-fourth to one-half that of drainage basins underlain by sedimentary rocks. There are exceptions. Limestone, which may be a massive rock, is highly resistant to erosion in arid regions, where mechanical or physical weathering is dominant. It is, however, highly susceptible to chemical weathering, especially solution, in humid regions. Most of the earth material removed from a limestone terrain will be transported as dissolved load, with some suspended load derived from erosion of the residual soil.

Another factor of importance in determining erosion rates is the permeability of earth materials. When soils are permeable, much of the water delivered to the surface infiltrates and does not produce surface runoff, thereby

inhibiting surface erosion. This condition is characteristic of very sandy soils. Conversely, when soil materials
are of low permeability (e.g., clayey soils), a greater part of
the precipitation runs off on the surface, thereby causing
greater erosion and higher sediment yields.

Most drainage areas are composed of more than one
rock type. In some areas the sedimentary rocks have been
folded, and rocks of different resistance are exposed, with
hard rocks forming ridges and mountains and weak rocks
forming valleys. The erosional development of such a terrain is complex, and the sediment produced by a drainage
basin of this kind will reflect the complex geologic situation, the greater part of the sediment yield being derived
from the areas underlain by the rocks that are most susceptible to erosion.

GEOMORPHIC VARIABLES

The character of the topography of a drainage basin significantly influences the quantity and type of runoff and
sediment yield. The steeper a slope, the greater is the
gravitational force acting to remove earth materials from
the slope. In fact, the rate of movement of rocks and soil
particles is directly related to the sine of the angle of slope
inclination.

Steep slopes are readily eroded, and it follows that
drainage basins with a great range of relief or steep average slope will produce not only higher sediment yields but
coarser sediment. The average slope of a drainage basin
can be expressed simply as a ratio of basin relief to basin
length. Sediment yields increase exponentially with an
increase in this relief–length ratio.

Another important characteristic of a drainage system
is the spacing and distribution of drainage channels within

the drainage basin. This is referred to as the texture of the topography, and it can be described by a ratio of total channel length to drainage area. This ratio is the drainage density of the system. High drainage density indicates numerous, closely spaced channels that provide an escape route for both runoff and its entrained sediment load.

When relief–length ratio (*r*), expressing the role of gravity, is combined with drainage density (*d*), expressing the efficiency of the drainage system, this yields a texture-slope product (*rd*), a parameter that describes the gross morphology of a drainage system. Hence it is not surprising that it is closely related to sediment yield of small drainage basins of similar geology and land use.

The relation between the texture-slope product and sediment yield is such that a high sediment yield can be expected from basins with a large drainage density and steep slope. For basins with similar relief–length ratios, those with the highest drainage density produce the greater quantity of sediment. In general, however, the basins with the highest drainage density are also those with the steepest slope.

Many geomorphic characteristics can be related to sediment yield, but it can be stated with assurance that the steeper and the better drained the system, the greater will be the quantity of sediment produced per unit area.

The relationship may be used to estimate yield from other drainage basins in the region from which these data were obtained. Similar relations may be developed for other regions when sufficient geomorphic data become available.

In all studies, the sediment yield per unit area has been found to decrease as the size of the drainage basin increases. This reflects the previously discussed downstream decrease in gradient and slope and the increase in area available for temporary storage of sediment. Therefore total sediment yield per unit area invariably is related inversely to drainage area. Several other factors are involved, of course, but the largest drainage basins do not produce the largest quantity of sediment per unit area of drainage basin.

The morphology of a drainage basin is significantly related to sediment yield, but scientists have not yet done sufficient research to enable the prediction of sediment yields from drainage basins in the diverse regions of the world.

It is difficult to separate the influences of climate and vegetation on erosion and sediment yield, because the primary effect of climate on sediment yield is determined by the interaction between vegetation and runoff. This effect is displayed by the contrast between the dissolved load and the suspended load and bed load transported by streams. Dissolved load increases from a negligible amount in arid regions to 60 tons per square km (155 tons per square mile) in humid regions, where chemical weathering and groundwater contribution to river flow is greatest. The dense vegetational cover of humid regions retards runoff and aids infiltration, thereby enhancing the effects of chemical decomposition of the rocks and soils to produce soluble material. The available data also show a sharp increase in sediment yield (suspended and bed load) as precipitation increases from low to moderate amounts. In semiarid regions, however, the increase of vegetation density with increased precipitation exerts a significant influence on erosion; and sediment transport and sediment yield decrease as the climate becomes increasingly humid. This relationship can, of course, be significantly modified by human activities. As the previously mentioned effect of urbanization demonstrates, removal of vegetation from the land in humid regions greatly accelerates erosion, and it may increase sediment yield to the maximum expected in semiarid regions.

Average temperature also affects sediment yields. The hotter the climate, the more water is lost to evapotranspiration, and the critical zone where vegetation becomes dominant consequently shifts to areas of higher precipitation.

The effect of vegetational cover on sediment yield has been discussed previously for areas where fires have destroyed much of the cover and catastrophically increased erosion and export of sediment from the system. Additional data on the effect of vegetation on erosion rates reveal that with a 65 percent plant cover little erosion will occur, but as plant cover decreases erosion increases significantly.

Although erosion increases greatly with a decrease in plant cover between 20 and 15 percent, it cannot continue to increase at this high rate. At some point, the maximum rate of erosion of the soil will be achieved. At some value of low-plant-cover density, the influence of vegetation must be negligible. Erosion then will be determined only by soil erodibility.

Although average precipitation significantly influences vegetation type and density and the sediment yield, it has been demonstrated that, for a given quantity of annual precipitation, sediment yields will be greatest where highly seasonal (e.g., monsoonal) climatic conditions prevail. Precipitation, when concentrated during a few months of the year, produces large quantities of sediment because of the higher intensity of the precipitation events and the long dry season when vegetational cover is severely weakened by drought.

Climate also plays a role in determining the type of sediment produced by a drainage basin. A study of the type of sediment deposited on the inner continental shelf reveals that the type of sediment (mud, sand, or gravel) is indeed influenced by climate. Mud, for example, is most abundant off shores of high temperature and rainfall, where chemical weathering is important. Gravel is common off areas of both low temperature and rainfall, where mechanical weathering is dominant. Sand is found everywhere, but it is most abundant in areas of moderate climate and in arid areas. Average temperature also may be important where the annual temperature is below the freezing point.

CHAPTER 4

RIVERS AS AGENTS OF LANDSCAPE EVOLUTION: VALLEYS, CANYONS, FLOODPLAINS, AND RIVER TERRACES

Every landform at the Earth's surface reflects a particular accommodation between properties of the underlying geologic materials, the type of processes affecting those materials, and the amount of time the processes have been operating. Because landforms are the building blocks of regional landscapes, the character of the local surroundings is ultimately controlled by those factors of geology, process, and time—a conclusion reached in the late 19th century by the noted American geologist and geographer William Morris Davis. In some regions, severe climatic controls cause a particular process agent to become preeminent. Deserts, for example, are often subjected to severe wind action, and the resulting landscape consists of landforms that reflect the dominance of erosional or depositional processes accomplished by the wind. Other landscapes may be related to processes operating beneath the surface. Regions such as Japan or the Cascade Range in the northwestern part of the United States clearly have major topographic components that were produced by repeated volcanic activity. Nevertheless, rivers are by far the most important agents in molding landscapes because their ubiquity ensures that no region of the Earth can be totally devoid of landforms developed by fluvial processes.

Rivers are much more than sluiceways that simply transport water and sediment. They also change a nondescript geologic setting into distinct topographic forms. This happens primarily because movement of sediment-laden water is capable of pronounced erosion, and when transporting energy decreases, landforms are created by the deposition of fluvial sediment. Some fluvial features are entirely erosional, and the form is clearly unrelated to the transportation and deposition of sediment. Other features may be entirely depositional. In these cases, topography is constructed of sediment that buries some underlying surface that existed prior to the introduction of the covering sediment. Realistically, many fluvial features result from some combination of both erosion and deposition, and the pure situations probably represent end members of a continuum of fluvial forms.

VALLEYS AND CANYONS

River valleys constitute a major portion of the natural surroundings. In rare cases, spectacular valleys are created by tectonic activity. The Jordan River and the Dead Sea, for example, occupy a valley that developed as a fault-bounded trough known as a rift valley. The distinct property of these and other tectonically controlled valleys is that the low topographic zone (valley) existed before the river. Notwithstanding tectonic exceptions, the overwhelming majority of valleys, including canyons and gorges, share a common genetic bond in that their characteristics are the result of river erosion (i.e., rivers create the valleys in which they flow). In most cases, erosion was accomplished by the same river that occupies the valley bottom, although sometimes rivers are diverted from one valley into another by a process known as stream piracy, or stream capture. Piracy of a large river into another valley often creates a situation where the original expansive valley is later occupied by a river that is too small to have created such a large valley. The opposite case also may occur. The implication here is that valley size is directly related to river size, an observation that generally holds true. Exceptions to this rule arise because of capture events during the evolution of a valley and because valley morphology is strongly influenced by variations in the bedrock into which the valley is carved.

A genuine bedrock valley is usually covered by valley-fill deposits that obscure the actual configuration of the valley floor. Therefore, little is known about valley morphology unless drill holes or geophysical techniques are employed to document the buried bedrock-alluvium contact. Where information is available, it suggests that the deepest part of most valleys is not directly beneath the river. Commonly, the influx of load at a tributary junction forces the river to the opposite side of the valley, a phenomenon demonstrated clearly in the upper Mississippi River Valley between St. Louis, Mo., and St. Paul, Minn.

Where a valley is devoid of thick deposits and is completely occupied by a river, the bedrock valley floor often develops an asymmetrical configuration such that the deepest part of the valley occurs on the inside of bends. This general rule is not inviolate because the position of incision depends on the amount of load entrained by the river. When sediment load is totally entrained and velocity is high, entrenchment will most likely occur on the inside of the bend. If deposition occurs or sediment cannot be entrained, however, incision will normally be on the outside of the bend. In straight reaches the deepest part of the valley floor is normally associated with an inner channel cut into bedrock. Its position is determined by where the river was at the time that it flowed at the level of the valley floor. Inner channels form as the culmination of a progressive change in erosional features during the initial phase of incision. Scour features gradually coalesce until a distinct channel appears that is able to contain the entire river flow. Inner channels are rarely seen except when exposed during excavation associated with dam construction. Where observed, such channels commonly have a narrow, deep gorgelike shape. For example, at the site of the Prineville Dam in the state of Oregon, the inner channel averages 21 metres (about 70 feet) wide and as much as 18 metres (60 feet) deep.

VALLEY EVOLUTION

The ultimate form assumed by any valley reflects events that occurred during its developmental history and the characteristics of the underlying geology. During initial valley development in areas well above regional baselevel, valley relief tends to increase as rivers expend most of their energy in vertical entrenchment. Valleys are generally narrow and deep, especially in areas where they are cut into unfractured rocks with lithologic properties that resist erosion (most igneous rocks, well-indurated sedimentary rocks such as quartzites, and high-rank, silica-rich metamorphic rocks). Abrupt changes in river and valley bottom gradients, such as knickpoints and waterfalls, are common in the initial developmental phase. As downcutting continues, however, rivers gradually smooth out the longitudinal profile of the valley floor. Eventually most, if not all, waterfalls are eliminated, and rivers reach an elevation close to their baselevel. In this condition, more energy is expended laterally than vertically, and a river progressively broadens its valley floor. As a result, most river valleys change over time from narrow forms to broader ones, the shape at any time being dependent on baselevel, rock type, and rock structures.

In areas where pronounced macrostructures such as major folds or faults exist in the geologic framework, the position and character of valleys are controlled by those structures. For example, the folds in the Appalachian Mountains in the eastern United States exert a very strong control on the orientation and form of many valleys developed in the region.

FORMATION OF CANYONS AND GORGES

The most spectacular valley forms are canyons and gorges that result from accelerated entrenchment prompted by recent tectonic activity, especially vertical uplift. Canyons and gorges are still in the initial phase of valley development. They range in size from narrow slits in resistant bedrock to enormous trenches. Where underlying bedrock is composed of flat-lying sedimentary rocks, regional uplift creates high-standing plateaus and simultaneously reinvigorates the erosive power of existing rivers, a phenomenon known as rejuvenation. Vertical entrenchment produces different valley styles depending on the size of the river and the magnitude and rate of uplift. The Grand Canyon of the Colorado River, located in the southwestern United States and formed in response to uplift of the Colorado Plateau, has entrenched about 1,800 metres (5,900 feet) and widened its walls 6 to 29 km (3.7 to 18 miles) during the past 10 million years. The Grand Canyon is only one of many spectacular canyons that developed in response to uplift of the Colorado Plateau. Uplift of the Allegheny Plateau in the eastern United States has led to the creation of the narrow, deep valleys that are so prominent in West Virginia and western Pennsylvania.

Canyons and gorges frequently develop across the trends of underlying macrostructures. In normal situations, valleys should follow the orientation of the major folds and faults. However, the geologic setting prior to uplift and the processes associated with tectonic activity

Vertical uplift in the Colorado Plateau created the Grand Canyon of the Colorado River, which has exhibited remarkable entrenchment and widening over the past 10 million years. Photos.com/Thinkstock

permit the development of transverse canyons. Transverse canyons, gorges, or water gaps are most easily explained in terms of accelerated headward erosion of rivers along faults cutting across the trend of resistant ridges. In such cases, the fault zone allows rivers to preferentially expand through an already existing ridge of resistant rocks, thereby creating a canyon.

Most transverse canyons, however, are not associated with faults. When faults are absent, transverse canyons are usually interpreted as developing in one of two ways. First, valleys may have been eroded into the landscape before the tectonic features (folds and faults) were developed. Such macrostructures rise across the trend of these valleys, and if the rate of river downcutting can keep pace with the rate at which the structures rise, gorges or canyons will be developed transverse to the structural trend. Because the valleys are older than the tectonic displacement, they are called antecedent. Antecedent canyons have been identified in the Alps, the Himalayas, the Andes, the Pacific coastal ranges of the United States, and every other region of the world that has experienced recent or ongoing tectonism. Second, complexly folded and faulted terranes are sometimes buried by a variable thickness of younger sediment. Drainage patterns develop on the sedimentary cover in a manner similar to those formed in any basin where there is no structural control. If the region is vertically uplifted, the rejuvenated rivers begin to entrench and will eventually be let down across the trends of resistant rocks in the underlying complex of folds and faults. Canyons and their formative rivers following this evolutionary path are said to be superimposed. The concept of superimposition was first used to explain water gaps in the Appalachians, but superimposition has since been employed as a model for drainage evolution in most areas of the world that have experienced uplift during the Cenozoic Era (the past 65.5 million years).

In light of the aforementioned information, it is well to note that detailed studies of physiography are indeed rare in mountain belts where the initial topography created by deformation is still preserved. One area that has been investigated is the Zagros Mountain system near the borderlands of Iraq and Iran from eastern Turkey to the Gulf of Oman. In this region, none of the accepted models for the creation of transverse canyons is totally acceptable, even though all of them may be involved to a certain degree. Instead, it seems likely that drainage development associated with normal processes of denudation can produce canyons transverse to a fold belt (given some heterogeneity in the geologic framework) without requiring some unique preexisting condition in the system.

FLOODPLAINS

Floodplains are perhaps the most common of fluvial features in that they are usually found along every major river and in most large tributary valleys. Floodplains can be defined topographically as relatively flat surfaces that stand adjacent to river channels and occupy much of the area constituting valley bottoms. The surface of a floodplain is underlain by alluvium deposited by the associated river and is partially or totally inundated during periods of flooding. Thus, a floodplain is not only constructed by but also serves as an integral part of the modern fluvial system, indicating that the surface and alluvium must be related to the activity of the present river.

The preceding definition suggests that, in addition to being a distinct geomorphic feature, a floodplain has a significant hydrologic role. A floodplain directly influences the magnitude of peak discharge in the downstream reaches of a river during episodes of flooding. In extreme precipitation events, runoff from the watershed enters the trunk river faster than it can be removed from the system. Eventually, water overtops the channel banks and is stored on the floodplain surface until the flood crest passes a given locality farther downstream. As a consequence, the flood crest on a major river would be significantly greater if its floodplain did not store water long enough to prevent it from becoming part of the downstream peak discharge. The capacity of a floodplain system to store water can be enormous. The volume of water stored during the 1937 flood of the Ohio River in the east-central United States, for example, was roughly 2.3 times the volume of Lake Mead, the largest artificial reservoir in North America. The natural storage in the Ohio River watershed during this particular event represented approximately 57 percent of the direct runoff.

Because a floodplain is so intimately related to floods, it also can be defined in terms of the water level attained during some particular flow condition of a river. In that sense a floodplain is commonly recognized as the surface corresponding to the bank-full stage of a river (i.e., the water level at which the channel is completely filled). Numerous studies have shown that the average recurrence interval of the bank-full stage is 1.5 years, though this value might vary from river to river. Nonetheless, this suggests that most floodplain surfaces will be covered by water twice every three years. It should be noted, however, that the water level having a recurrence interval of 1.5 years will cover only a portion of the relatively flat valley bottom surface that was defined as the topographic floodplain. Clearly, parts of the topographic floodplain will be inundated only during river stages that are considerably higher than bankfull and occur less frequently. Thus, it seems that the definition of a hydrologic floodplain is different from that of the topographic floodplain, and how one ultimately studies a floodplain surface depends on which point of view concerning the feature is considered of greatest significance.

FLOODPLAIN DEPOSITS, ORIGINS, AND FEATURES

Although valley-bottom deposits result from processes operating in diverse sub-environments, including valley-side sheetwash, the most important deposits in the floodplain framework are those developed by processes that function in and near the river channel. These deposits are normally referred to as (1) lateral accretion deposits, which develop within the channel itself as the river migrates back and forth across the valley bottom, and (2) vertical accretion deposits, which accumulate on the floodplain surface when the river overflows its channel banks.

In any valley where the river tends to meander, maximum erosion will occur on the outside bank just downstream from the axis of the meander bend. Detailed studies have shown, however, that deposition occurs simultaneously on the inside of the bend, the volume of deposition being essentially equal to the volume of bank erosion. Thus, a meandering river can shift its position laterally during any interval of time without changing its channel shape or size. Deposition on the inside of the meander bend creates a channel feature known as a point bar, which represents the most common type of lateral accretion. Over a period of years point bars expand laterally as the opposite bank is continually eroded backward. The bars progressively spread across the valley bottom, usually as a thin sheet of sand or gravel containing layers that dip into the channel bottom. Point bars tend to increase in height until they reach the level of older parts of the floodplain surface, and the maximum thickness of laterally accreted deposits is controlled by how deeply a river can scour its bottom during recurrent floods. A general rule of thumb is that river channels are probably scoured to a depth 1.75 to two times the depth of flow attained during a flood. Because bank-full depth increases in the downstream direction, the thickness of lateral accretion deposits should increase gradually down the valley.

Vertical accretion (also called overbank deposition) occurs when rivers leave their channel confines during periodic flooding and deposit sediment on top of the floodplain surface. The floodplain, therefore, increases in elevation during a flood event. Overbank deposition is usually minor during any given flood event. The insignificant deposition reflects the documented phenomenon that maximum concentration of suspended load occurs during the rising phase of any flood. Thus, much of the potential overbank sediment is removed from the system before a river rises to bank-full stage.

INCREMENT RATES OF OVERBANK DEPOSITION IN MAJOR FLOODS		
RIVER BASIN	FLOOD	AVERAGE THICKNESS OF DEPOSITION (METRES)
Ohio River	January–February 1937	0.0024 (0.0945 inches)
Connecticut River	March 1936	0.0347 (1.37 inches)
Connecticut River	September 1938	0.0223 (0.878 inches)
Kansas River	July 1951	0.0299 (1.18 inches)

Source: Adapted from M.G. Wolman and L.B. Leopold, "River Flood Plains: Some Observations on Their Formation," U.S. Geological Survey professional paper no. 282-C, 1957, courtesy of the U.S. Department of the Interior, U.S. Geological Survey

Because lateral and vertical accretionary processes occur during the same time interval, alluvium beneath a floodplain surface usually consists of both type of deposits. The two types often differ in their particle-size characteristics, with lateral accretion deposits having larger grain sizes. These textural differences, however, are not always present. In fact, suspended-load rivers that transport mostly silt and clay develop point bars composed of fine-grained sediment. Conversely, mixed-load rivers with cohesive banks may deposit sand and gravel on a floodplain surface as vertical accretion deposits.

Floodplains also are developed by braided rivers, but the fluvial processes are more dynamic and less regular. Bars and bank erosion, for example, are not confined to one particular side of the channel, and the river often changes its position without laterally eroding the intervening material. Channels and islands associated with the braided-stream pattern become abandoned, and these eventually coalesce into a continuous floodplain surface when old channels become filled with overbank sediment. The result is that floodplain sediments in a braided system are often irregular in thickness, and recognition of the true floodplain sequence may be complicated because braided streams are often associated with long-term valley aggradation. In this case, the total deposit might appear to be very thick, but the actual floodplain sediment relates only to the present river hydrology. The true floodplain deposit, therefore, is merely a thin cap on top of a thick, continuous valley fill.

Topography developed on a floodplain surface is directly related to depositional and erosional processes. The dominant feature of lateral accretion, a point bar, is subjected to erosion during high discharge when small channels called chutes are eroded across the back portion of the point bar. As the river shifts laterally and chutes continue to form, point bars are molded into alternating ridges and swales that characterize a distinct topography known as meander scrolls. As the river changes its position, meander-scroll topography becomes preserved as part of the floodplain surface itself. Overbank processes also create microtopography. The latter includes natural levees, which are elongate narrow ridges that form adjacent to channels when the largest particles of the suspended load are deposited as soon as the river leaves the confines of its channel. Natural levees build vertically faster than the area away from the channel, which is known as a backswamp. For example, during the 1973 flood on the Mississippi River, 53 cm (21 inches) of sediment were deposited on natural levees, while only 1.1 cm (0.4 inch) accumulated in the backswamp area. The backswamp area of a floodplain is usually much more regular, and its flatness is disrupted only by oxbow channels (abandoned river channels) or by ridgelike deposits known as splay deposits that have broken through natural levees and spread onto the back-swamp surface. Oxbows, or oxbow lakes, gradually fill in with silts and clays during normal overbank deposition, leaving that surface more regular than might be expected.

TIME AND THE FLOODPLAIN SYSTEM

The variety of floodplain deposits and features raises the question as to which process, lateral river migration or overbank flow, is the most important in floodplain development. There is probably no universal answer to this question, but rates of the depositional processes suggest that most floodplains should result primarily from the processes and deposition associated with lateral migration. In addition, there is an assumption that the level of a floodplain constructed entirely by overbank deposition should rise at a progressively decreasing rate. This follows because as the floodplain surface is elevated relative to the channel floor, the river stage needed to overtop the banks is also increasing. The floodplain surface, therefore, is inundated less frequently, and the growth rate necessarily decreases. Indeed, studies have shown that the initial phase of floodplain elevation by vertical accretion is quite rapid because flooding occurs frequently. It is generally accepted that 80 to 90 percent of floodplain construction by vertical accretion would take place in the first 50 years of the process. A 3-metre (10-foot) thick overbank deposit would probably take several thousand years to accumulate.

Given the preceding information, it seems certain that the total thickness of vertically accumulated sediment will depend primarily on the rate at which the river migrates laterally. In fact, the total thickness of overbank deposition will be controlled by the amount of time it takes a river to migrate across the entire width of the valley. For example, if a floodplain is 1 km (0.6 miles) wide and the river shifts laterally at a rate of 2 metres (about 7 feet) a year, it will take approximately five hundred years for the river to migrate completely across the valley bottom. At any given point in the valley bottom, several metres of overbank sediment may accumulate in that five-hundred-year interval, but the entire deposit will be reworked by lateral erosion when the river once again reoccupies that particular position. Thus the lateral migration rate becomes a limiting factor on the thickness of vertical accretion deposits. This conclusion, however, cannot be considered as an inviolate rule. Many rivers have extremely slow rates of lateral migration when geologic conditions prevent bank erosion. In these cases, vertical accretion may be the dominant process of floodplain development.

RIVER TERRACES

Terraces are flat surfaces preserved in valleys that represent floodplains developed when the river flowed at a higher elevation than its present channel. A terrace consists of two distinct topographic components: (1) a tread, which is the flat surface of the former floodplain, and (2) a scarp, which is the steep slope that connects the tread to any surface standing lower in the valley. Terraces are commonly used to reconstruct the history of a river valley. Because the presence of a terrace scarp requires river downcutting, some significant change in controlling factors must have occurred between the time that the tread formed and the time that the scarp was produced. Usually the phase of trenching begins as a response to climatic change, tectonics (movement and deformation of the crust), or baselevel lowering. Like most floodplains, abandoned or active, the surface of the tread is normally underlain by alluvium deposited by the river. Strictly speaking, however, these deposits are not part of the terrace because the term refers only to the topographic form.

The extent to which a terrace is preserved in a valley usually depends on the age of the surface. Old terraces are those that were formed when the river flowed at very high levels above the present-day river channel, while terraces of even greater age are those usually cut into widely separated, isolated segments. In contrast, very young terraces may be essentially continuous along the entire length of the trunk valley, being dissected only where tributary streams emerge from the valley sides. These young terraces may be close in elevation to the modern floodplain, and the two surfaces may be difficult to distinguish. This difficulty emphasizes the importance of how a floodplain and terrace are defined. Presumably the surface of a terrace is no longer related to the modern hydrology in terms of frequency and magnitude of flow events. Thus, any flat surface standing above the level inundated by a flow having a recurrence interval of 1.5 years is by definition a terrace. The complication arises, however, because some low terraces may be covered by floodwater during events of higher magnitude and lower frequency. These terrace surfaces are inundated by the modern hydrologic system but less frequently than the definition of a hydrologic floodplain would allow. In some cases, a low terrace may be underlain by sediment that has been continuously deposited for thousands of years during infrequent large floods.

Terraces are most commonly classified on the basis of topographic relationships between their segments. Where terrace treads stand at the same elevation on both sides of the valley, they are called paired terraces. The surfaces of the paired relationship are presumed to be equivalent in age and part of the same abandoned flood-plain. Where terrace levels are different across the valley, they are said to be unpaired terraces. In most cases the staggered elevations in these systems were formed when the river eroded both laterally and vertically during the phase of degradation. Levels across the valley, therefore, are not precisely the same age but differ by the amount of time needed for the river to cross from one side of the valley to the other. Actually, the topographic classification is purely descriptive and is not intended to be used as a method for determining terrace origin. A more useful classification provides a genetic connotation by categorizing terraces as either erosional or depositional. Erosional terraces are those in which the tread (abandoned floodplain) has been formed primarily by lateral erosion under the conditions of a constant baselevel. Where erosion cuts across bedrock, the terms bench, strath, or rock-cut terrace are employed. The terms fill-cut or fillstrath are used to indicate that the lateral erosion has occurred across unconsolidated debris. Depositional terraces are those in which the tread represents the upper surface of a valley fill.

Rock-cut terraces and depositional terraces can be distinguished by certain properties that reflect their mode of origin. Rock-cut surfaces are usually capped by a uniformly thin layer of alluvium, the total thickness of which is determined by the depth of scour of the river that formed the terrace tread. In addition, the surface eroded across the bedrock or older alluvium is remarkably flat and essentially mirrors the configuration of the tread. In contrast, alluvium beneath the tread of a depositional terrace can be extremely variable in thickness and usually exceeds any reasonable scouring depth of the associated river. Moreover, the eroded surface in the bedrock beneath the fill can be very irregular even though the surface of the terrace tread is flat. The most difficult terrace to distinguish by these criteria are erosional terraces that are cut across a thick, unconsolidated valley fill.

THE ORIGIN OF RIVER TERRACES

The treads of river terraces are formed by processes analogous to those that produce floodplains. In depositional terraces, however, the origin of the now abandoned floodplain is much less significant than the long-term episode of valley filling that preceded the final embellishment of the tread. The thickness of valley-fill deposits is much greater than anything that could be produced by vertical accretion on a floodplain surface. In fact, most of the valley fill is composed of channel deposits rather than floodplain deposits. Thus, the sediment beneath a depositional terrace reflects a continuously rising valley floor. The tread represents the highest level attained by the valley floor as it rose during this episode of aggradation, and the upper skim of the deposit is that affected by processes of floodplain origin. What caused the extended period of valley filling is thus the important aspect of depositional terraces rather than the processes that developed the final character of the tread.

Valley filling that creates the underpinning of a depositional terrace occurs when the amount of sediment produced in a basin over an extended period of time is greater than the amount that the river system can remove from the basin. Usually this phenomenon is produced by climate change, influx of glacial outwash, uplift in source areas, or rises in baselevel that trigger deposition in the lower portions of the basin. Development of the actual terrace requires an interval subsequent to valley filling during which the river entrenches into the fill. Many of the same factors that trigger valley filling are those which, oppositely impressed, initiate the episode of entrenchment.

The relationship between glaciation and depositional terraces constitutes the cornerstone of reconstructing geomorphic history in valleys that have been glaciated. The balance between load and discharge that ultimately determines whether a river will deposit or erode is severely altered during glacial episodes. An enormous volume of coarse-grained bed load is carried by an active glacier and released at the glacial margin. This influx of sediment simply overwhelms the downstream fluvial system, even though meltwater produced near the ice margin provides greater than normal transporting power to a river emerging from the glacier. As a result, valley reaches downstream from the ice margin begin to fill with coarse debris (outwash), which cannot be transported on the channel gradient that existed prior to the glacial event. Deposition ensues, and the valley aggrades until the gradient, load, and discharge conditions are modified enough to allow transport of the entire load or to initiate river entrenchment into the fill.

Valley fills composed of outwash and the depositional terraces that result from later entrenchment are closely associated with moraines (ridges composed of rock debris deposited directly by ice) developed simultaneously at the ice margin. Characteristically the gradient on the terrace surface increases drastically near the moraine, and outwash beneath the terrace tread thickens significantly and becomes notably more coarse-grained. The terrace and its associated alluvium end at the moraine, being totally absent up the valley from the morainal position. This allows the location of an ice margin to be determined as the upstream extremity of an outwash terrace even if the associated moraine has been removed by subsequent erosion.

Accumulations of rock debris directly set down by ice—known as moraines and shown here in Glacier National Park, Mont.—develop at the same time as valley fills. U.S. Geological Survey

In unglaciated river systems, valley fills are most commonly associated with climatic changes, tectonics, or rising sea levels. Climatically produced valley aggradation is controlled by very complex interrelationships between precipitation, vegetation, and the amount of sediment yielded from basin slopes. Every climatic regime has a particular combination of precipitation and vegetation type and density that will produce a maximum value of sediment yield. The effect of a particular climate change can increase or decrease sediment yield in a basin, depending on what conditions existed prior to the climate change with respect to the values that would produce the maximum yield.

In contrast to depositional terraces, erosional terraces are specifically related to the processes of floodplain development. Erosional terraces are those in which lateral river migration and lateral accretion are the dominant processes in constructing the floodplain surface that subsequently becomes the terrace tread. Most of the terrace surface is underlain by point bar deposits. These deposits are usually thin and maintain a constant thickness of sediment that rests on a flat surface eroded across the underlying bedrock or unconsolidated debris. The thickness of the point bar deposits is controlled by the depth to which the formative river was able to scour during the formation of the floodplain. Any thickness greater than the depth of scour indicates that deposits underlying the tread represent a valley fill (depositional terrace) rather than an erosional terrace. Rock-cut terraces were first and best described in the Big Horn Basin of Wyoming, although some of the terraces in that area may be depositional in origin.

OUTWASH

Outwash is a deposit of sand and gravel carried by running water from the melting ice of a glacier and laid down in stratified deposits. An outwash may attain a thickness of 100 metres (328 feet) at the edge of a glacier, although the thickness is usually much less; it may also extend many kilometres in length. For example, outwash deposits from the Wisconsin Glaciation can be traced to the mouth of the Mississippi River, 1,120 km (700 miles) from the nearest glacial terminus.

The sheet of outwash may be pitted with undrained kettles or dissected by postglacial streams. Outwash plains are commonly cross-bedded with units of alternating grain size. The ordinarily gentle slope causes the larger material to be dropped nearest the glacier, while the smaller grain sizes are spread over greater distances. Striated pebbles are uncommon because the striations are worn away during transport. Outwashes are the largest of the fluvioglacial deposits and provide a considerable source of windblown material. When confined within valley walls, the outwash deposit is known as a valley train.

TERRACES AND GEOMORPHIC HISTORY

The use of terraces to determine regional geomorphic history requires careful field study involving correlation of surfaces within a valley or between valleys. The process is not easy, because each terrace sequence must be examined according to its own climatic, tectonic, and geologic setting. Terraces that have been dissected into segments often have only isolated remnants of the original surface. These remnants are commonly separated by considerable distances, often many kilometres. Reconstruction of the original terrace surface requires that the isolated remnants be correctly correlated along the length of the valley, and every method used in this procedure has fundamental assumptions that may or may not be valid. Furthermore, errors in physical correlation of surfaces lead to faulty interpretation of valley history. This problem is exacerbated because fluvial mechanics may be out of phase in different parts of a valley or from one valley to its adjacent neighbour. For example, pronounced filling by outwash deposition (discussed earlier) may be occurring in the upper reaches of a major valley such as the Mississippi during the maximum of a glacial stage. At the same time, however, near the Gulf of Mexico, the lower reaches of the Mississippi River would be actively entrenching because baselevel (sea level) is drastically lowered during glacial periods when storage of ice on the continents upsets the balance in the hydrologic cycle. Deposition and entrenchment involved in terrace formation is clearly not synchronous along the entire length of such a river system.

In addition, it is now known that more than one terrace can result during a period of entrenchment. This indicates that the downcutting that presumably results during a change in climate or some other controlling factor may not be a continuous unidirectional event. Instead, the response to that change is complex. It often involves pauses in vertical entrenchment during which the river may form erosional terraces by lateral planation or depositional terraces by short intervals of valley alluviation. The complicating factor with regard to valley history is that multiple terraces may be formed during an adjustment to one equilibrium-disrupting change in factors that control fluvial mechanics.

CHAPTER 5

RIVERS AS AGENTS OF LANDSCAPE EVOLUTION: ALLUVIAL FANS, DELTAS, AND ESTUARIES

Other landscape features occurring at the fringes of watersheds are heavily influenced by the activities of rivers. Alluvial fans, which are concentrations of sediment that accumulate at the mouth of a mountain canyon, are the result of rivers that cease or slow the delivery of sediment. Deltas, on the other hand, are low-lying plains formed from the continual deposition of sediment by the river. They occur where the river empties into the ocean. Estuaries also occur where rivers meet a larger water body. Estuaries are, however, partially enclosed by land and characterized by the brackish conditions that result when river water mixes with seawater.

ALLUVIAL FANS

Alluvial fans are depositional features formed at one end of an erosional-depositional system in which sediment is transferred from one part of a watershed to another. Erosion is dominant in the upper part of the watershed, and deposition occurs at its lower reaches where sediment is free to accumulate without being confined within a river valley. The two areas are linked by a single trunk river. Fans are best developed where erosion occurs in a mountain area and sediment for the fan is placed in an adjacent basin. A fan is best described

Although alluvial fans are predominant in arid areas such as Death Valley, Calif., they can form in nearly any climatic zone with analogous physiographic controls. Dr. Marli Miller/Visuals Unlimited/Getty Images

topographically as a segment of a cone that radiates away from a single point source. The apex of the cone stands where the trunk river emerges from the confines of the upland area. It is possible, however, that the point source can shift to a position well down the original fan surface. This occurs when the trunk stream entrenches the fan surface, and the mountain-bred flow, still confined in the channel cut into the fan, eventually emerges at a location far removed from the mountain front. The location where the stream emerges onto the fan surface then becomes the point source for a still younger fan segment. Fans also expand upward and laterally. In many cases, adjacent fans merge at their lateral extremities, and the individual cone or fan shape becomes obliterated. Widespread coalescing of fans produces a rather nondescript topography that covers an entire piedmont area (stretch of land along the base of mountains) and is commonly referred to as a bajada, alluvial plain, or alluvial slope.

Alluvial fans have been studied in greatest detail in areas of arid or semiarid climate, where they tend to be larger and better preserved. This is especially true where considerable relief exists between the erosional part of the basin and the zone of deposition. Fans in this particular climatic setting have been described in various parts of the world, including the western United States, Afghanistan, Pakistan, Peru, Central Asia, and many other semiarid regions where mountains exist adjacent to well-defined basins. The dominance of fans in arid and semiarid regions does not mean that fans are absent in other climatic zones. On the contrary, fans can develop in almost any climatic zone where the physiographic controls are similar. For example, fans have been identified in Canada, Sweden, Japan, Alaska, and very high mountain areas such as the Alps and Himalayas. The one common factor that links these fans together, regardless of their climatic setting, is the similar plan-view geometry. Other characteristics, such as morphology and depositional processes, may be significantly different, however. The widespread distribution of fans has led to the characterization of these features as being one of two types—either dry or wet. Dry fans are those that seem to form under conditions of ephemeral flow, while wet fans are those that are created by streams that flow constantly. This classification suggests that fan type is climatically controlled, because ephemeral flow is normally associated with the spasmodic rainfall typical of arid climates, and perennial streamflow is more dominant in humid climates.

SIZE, MORPHOLOGY, AND SURFACE CHARACTERISTICS

The size of an alluvial fan seems to be related to many factors, such as the physiography and geology of the source area and the regional climate. There appears to be no lower limit to the size of fans as the feature may appear on a microscale in almost any environment. It is known from studies in various parts of the world that a large number of modern-day fans have a radius from 1.5 to 10 km (0.9 to 6 miles). Some fans have a radius as large as 20 km (about 12 miles), but these are rare because fans of that size tend to merge with their neighbours, and limited space in depositional basins often prevents free expansion. It is now firmly established that the area of a dry fan seems to be closely related to the area of the basin supplying the fan sediment. For example, in the western part of the United States, area of the fan and source basin area are related by a simple power function $A_f = cA_d^n$, where A_f is the area of the fan and A_d is the area of the drainage basin. The value of the exponent n is reasonably constant for fans in California and Nevada, with a value of approximately 0.9 when the measurements are made in square miles. The coefficient c in the equation, however, varies widely and reflects the effect of other geomorphic factors on fan size. The most important of these factors are climate, lithology of source rock, tectonics, and the space available for fan growth. Fans studied in Fresno County, Calif., for example, showed that for a given drainage basin area fans derived from basins underlain by mudstones and shale are almost twice as large as those that receive sediment from basins underlain by sandstone. In basins underlain by different rocks, the value of n was approximately the same, but the effect of particle size was seen clearly in the value of the coefficient c, which varied from 0.96 for sandstone basins to 2.1 in mudstone drainage basins. Presumably basins underlain by fine-grained sediments are much more erodible and produce a much greater sediment load.

Fans are, by the very nature of their semi-conical shape, convex upward across the fan surface. The longitudinal slope of a fan usually decreases from the apex to the toe even though its value at any particular location depends on the load-discharge characteristics of the fluvial system. Near the mountain front in the apical area, slopes on fans are commonly very steep, though they probably never exceed 10°. In their distal margins near the toe, gradients may be as low as two metres per kilometre , or about 10.5 feet per mile (<1°). The steepest gradients are often associated with coarse-grained loads, high sediment production, and transport processes other than normal streamflow. These same factors may often counteract one another within any given region. The aforementioned fans derived from basins underlain by the mudstones are much steeper than fans of the same size related to sandstone basins. The small particle size would presumably create a more gentle slope, but this expectation is offset by the high rate of sediment production in the mudstone basins which produces a much greater total load.

Fan gradients are often known to have special characteristics. First, the gradient of most fans at the apex is approximately the same as that of the trunk river where it moves from the mountain area onto the fan itself. This indicates that deposition on the fan is not caused by a dramatic decrease in gradient as the trunk river passes from the source area to the fan apex. The decrease in velocity required for deposition to occur is caused by some change in hydraulic geometry or because total river discharge decreases as water infiltrates from the channel bottom into the fan material itself. Second, the normal concave-up longitudinal profile that exists on most fans between the apex and the toe is not a smooth exponential curve. Instead, on many fans such as some found in Canada, New Zealand, and the western United States, concavity is produced by the junction of several relatively straight segments, each successive down-fan segment having a lower gradient. Each of the individual segments is probably related to changes imposed on the channel of the trunk river upstream from the fan apex. On some fans, intermittent uplifts of the source area have increased stream gradients, and, in response to these spasmodic tectonic events, there formed a new fan segment that gradually adjusted its slope until it was essentially the same as the newly developed steeper slope of the trunk river. Segmentation, however, may also result from other factors, such as a climatic change that produces a different load/discharge balance. The overall longitudinal profile may be a sensitive indicator of changes that have occurred in the balance between erosional and depositional parts of the fluvial system.

Although fan size and gradients appear to be related to the characteristics of the drainage basin, considerable variation exists on the surface of fans that have been developed under the same physiographic, geologic, and climatic controls. Surface characteristics of dry fans can often be subdivided into major zones called modern washes, abandoned washes, and desert pavements. These different zones seem to reflect areas that are involved to a greater or lesser degree in modern fan processes. For example, on the Shadow Mountain fan in Death Valley, Calif., washes of various types make up almost 70 percent of the surface area, but only a few of them are occupied by present-day streamflow. These are modern washes and represent the primary areas of deposition on the fan surface under the present discharge regime. They normally contain unweathered sediment particles and have virtually no vegetation.

The large majority of washes are now abandoned, meaning that they are no longer occupied by flow coming from the mountain basins. Abandoned washes have a scrub vegetation, and the gravel in the channels tends to be coated with a dark surface veneer known as desert varnish. Most authorities believe that desert varnish, a brownish-black veneer of iron and manganese oxides, requires several thousand years to develop. This indicates that washes recognized as abandoned have not been occupied by water for millennia.

Desert pavements are surfaces composed of tightly packed gravel, the particles of which are covered by a thick varnish coating. The gravel usually exists as a thin surface cover or armour, which protects an underlying layer of silt that formed under long weathering of the original deposits. Silt that was originally in the spaces between the gravel at the surface has been blown away by wind action, leaving behind a lag deposit composed entirely of gravel. Areas of desert pavement are commonly cut by gullies that head within the pavement area itself. The gullies carry a fine-grained load, which is locally derived from the silt layer beneath the surface gravel cap. Because of this, they often meander and may stand at lower elevations than adjacent modern washes that originate in the mountains. This topographic relationship sets up a geomorphic situation that allows water flowing down modern washes to be diverted periodically into the gullies. With time, part of the desert pavement area may revert back into an active wash by shifting the entire position of the river draining from the mountain. When this occurs, the segment of the wash downstream from where it is diverted gradually turns back into an area of an abandoned wash. What results from these activities is the possibility that processes functioning on dry fans are continuously creating and destroying the various surface areas mentioned above. This means that modern washes will eventually become abandoned washes, and, with time, such abandoned washes will gradually turn into the smooth, heavily varnished surface of a desert pavement. At other places on the same fan, desert pavement areas are being converted back into modern washes, so that the history of the fan becomes a complex continuum of change referred to as dynamic equilibrium.

The dynamic equilibrium model is not accepted by all fan experts. Some believe fans are formed and destroyed (i.e., deposited and eroded) in response to climatic changes that produce different load/discharge relationships. Others hold that some fans have been building continuously for a long time and are approaching some type of equilibrium condition but as yet have not attained that condition. It should be noted that these diverse opinions have been produced by examination of the same fans. Thus, the significance of features and materials found on a fan surface is not so readily discernible that everyone will arrive at the same conclusion as to how they formed.

FAN DEPOSITS AND DEPOSITIONAL PROCESSES

Transfer of sediment from source basins to depositional sites on a fan surface involves flow consisting of several types, ranging from high-viscosity debris or mudflows to flows involving normal water. The type of flow experienced on any fan depends primarily on the geologic characteristics of the basin and on the magnitude of precipitation that initiates the flow event. In arid regions the ephemeral nature of rivers and the character of rainfall results in spasmodic rather than continuous deposition on the fan surface. The location of deposition tends to change repeatedly. Deposits of any single flow usually are confined to shallow channels and because of this assume a long, linear distribution. Each deposit may be up to several kilometres long and only 100 to 700 metres (330 to 2,300 feet) wide. The dimensions of each deposit depend on the viscosity of flow, the permeability of surface material, and how far down the fan flow can be held within a distinct channel. Although flow emerging onto the fan surface follows well-defined channels near the apex, water overflows the banks and spreads outward as diffuse flow at some point along the down-fan path of movement. Where the channel is capable of shifting laterally, the location of deposition tends to develop a sheet of rather poorly bedded sand and gravel in which individual layers can be traced for some distance away from the channel. Commonly these sheets are interrupted by thick deposits that represent entrenchment and backfill into the fan surface.

Debris flows or mudflows must follow well-defined channels because a greater depth of flow is needed to offset the high viscosity of the fluid. Nonetheless, debris flows may overflow banks and spread out as sheets, though their viscosity suggests that they will not spread as far laterally as normal water flows. Debris flows are so dense that they are capable of transporting large boulders for considerable distances. The distance of transport, however, is limited by the high viscosity of the fluid, and so movement down the channel may simply stop, even though the fluid is still confined within the channel. Fan deposits that result from debris flows are characteristically unsorted, having clast sizes that range from clay to boulders. Usually no sedimentary structures such as bed forms or cross-beds are observed in deposits of this type. Also, the deposits of debris flows are usually lobate and have well-defined margins often marked by distinct ridges. Some fans are built almost entirely by debris flows. The flow characteristics seem to be generated most commonly in arid or semiarid climates, where torrential rains are separated by periods of little or no precipitation. This pattern allows material to collect on the slopes of the source basin and provides the load necessary to generate a debris-flow pattern.

This does not mean that debris flows are restricted only to those climatic regions. Fans developed primarily by debris-flow action have been described in humid-temperate regions, such as New Zealand and Virginia in the United States. In general, fans in Virginia, found on the east flank of the Blue Ridge Mountains, are smaller than arid fans and do not have the same areal relationships as the dry fans in California. They are typically elongate and rather irregular. Such fans probably result from major storm events, which in some cases erode deep trenches near the apex and deposit coarse debris across the lower fan surface. Geologic evidence suggests that the interval between depositional events can be extremely long, some possibly having a depositional recurrence interval from three thousand to six thousand years. Therefore, alluvial fans developed by these processes may be extremely old and not necessarily related to the modern climate. This also is demonstrated in some fans in the White Mountains of California, which have been continuously accumulating for more than 700,000 years and appear to be totally composed of debris-flow deposits.

Deposition on true wet fans seems to be considerably different from that associated with dry fans. Fans developed in the Kosi River basin in India contrast drastically with classic dry fans. The Kosi fan has as its source the Himalayas, and sediment derived from that source is being collected in the piedmont area. During the last several hundred years, the Kosi River has shifted approximately 100 km (60 miles) while creating its large wet fan. At the fan apex, sediment is characteristically coarse gravel, which is rarely transported far downstream. The river tends to widen drastically in a downstream direction, and braiding becomes the dominant channel pattern spread over an extremely wide area of the fan—approximately 6 km (about 4 miles). The shift in channel location seems to be a progressive event rather than the almost random shifting noted on dry fans. Fans developed by this perennial flow should have rather well-defined stratification and be very well sorted. Both of these characteristics have been demonstrated by experimental flume studies of wet fans, and such characteristics are occasionally shown in the natural field setting.

Although lateral shifting of modern washes is necessary for the development of some fan characteristics, it is equally important to recognize that the loci of deposition also migrate along radial lines during fan development. Such longitudinal shifting is facilitated by entrenching and/or backfilling the channel that links the source area to the fan. Incision at the fan apex produces a fan-head trench, which has a lower gradient than the fan surface. The trench is thus deepest at the apex and becomes shallower as it progresses down the fan. It eventually becomes part of the normal drainage system on the fan surface. This property is significant because sediment may be transported and deposited farther down fan in the confines of a trench than it would be in a normal surface channel. The location of fan deposition may thus depend on where the trench channel emerges onto the fan surface. Entrenchment near the fan apex can be temporary or permanent. Distinguishing between these two possibilities is critical in an analysis of fan origin, and it often demands an understanding of whether the fan surface is still part of the active system. Many fan-head trenches appear to be short-term features in that they show evidence of alternating episodes of trenching and filling. In that sense, the entrenchment is temporary in nature. Experimental studies of wet fans and field observations have increased scientific perception of how the temporary nature of fan-head trenches is controlled. In wet fans, sediment is spread as a sheet over most of the area near the fan apex. Deposition in the down-fan area, however, occurs in numerous braided channels. This depositional pattern will continue until the fan slope near the apex becomes so steep that it initiates vertical incision by the trunk river. The result of incision is the fan-head trench. Flow becomes confined within that channel rather than being spread evenly across the upper part of the fan. Thus, the fan surface near the apex is temporarily starved of sediment, and most of the water and debris coming from the source area is transported down the fan in the entrenched channel. As entrenchment migrates upstream into the source area, increased load is derived as the trunk river is rejuvenated. The load is subsequently transported downstream and deposited in the fan-head trench. This initiates a phase of deposition within the trench that raises the channel floor until the trench is totally filled, and deposition begins again over the entire apical area. Eventually the gradient becomes over-steepened and the process repeats itself. In this case, it is clear that the fan-head trench is temporary. The entire fan may continue to grow with time, but the apex area experiences episodes of entrenchment during which sediment is reworked and moved farther down the fan. These episodes alternate with filling of the channel until the slope of the fan near the apex is increased to a threshold condition.

Temporary entrenchment may result from processes other than the built-in system described above. It may be that alternating trenching and filling results when fan processes change during variations of climate that produce different amounts of sediment, rainfall, and discharge. In such a case, the primary driving force is external to the system and is involved more with characteristics of the drainage basin than with processes operating at the fan apex.

In some cases, entrenchment on a fan surface is permanent or certainly long-term. Depths of incision are often greater than 30 metres (100 feet) below the fan surface, making trenches of that magnitude very difficult to refill. The cause of incision of this magnitude is usually external to the fan system itself. In basins of deposition that are open, the most common cause of permanent entrenchment is a decline in baselevel by the river flowing through the basin. This will initiate a wave of fan incision that is propagated up the fan from the toe. Eventually the entire fan is dissected when entrenchment reaches the apex and proceeds into the drainage basin. When this occurs, the fan surface standing above the trench is no longer part of the active fan. In fact, soils will develop on the alluvium, and drainage networks will be established on the old fan surface.

ECONOMIC SIGNIFICANCE

Alluvial fans are important for a variety of practical reasons. In some cases, particularly porous and permeable fan deposits are the primary source of groundwater, which is used for irrigation and for water supply. This is especially true in arid or semiarid climates. Wet fans are known to have economic significance because their process mechanics tend to concentrate heavy mineral particles in placer deposits. As discussed earlier, experimental work on wet fans shows that water tends to spread as a sheet near the fan head, but flow down the fan is subdivided into many braided channels that shift their position laterally. This flow pattern is periodically interrupted by fan-head trenching. Therefore, as noted both in nature and in experimental flume studies, wet fans grow progressively with time, but processes producing alternating trenching and filling at the fan head tend to rework and distribute the sediment down the fan. Experimental studies in the United States have shown that heavy minerals derived from a source area are preferentially concentrated in the area of the fan head by repeated trenching and filling. The concentration is great enough to expect economic placer deposits to develop at the fan head and at the base of backfilled channels.

Perhaps the classic example of the connection between wet-fan processes and the concentration of valuable metals is the Witwatersrand Basin in South Africa, which ranks as one of the greatest gold-producing areas of the world. Although the six major goldfields in the basin and their sedimentary deposits are not entirely fluvial, gold seems to be concentrated in ancient fan deposits from the source areas of granite that originally contained the gold. Evidence suggests that each of these fields is associated with a wet fan that developed where a large river discharged from the source rocks.

DELTAS

The most important landform produced where a river enters a body of standing water is known as a delta. The term is normally applied to a depositional plain formed by a river at its mouth, with the implication that sediment accumulation at this position results in an irregular progradation of the shoreline. This surface feature was first recognized and named by the ancient Greek historian Herodotus, who noted that sediment accumulated at the mouth of the Nile River resembled the Greek letter Δ (delta). Even though a large number of modern deltas have this triangular form, many display a variety of sizes and shapes that depend on a number of environmental factors. Thus, the term now has little, if any, shape connotation. Deltas, in fact, exhibit tremendous variation in their morphological and sedimentologic characteristics and also in their mode of origin. Most of the variation results from (1) characteristics within the drainage basin that provides the sediment (e.g., climate, lithology, tectonic stability, and basin size); (2) properties of the transporting agent, such as river slope, velocity, discharge, and sediment size; and (3) energy that exists along the shoreline, including such factors as wave characteristics, longitudinal currents, and tidal range. The shoreline zone, therefore, becomes the battleground between variable amounts and sizes of sediment delivered to the river mouth and the energy of the ocean waters at that site. The balance between these two factors determines whether accumulation of the river-borne sediment will occur or whether ocean processes will disperse the sediment or prevent its deposition. The combination of these numerous variables tends to create deltas that occur in a complete spectrum of form and depositional style.

Deltas are distributed over all portions of the Earth's surface. They form along the coasts of every landmass and occur in all climatic regimes and geologic settings. The largest deltas of the world are those created by major river systems draining regions that are subcontinental in size and yield abundant sediment from the watershed.

CLASSIFICATION OF DELTAS

Deltas come in a multitude of plan-view shapes, as their characteristics are determined by the balance between the energy and sediment load of a fluvial system and the dynamics of the ocean. Various ways of classifying deltas have been devised. One of the more widely used schemes is based on deltaic form as it reflects controlling energy factors. This scheme divides deltas into two principal classes: high-constructive and high-destructive.

High-constructive deltas develop when fluvial action and depositional process dominate the system. These deltas usually occur in either of two forms. One type, known as elongate, is represented most clearly by the modern bird-foot delta of the Mississippi River. The other, called lobate, is exemplified by the older Holocene deltas of the Mississippi River system. Both of these high-constructive types have a large sediment supply relative to the marine processes that tend to disperse sediment along the shoreline. Normally, elongate deltas have a higher mud content than lobate deltas and tend to subside rather rapidly when they become inactive.

High-destructive deltas form where the shoreline energy is high and much of the sediment delivered by the river is reworked by wave action or longshore currents before it is finally deposited. Deltas formed by rivers such as the Nile and the Rhône have been classified as wave-dominated. In this class of high-destructive delta, sediment is finally deposited as arcuate sand barriers near the mouth of the river. In another subtype, called tide-dominated, tidal currents mold the sediment into sandy units that tend to radiate in a linear pattern from the river mouth. In such a delta, muds and silts are deposited inland of the linear sands, and extensive tidal flats or mangrove swamps characteristically develop in that zone.

Considerable attention has been given to deltas that are composed of very coarse deposits—those of sand and gravel. Deltas developing from this type of material are commonly classified as either fan deltas or braid deltas. A fan delta is a depositional feature that is formed where an alluvial fan develops directly in a body of standing water from some adjacent highland. A braid delta is a coarse-grained delta that develops by progradation of a braided fluvial system into a body of standing water. The two are related by the fact that they are composed primarily of very coarse sediment. However, they differ in that braid deltas result from well-defined, highly channelized braided rivers that are deeper and have more sustained flow than streams which develop alluvial fans. In addition, the braided system that ultimately forms the braid delta may have its source far removed from the body of standing water and may in fact consist of large alluvial plains rather than the restricted areal and longitudinal extent associated with alluvial fans.

MORPHOLOGY OF DELTAS

Deltas consist of three physiographic parts called the upper delta plain, the lower delta plain, and the subaqueous delta. The upper delta plain begins as the river leaves the zone where its alluvial plain is confined laterally by valley walls. When the valley wall constraint ends, the river breaks into a multitude of channels, and the depositional plain widens. This point source of the upper delta plain can be thought of as the apex of the entire delta, which is analogous to the same reach of an alluvial fan. The entire upper delta plain is fluvial in origin except for marshes, swamps, and freshwater lakes that exist in areas between the many river channels. The surface of the upper delta plain is above the highest tidal level and thus is not affected by marine processes. In contrast, the lower delta plain is occasionally covered by tidal water. For this reason, the boundary between the upper delta plain and the lower delta plain is determined by the maximum tidal elevation. Features and deposits in the lower delta plain are the result of both fluvial and marine processes. Tidal flats, mangrove swamps, beach ridges, and brackish-water bays and marshes are common in this zone.

Deltas affected by high tidal ranges, such as those constructed by the Niger River and the Ganges–Brahmaputra system, are dominated by marine incursions and expansive lower delta plains. For example, the Ganges–Brahmaputra system in Bangladesh has a lower delta plain that occupies more than half of its total surface area of 60,000 square km (23,000 square miles) and is characterized by enormous mangrove swamps. Low tidal ranges result in deltas having much better developed upper delta plains (e.g., the Nile of Egypt and the Volga of Russia).

A subaqueous delta plain is located entirely below sea level, and marine processes dominate the system. This part of the delta is responsible for the topographic bulge seen on the continental shelf seaward of channels that flow across the exposed delta plains. Sediment-laden river flow entering the ocean in well-defined channels loses transporting power where the channels end, and sediment is deposited as the subaqueous delta plain. Large

Russia's Volga Delta has a well-developed upper plain owing to low tidal ranges. Reza/Getty Images

subaqueous plains are best developed where the continental shelf is shallow and gently sloping and where sediment loads derived from source basins are great. The subaqueous deltas of the Amazon, the Orinoco, and the Huang He are broad and widespread in response to these controls. It is true, however, that even if these ideal conditions exist, a broad subaqueous delta does not always result. This is especially true where large submarine canyons exist near the terminations of river channels. In these cases, sediment delivered to the ocean is funneled down the canyon and deposited beyond the margin of the continental shelf. If a subaqueous delta develops in such situations, it is usually very small.

River channels that traverse the subaerial portion of a delta (upper and lower delta plain) serve as the conduits through which sediment is delivered to the subaqueous component. The channels assume any one of three patterns: (1) long, straight single channels, (2) braided or anastomotic (veinlike) multiple channels, or (3) channels that bifurcate (branch) in a downstream direction. In general, the channel pattern is controlled both by source basin characteristics (sediment size and volume, flood-discharge features, etc.) and marine properties (tidal range and wave energy, for example). Rivers transporting fine-grained sediment tend to develop either single channels or downstream bifurcating patterns. The single-channel pattern results where offshore wave energy is high (e.g., the Mekong and Congo deltas). Braided or anastomotic channels develop best where rivers carry a large volume of coarse-grained bed load. Branching distributaries form most commonly where tidal range and wave energy is low (e.g., the Mississippi and Volga deltas).

Most delta channels are bordered by natural levees that resemble those found on floodplains. These features are best developed by rivers that flood frequently and transport large volumes of suspended load, as, for example, the Mississippi. Interfluve areas (those between adjacent streams flowing in the same direction) are variable in character, depending on climate, tidal range, and offshore wave energy.

DEPOSITS AND STRATIGRAPHY

Delta growth indicates that a river delivers sediment to the shore faster and in greater volume than marine processes can remove the load. During the delta-building process, sediment is distributed in such a way that the feature develops a unique form. Under normal discharge conditions, sediment remains within the channel until it reaches the river mouth. No lateral dispersion of the load occurs on the subaerial delta plain, and because river velocity is so low, waves and currents spread the fine-grained portion of the sediment laterally along the delta front. During floods, however, suspended sediment and organic matter are deposited in the interfluve areas, causing those portions of the subaerial delta to aggrade. The high river velocity at the mouth offsets wave and current action, allowing sediment to be transported farther seaward. This facilitates accumulation at the delta front and causes the subaqueous delta to prograde.

The dispersal of sediment during floods and normal discharges creates a well-defined horizontal and vertical depositional sequence. On the subaerial delta plain, silts and clays accumulate vertically in inter-distributary zones. At the mouths of deltaic rivers, marine processes rework fine-grained sediment, but more coarse deposits of sands and silts usually build forward while maintaining a steep seaward slope. Smaller clay particles pass over the delta slope and are deposited on the continental shelf in front of the subaqueous delta plain. Therefore, in a horizontal sense, many deltas have silty, organic-rich deposits in their subaerial portion, though channel sands and levee deposits interrupt the fine-grained interfluve sequence. More coarse sediment is deposited at the river mouth, and very fine-grained materials (clays) accumulate beyond the delta front. The vertical sequence is essentially the same with marine clays at the lowest elevation (greatest depth), silts and sands at nearshore depths, and silts, clays, and organics—along with associated channel and levee sands—at the highest (subaerial) elevations. This model of alluviation does not accommodate very coarse (gravel and sand) deposition on the subaerial delta plain, which provides the special deltaic types known as fan deltas or braid deltas, but it is representative of most of the major deltas of the world.

Deposits found in the deltaic stratigraphic sequence were named topset, foreset, and bottomset by the American geologist Grove K. Gilbert in his 1890 report on Lake Bonneville, the vast Pleistocene ancestor of what is now the Great Salt Lake of Utah. Although Gilbert examined small deltas along the margins of the ancient lake, the stratigraphic sequence he observed is similar to that found in large marine deltas. Topset beds are a complex of lithologic units deposited in various sub-environments of the subaerial delta plain. Layers in the topset unit are almost horizontal. Foreset deposits accumulate in the subaqueous delta front zone. The deposits are usually coarser at the river mouth and become finer as they radiate seaward into deeper water. Strata in the foreset unit are inclined seaward at an angle reflecting that of the delta slope or front. In large marine deltas the beds rarely dip more than 1°, but where bed load is coarse, such as in braid deltas, foreset beds may be inclined at angles greater than 20°. Foreset layers are beveled at their landward positions by topset beds, which expand horizontally as the entire delta advances into the ocean. At their seaward extremity, fore-set beds grade imperceptibly into the bottomset strata. Bottomset deposits are composed primarily of clays that were swept beyond the delta front. These beds usually dip at very low angles that are consistent with the topography of the continental shelf or lake bottom in front of the subaqueous delta. This depositional environment is commonly referred to as the prodelta zone.

DELTAS AND TIME

One of the most important perceptions needed to understand deltas is how their depositional framework changes with time. Because delta characteristics are controlled by factors that are subject to change, it follows that deltaic growth patterns are dynamic and variable.

The most significant effect is that the site of deposition shifts dramatically with time. This occurs because the channel gradient and transporting power of a delta river decreases as the deltaic lobe extends farther seaward and shorter routes to the ocean become available. These shorter pathways may begin far inland, usually being occupied when the river is diverted through breaches in levees called crevasses. This process effectively shifts the locus of deposition and initiates the development of a new deltaic lobe. For example, the Mississippi Delta actually consists of the coalescence of seven major lobes constructed at different times and positions during the last five thousand years. In fact, the modern bird-foot delta of the Mississippi River is only a small part of the entire deltaic system, and there is good reason to believe that another major shift in the depositional position is imminent. The Atchafalaya River, a major distributary, branches from the Mississippi upstream from Baton Rouge, La., and its route to the ocean is approximately 300 km (about 185 miles) shorter than the present course of the Mississippi. This channel carries 30 percent of the Mississippi flow, and sediment reaching Atchafalaya Bay (160 km [100 miles] west of New Orleans) is actively building a new delta lobe. Complete diversion of the Mississippi discharge into the Atchafalaya will accelerate growth of the new delta. The present bird-foot delta will be abandoned and, starved of any incoming sediment, will become severely eroded by the unopposed attack of marine processes.

Even within a modern delta, water and sediment, funneled through crevasses, build smaller subdeltas, which are ephemeral in space and time. What emerges is a picture of a dynamic system in which depositional sites change over different time scales. On a short-term basis (years to decades), a limited area (subdelta) may receive sediment, but the position of accumulation shifts rapidly. On a longer time scale (hundreds to thousands of years), the position of an entire active delta may migrate over a considerable distance.

ESTUARIES

Estuaries are partially enclosed bodies of water located along coastal regions where flow in downstream reaches of rivers is mixed with and diluted by seawater. The landward limit of an estuary is defined in terms of salinity, often where chlorinity is 0.01 parts per thousand. The inland extent of this chemical marker, however, varies according to numerous physical and chemical controls, especially the tidal range and the chemistry of river water. Actually, the term estuary is derived from the Latin words *aestus* ("the tide") and *aestuo* ("boil"), indicating the effect generated when tidal flow and river flow meet. Nonetheless, if estuaries are defined on the basis of salinity, many coastal features such as bays, tidal marshes, and lagoons can be regarded as estuaries.

Estuaries have always been extremely important to humankind. From early times, they have served as centres of shipping and commerce. In fact, many seaports were originally founded at the seaward margin of major river systems. Concomitantly, some of the oldest civilizations developed in estuarine environments. In addition to shipping, much of the world's fishing industry is dependent on the estuarine environment. Many species of fish and shelled bottom dwellers spend much of their life cycle there. In most cases, these animals have a tolerance for wide ranges in salinity and temperature. Pollutants introduced by humans, however, can affect such forms of marine life significantly if large enough amounts of the contaminants accumulate among bottom sediments.

ORIGIN AND CLASSIFICATION

Most modern estuaries formed as the result of a worldwide rise in sea level, which began approximately 18,000 years ago during the waning phase of the Wisconsin Glacial Stage. When glaciation was at its maximum, sea level was significantly lower than it is today because much of the precipitation falling on the continents was locked up in massive ice bodies rather than returning to the ocean. In response, rivers entrenched their downstream reaches as baselevel (sea level) declined. As the ice began to dissipate, sea level rose, and marine waters invaded the entrenched valleys and inundated other portions of the coastal zone, such as deltas and coastal plains. It is known that the subsidence of a coast produces the same effect as a rise in sea level. Thus tectonic activity sometimes creates estuaries.

In general, estuaries develop in one of three ways. First, estuaries represent drowned valleys. The valleys may have been formed by normal river entrenchment (e.g., Chesapeake Bay in the eastern United States) or as the result of glacial erosion. The latter type, called fjords, are deep, narrow gorges cut into bedrock by tongues of glacial ice advancing down a former stream valley. Fjords are most common in Norway and the coastal margins of British Columbia, Can. Both valley types (river and glacial) became estuarine environments with the postglacial rise in sea level. Second, some estuaries develop when barrier islands and/or spits enclose large areas of brackish water between the open ocean and the continental margin. These depositional features restrict free exchange between river and marine water and create lagoons or partially enclosed bays that develop the chemical characteristics of an estuarine

Scenic fjord, or sea inlet, winding deep into the mountainous coast of western Norway. Bob and Ira Spring

environment. Such settings are best exemplified in the Gulf Coast region of the United States (e.g., Galveston Bay), the Vadehavet tidal area of Denmark, the Swan Estuary of Western Australia, and the Waddenzee of the Netherlands. Third, some estuaries are clearly submerged in response to tectonic activity, such as down-faulted coastal zones or isostatically controlled subsidence (e.g., San Francisco Bay).

Physical oceanographers commonly classify valley-type estuaries by the process and extent of mixing between fresh water and seawater. A salt-wedge estuary is dominated by river discharge, and tidal effects are negligible. In this situation, fresh water floats on top of seawater as a distinct layer, which thins toward the ocean. A wedge-shaped body of seawater underlies the fresh-water layer and thins toward the continent. The interface between the two water types is well defined, and very little mass transfer or mixing of the two waters occurs. Partially mixed estuaries are characterized by an increased tidal effect to a condition where river discharge does not dominate the system. Mixing of the two water types is prominent in this system and is caused by increased turbulence. Mass transfer of water involves movement in both directions across a boundary that becomes less distinct than the one found in the salt-wedge estuaries. In vertically homogeneous estuaries, the velocity of tidal currents is large enough to produce total mixing and eliminate the fresh/salt water boundary. The water salinity is constant in the vertical sense and tends to decrease toward the continent. In general, the classification of estuaries by mixing indicates that the more substantial the river discharge, the weaker is the mixing. In addition, the dominance of river flow causes a greater salinity gradient. This indicates that sizable fluvial activity tends to block the entrance of seawater into the estuary environment.

FJORDS

Fjords, which is also spelled fiords, are long narrow arms of the sea that commonly extend far inland and result from marine inundation of a glaciated valley. Many fjords are astonishingly deep. Sogn Fjord in Norway is 1,308 metres (4,290 feet) deep, and Canal Messier in Chile is 1,270 metres (4,167 feet). The great depth of these submerged valleys, extending thousands of feet below sea level, is compatible only with a glacial origin. It is assumed that the enormous, thick glaciers that formed in these valleys were so heavy that they could erode the bottom of the valley far below sea level before they floated in the ocean water. After the glaciers melted, the waters of the sea invaded the valleys.

Fjords commonly are deeper in their middle and upper reaches than at the seaward end. This results from the greater erosive power of the glaciers closer to their source, where they are moving most actively and vigorously. Because of the comparatively shallow thresholds of fjords, the bottoms of many have stagnant water and are rich in black mud containing hydrogen sulfide.

Glacial erosion produces U-shaped valleys, and fjords are characteristically so shaped. Because the lower (and more horizontally inclined) part of the U is far underwater, the visible walls of fjords may rise vertically for hundreds of feet from the water's edge, and close to the shore the water may be many hundreds of feet deep. In some fjords small streams plunge hundreds of feet over the edge of the fjord; some of the world's highest waterfalls are of this type. Fjords commonly have winding channels and occasional sharp corners. In many cases the valley, floored with glacial debris, extends inland into the mountains. Sometimes a small glacier remains at the valley's head. The river that formed the original valley commonly reestablishes itself on the upper valley floor after the disappearance of the ice and begins to build a delta at the fjord's head. Often this delta is the only place on the fjord where villages and farms can be established.

SEDIMENTATION IN ESTUARIES

The bedrock floor near the mouth of most estuaries is usually buried by a thick accumulation of sediment. The texture and composition of sediment in estuaries in the United States is known to be a function of river-basin geology, bathymetry, and hydrologic setting. Where sediment supply is inadequate to fill drowned valleys, clay and silt are usually deposited in the central part of bays and grade shoreward and seaward into bodies of sand. Where sediment supply and tidal range are both large, such as in Oregon and northern California in the western United States, the clay and silt are commonly swept from the channels and deposited on the marginal flats. In the Gulf Coast region, small tides and abundant fine-grained sediment tend to create very shallow estuaries. Silt and clay are usually deposited in lagoons behind barrier bars, although these grade into sands around the lagoonal margins.

The character and distribution of estuarine sediment are influenced by many physical, chemical, and biologic processes, such as tidal currents, flocculation, bioturbation (the reworking and alteration of sediment by organisms), storms, morphology of the estuary, and human activities. The sediment type that is deposited, therefore, depends on the dynamics of the system, which in turn are controlled by an equilibrium between river and tidal flow. River discharge develops inertia, which results in the collision of river and ocean waters in the estuary itself. Most sediment is derived from the river system, and whether or not it is deposited within the estuary depends on how quickly the velocity is diminished by the effect of tidal currents and by the extent of the tidal range. Notwithstanding the above, it has been long recognized that net sediment transport in many open estuaries can be from the sea toward the land.

CHAPTER 6
MAJOR RIVERS OF AFRICA

Africa is home to several great rivers. The Nile, the longest river in the world, winds its way from its headwaters in East Africa to empty into the eastern Mediterranean Sea. Africa's second longest river, the Congo, begins in Zambia, but it flows westward through dense rainforests into the Atlantic Ocean. The Niger River drains a large part of West Africa, flowing into the Atlantic Ocean by way of a wide delta in southern Nigeria.

THE CONGO RIVER

The Congo River (formerly the Zaire River) is a river in west-central Africa. With a length of 4,700 km (2,900 miles), it is the continent's second longest river, after the Nile. It rises in the highlands of northeastern Zambia between Lakes Tanganyika and Nyasa (Malawi) as the Chambeshi River at an elevation of 1,760 metres (5,760 feet) above sea level and at a distance of about 700 km (430 miles) from the Indian Ocean. Its course then takes the form of a giant counterclockwise arc, flowing to the northwest, west, and southwest before draining into the Atlantic Ocean at Banana (Banane) in the Democratic Republic of the Congo. Its drainage basin, covering an area of 3,457,000 square km (1,335,000 square miles), takes in almost the entire territory of that country, as well as most of the Republic of the Congo, the Central African Republic, eastern Zambia, and northern Angola and parts of Cameroon and Tanzania.

With its many tributaries, the Congo forms the continent's largest network of navigable waterways. Navigability, however, is limited by an insurmountable obstacle: a series

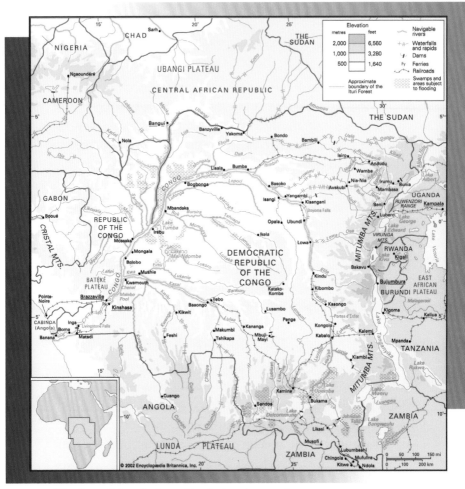

The Congo River basin and its drainage network.

of 32 cataracts over the river's lower course, including the famous Inga Falls. These cataracts render the Congo unnavigable between the seaport of Matadi, at the head of the Congo estuary, and Malebo Pool, a lakelike expansion of the river. It was on opposite banks of Malebo Pool—which represents the point of departure of inland navigation—that the capitals of the former states of the French Congo and the Belgian Congo were founded: on the left bank Kinshasa (formerly Léopoldville), now the capital of the Democratic Republic of the Congo, and on the right bank Brazzaville, now the capital of the Republic of the Congo.

The Amazon and the Congo are the two great rivers of the world that flow out of equatorial zones where heavy rainfall occurs throughout all or almost all of the year. Upstream from Malebo Pool, the Congo basin receives an average of about 150 cm (60 inches) of rain a year, of which more than one-fourth is discharged into the Atlantic. The drainage basin of the Congo is only about half the size of that of the Amazon, however. And the Congo's rate of flow—41,000 cubic metres (1.45 million cubic feet) per second at its mouth—is considerably less than the Amazon's flow of more than 175,000 cubic metres (6.18 million cubic feet) per second.

While the Chambeshi River, as the remotest source, may form the Congo's original main stream in terms of the river's length, it is another tributary—the Lualaba, which rises near Musofi in southeastern Democratic Republic of the Congo—that carries the greatest quantity of water and thus may be considered as forming the Congo's original main stream in terms of water volume.

When the river first became known to Europeans at the end of the 15th century, they called it the Zaire, a corruption of a word that is variously given as *nzari*, *nzali*, *njali*, *nzaddi*, and *niadi* and that simply means "river" in local African languages. It was only in the early years of the 18th century that the river was first called the "Rio Congo," a name taken from the kingdom of Kongo that had been situated along the lower course of the river. During the period (1971–97) when the Democratic Republic of the Congo was called Zaire, the government also renamed the river the Zaire. Even during that time, however, the river continued to be known throughout the world as the Congo. To the literary-minded the river is evocative of the famous 1902 short story "Heart of

Darkness" by Joseph Conrad. His book conjured up an atmosphere of foreboding, treachery, greed, and exploitation. Today, however, the Congo appears as the key to the economic development of the central African interior.

PHYSIOGRAPHY

The expression "Congo basin," strictly speaking, refers to the hydrographic basin. This is not only vast but is also covered with a dense and ramified network of tributaries, subtributaries, and small rivers—with the exception of the sandy plateaus in the southwest.

The Congo basin is the most clearly distinguished of the various geographic depressions situated between the Sahara to the north, the Atlantic Ocean to the south and west, and the region of the East African lakes to the east. In this basin, a fan-shaped web of tributaries flows downward along concentric slopes that range from 275 to 460 metres (900 to 1,500 feet) in elevation and that enclose a central depression. The basin itself stretches for more than 1,900 km (1,200 miles) from north to south (from the Congo–Lake Chad watershed to the interior plateaus of Angola) and also measures about 1,900 km (1,200 miles) from the Atlantic in the west to the Nile-Congo watershed in the east.

The central part of the Congo basin—often called the *cuvette* (literally "saucer" or "shallow bowl")—is an immense depression containing Quaternary alluvial deposits that rest on thick sediments of continental origin, consisting principally of sands and sandstones. These underlying sediments form outcrops in valley floors at the eastern edge of the *cuvette*. The filling of the *cuvette*, however, began much earlier. Boreholes have revealed that since late Precambrian times (i.e., since at least 570 million years ago) considerable sediment has accumulated, derived from the erosion of formations situated around the periphery of the *cuvette*. The arrangement of surface relief, thick depositional strata, and substratum in amphitheatre-like fashion around the main Congo channel, which has been uniform across time, is evidence of a persistent tendency to subsidence in this part of the continent. This subsidence is accompanied by uplifting on the edges of the *cuvette*, principally on its eastern side—which has also been influenced by the formation of the Western Rift Valley.

From its sources to its mouth, the Congo River system has three contrasting sections—the upper Congo, middle Congo, and lower Congo. The upper reaches are characterized by three features—confluences, lakes, and waterfalls or rapids. To begin with, several streams of approximately equal size unite to form the river. In a little more than 100 km (60 miles), the upper Lualaba joins the Luvua and then the Lukuga. Each stream for part of its course undergoes at least a lacustrine type of expansion, even when it does not form a lake. Thus, Lake Upemba occurs on the upper Lualaba; Lakes Bangweulu and Mweru occur on the Chambeshi–Luapula–Luvua system; and Lake Tanganyika, which is fed by the Ruzizi (flowing from Lake Kivu) and by the Malagarasi, itself flows into the Lukuga. Rapids occur not only along the headstreams but also in several places along the course of the main stream. Navigation thus is possible only along sections of the upper Congo by vessels of low tonnage. Even so, these stretches are in danger of being overgrown by aquatic vegetation, particularly water hyacinths.

Kisangani (formerly Stanleyville)—located just downstream of the Boyoma Falls, a series of seven cataracts—marks the real beginning, upriver, of the navigable Congo. This central part of the river flows steadily for more than 1,600 km (1,000 miles) to within 35 km (22 miles) of

Kinshasa. Its course at first is narrow but soon grows wider, after which many islands occur in midstream. This change in the character of the river corresponds to its entry into its alluvial plain. From that point onward, with the exception of a few rare narrow sections, the Congo divides into several arms, separated by strings of islands. It increases from a width of more than 5.5 km (3.5 miles) downstream from Isangi (where the Lomami enters the Congo) to a width of 8 to 11 km (5 to 7 miles) and on occasion—for example, at the mouth of the Mongala—to 13 km (8 miles). Beyond the natural levees (formed by silt deposits) occurring on either bank, some areas are subjected to extensive flooding that increases the river's bounds still further. It is not always easy to distinguish such areas from the "rain swamps" in regions lying between rivers. The middle course of the Congo ends in a narrow section called the Chenal ("Channel"), or Couloir ("Corridor"). Between banks no more than 0.8 to 1.6 km (0.5 to 1 mile) wide, the riverbed deepens and the current becomes rapid, flowing through a valley that cuts down several hundreds of yards deep into the soft sandstone bedrock of the Batéké Plateau. Along this central reach the Congo receives its principal tributaries, primarily the Ubangi and the Sangha on the right bank and the Kwa on the left bank. An enormous increase in the average rate of flow results, rising from less than 250,000 cubic feet (7,000 cubic metres) a second at Kisangani to nearly its maximum flow at Kinshasa.

Upon leaving the Chenal, the Congo divides into two branches, forming Malebo Pool, a vast lacustrine area about 24 by 27 km (15 by 17 miles), which marks the end of the middle Congo. Immediately downstream occur the first waterfalls of the final section of the river's course. Cataracts and rapids are grouped into two series, separated by a fairly calm central reach, in which the elevation drops from a little less than 275 metres (900 feet) to a few yards above sea level. The Congo's estuary begins at Matadi, downstream from the rapids that close off the interior Congo; 134 km (83 miles) in length, it forms the border between Angola and the Democratic Republic of the Congo. At first the estuary is narrow—less than 0.8 to 2.4 km (0.5 to 1.5 miles) in width—with a central channel 20 to 24 metres (65 to 80 feet) deep, but it widens downstream of Boma. There the river, obstructed by islands, divides into several arms, and in some places the depth does not exceed 6 to 7.5 metres (20 to 25 feet), which makes dredging necessary to allow oceangoing vessels to reach Matadi. Beyond the estuary's mouth, the course of the Congo continues offshore as a deep underwater canyon that extends for a distance of about 200 km (125 miles).

HYDROLOGY

The Congo has a regular flow, which is fed by rains throughout the year. At Kinshasa the flow has for many years remained between the high level of 65,000 cubic metres (2.31 million cubic feet) per second, recorded during the flood of 1908, and the low level of 21,000 cubic metres (756,000 cubic feet) per second, recorded in 1905. During the unusual flood of 1962, however, by far the highest for a century, the flow probably exceeded 73,000 cubic metres (2.6 million cubic feet) per second.

At Brazzaville and Kinshasa, the river's regime is characterized by a main maximum at the end of the year and a secondary maximum in May, as well as by a major low level during July and a secondary low level during March and April. In reality, the downstream regime of the Congo represents climatic influence extending over 20° of latitude on both sides of the Equator a distance of some 2,250 km (1,400 miles). Each tributary in its course modifies the level of the main stream. Thus, for example, the low level in July at Malebo Pool results from two factors: a drought that occurs for several months in the southern part of the basin at that time, as well as a delay before the floods of the Ubangi tributary flowing down from the north arrive, which does not happen before August. The Congo basin is so vast that no single meteorologic circumstance is capable of disturbing the slow movement of the waters' rise and fall. The annual fluctuations may alter drastically, however, when floodwaters from different tributaries that normally coincide with each other arrive at different times.

Lake Tanganyika, apart from brief seiches caused by wind drift and sudden changes in atmospheric pressure, may experience considerable variations in its water level from year to year. In 1960, for example, its waters flooded parts of Kalemi, Democratic Republic of the Congo, and Bujumbura, Burundi. A series of particularly rainy years followed by a blocking of the outlet by floating vegetation may explain this phenomenon.

CLIMATE

Typical climate in regions through which the Congo flows is that of Yangambi, a town situated on the river's right bank slightly north of the Equator and a little downstream of Kisangani. Humidity is high throughout the year, and annual rainfall amounts to 170 cm (67 inches) and occurs fairly regularly. Even in the driest month the rainfall totals more than 7.6 cm (3 inches). Temperatures are also uniformly high throughout the year, and there is little diurnal variability. The average temperature at Yangambi is in the mid-70s F (mid-20s C).

From the pluviometric equator (an imaginary east-west line indicating the region of heaviest rainfall), which is situated slightly to the north of the geographic equator, the amount of rainfall decreases regularly in proportion to latitude. The northernmost points of the basin, situated in the Central African Republic, receive only from 20 to 40 cm (8 to 16 inches) less during the course of a year than points near the Equator. The dry season, however, lasts for four or five months, and there is only one annual rainfall maximum, which occurs in summer. In the far southern part of the basin, at a latitude of 12° S, the climate becomes definitely Sudanic in character, with marked dry and wet seasons of approximately equal length and with rainfall of about 125 cm (49 inches) a year.

STUDY AND EXPLORATION

The question of the source of the Congo confronted European explorers from the time that the Portuguese navigator Diogo Cão encountered the river's mouth in 1482, which he believed to be a strait providing access to the realm of the mythical Prester John, a Christian priest-king. It is virtually certain that, well before the Welsh explorer Henry Morton Stanley arrived in 1877, some 17th-century Capuchin missionaries reached the shores of Malebo Pool. This exploit, however, was not followed up, even by the amply supplied expedition led by James Kingston Tuckey, which was sent out by the British Admiralty in 1816 but was decimated and had to retrace its footsteps even before it had surmounted the cataracts. Preposterous hypotheses about the river continued to be entertained, connecting, for example, the upper Niger to the Congo or maintaining that the Congo and the Nile both flowed from a single great lake in the heart of Africa.

Even after the European discovery of Lake Tanganyika by the British explorers Richard Burton and John Speke (1858), then of the Lualaba (1867) and of Lake Bangweulu (1868) by the Scottish explorer David Livingstone,

Lake Tanganyika near Bujumbura, Burundi. Kay Honkanen/Ostman Agency

uncertainty remained—uncertainty that Stanley was to dissipate in the course of his famous expedition in 1876 and 1877 that took him by water from the Lualaba to the Congo's mouth over a period of nine months. In the interior of the Congo basin and above all on the right bank, the final blank spaces on the map could not be filled in until about 1890, when the exploration of the upper course of the Ubangi was completed.

THE NIGER RIVER

The Niger River is the principal river of western Africa. With a length of 4,200 km (2,600 miles), it is the third longest river in Africa, after the Nile and the Congo. The Niger is believed to have been named by the Greeks. Along its course it is known by several names. These include

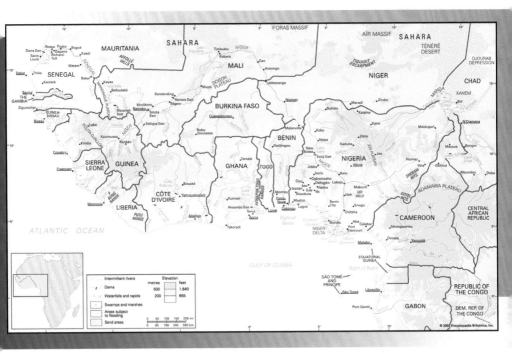

The Niger and Sénégal river basins and the Lake Chad basin and their drainage networks.

the Joliba (Malinke: "great river") in its upper course; the Mayo Balleo and the Isa Eghirren in its central reach; and the Kwarra, Kworra, or Quorra in its lower stretch.

PHYSIOGRAPHY

The Niger rises in Guinea at 9°05′ N and 10°47′ W on the eastern side of the Fouta Djallon (Guinea) highlands, only 240 km (150 miles) inland from the Atlantic Ocean. Issuing as the Tembi from a deep ravine 850 metres (2,800 feet) above sea level, it flows due north over the first 160 km (100 miles). It then follows a northeasterly direction, during the course of which it receives its upper tributaries—the Mafou, the Niandan, the Milo, and the Sankarani on the right and the Tinkisso on the left—and enters Mali. Just below Bamako, Mali's capital, the Sotuba Dam marks the end of the upper river. From there the Niger once dropped more than 300 metres (1,000 feet) in about 60 km (40 miles) into a valley formed by tectonic subsidence. The rapids in this stretch have been submerged by the waters backed up by the Markala Dam, however, located some 240 km (150 miles) downstream of the Sotuba Dam near Sansanding. In this stretch, at Koulikoro, the river takes a more east-northeasterly direction, and its bed becomes fairly free from impediments for about 1,600 km (1,000 miles).

At Mopti the Niger is joined by the Bani, its largest tributary on the right, after which it enters a region of lakes, creeks, and backwaters that is often called the "internal delta" of the Niger. These lakes are chiefly on the left bank and are connected to the river by channels that undergo seasonal changes in the direction of flow. At high water most of the lakes become part of a general inundation. Largest of the lakes in this region is Lake Faguibine, which is nearly 120 km (75 miles) long, 25 km (15 miles) wide, and more than 50 metres (160 feet) deep in places.

The labyrinth of lakes, creeks, and backwaters comes to an end at Kabara, the port of Timbuktu (Tombouctou). There, the river turns almost due east, passing its most northern point at latitude 17°05′ N. Some 400 km (250 miles) downstream from Timbuktu, a rocky ridge that obstructs the course of the river is pierced by a defile (narrow gorge) more than 1.6 k (1 mile) long, with an average width of about 240 metres (800 feet) and a depth of more than 30 metres (100 feet) in places. At low water the strong current there endangers navigation. A short way downstream the river turns to the southeast and widens considerably, flowing to Gao across a floodplain 5 to 10 km (3 to 6 miles) wide. This most northerly bend of the Niger flows through the southern fringe of the Sahara.

The middle course of the Niger River is navigable to small craft during high water as far downstream as Ansongo—some 1,770 km (1,100 miles) in all. Below Ansongo, 690 km (430 miles) downstream from Timbuktu, navigability is interrupted by a series of defiles and rapids. The river becomes navigable to small vessels again at Labbezanga—from which it flows into Niger—and continues to be navigable to the Atlantic Ocean. Navigation is seasonal, however, because of the fluctuations in the water level in the rainy and dry seasons.

Downstream from Jebba, in Nigeria, the Niger enters its lower course, flowing east-southeast through a broad and shallow valley 8 to 16 km (5 to 10 miles) wide. About 110 km (70 miles) from Jebba it is joined by the Kaduna River—an important tributary that contributes about one-fourth of the annual discharge of the river below the Niger-Kaduna confluence—and about 40 km (25 miles) above Lokoja the river turns to the south. At Lokoja the river receives the water of its greatest tributary, the Benue, thereby approximately doubling the volume of its annual discharge. At their confluence the Niger is about 1 km (0.75 mile) wide, and the Benue more than 1.6 km (1 mile). Together they form a lakelike stretch of water about 3.2 km (2 miles) wide that is dotted with islands and sandbanks. From Lokoja downstream to the town of Idah, the Niger flows in a restricted valley, enclosed by hills and in some places flanked by sandstone cliffs up to 45 metres (150 feet) high. Between Idah and Onitsha the banks are lower and the country flatter. At Onitsha, the largest town on the Niger's banks in Nigeria and the third largest riverine town after Bamako and Niamey (Niger), the valley narrows as the river flows through what is probably a fault in the area's sandstone. It emerges at Aboh, separating into many branches before reaching the Gulf of Guinea via Africa's largest delta.

The Niger delta, which stretches for nearly 240 km (150 miles) from north to south and spreads along the coast for about 320 km (200 miles), extends over an area of 36,000 square km (14,000 square miles). Within the delta the river breaks up into an intricate network of channels called rivers. The Nun River is regarded as the direct continuation of the river, but some of the other important channels include (from west to east) the Forcados, the Brass, the Sambreiro, and the Bonny. The mouths of these channels are almost all obstructed by sandbars. The Forcados, for instance, which supplanted the Nun as the most traveled channel in the early 20th century, was in turn displaced by the Escravos River in 1964. The delta is being gradually extended seaward by the increments of silt brought down by the river, and mangrove swamps extend beyond its outer edge.

The Benue (meaning "Mother of Water" in the Batta language) rises at 1,350 metres (4,400 feet) above sea level on the Adamawa Plateau in northern Cameroon at about 7°40′ N and 13°15′ E. In its upper course, which extends north-northwest to its confluence with the Mayo Kébi, close to the town of Garoua, it is a mountain torrent, falling more than 600 metres (2,000 feet) over a distance of 180 km (110 miles). The river then turns westward into Nigeria and, for the greater part of its course, flows over a broad and fertile floodplain. At Yola, a town 180 metres (600 feet) above sea level and some 1,370 km (850 miles) inland, the width of the river in flood is from 910 to 1,370 metres (3,000 to 4,500 feet). Near Numan, some 50 km (30 miles) downstream from Yola, the Benue is joined on its north bank by its most important tributary, the Gongola. Other important tributaries include the Shemankar, the Faro, the Donga, and the Katsina Ala.

Together with its tributaries, the Niger drains a total area of some 1.9 million square km (730,000 square miles).

The Niger drainage system is bounded in the south by such highlands as the Fouta Djallon, the Banfora Cliffs in Burkina Faso, the Plateau of Yorubaland, and the Cameroon highlands. This southern rampart forms a watershed separating the rivers of the Niger system from others that flow directly southward to the Atlantic Ocean. With the exception of such highlands as the Jos Plateau, the Iforas and Aïr massifs, and the Ahaggar Mountains to the north and east, the northern edge of the Niger basin is less clearly defined than the southern edge.

CLIMATE

Within the Niger basin, climate shows great variability. Mean annual precipitation levels decrease northward from more than 410 cm (160 inches) in the delta area to less than 25 cm (10 inches) in Timbuktu. Both the upper and the lower stretches of the river, however, drain areas with more than 130 cm (50 inches) of precipitation per year. The middle Niger is an area where precipitation decreases and is also the sector where the greatest amount of evaporation takes place. It is estimated that in the lake region the Niger loses some two-thirds of the annual volume of discharge that flows past Mopti.

HYDROLOGY

Because of climatic variations the annual river flood does not occur at the same time in different parts of the basin. In the upper Niger the high-water discharge occurs in June, and the low-water season is in December. In the middle Niger, a first high-water discharge—the white flood (so called because of the light sediment content of the water)—occurs soon after the rainy season between July and October. A second rise—the black flood (so called because of the greater sediment content)—begins in December with the arrival of floodwaters from upstream. May and June are the low-water months in the middle stretch. On the Benue there is only one high-water season. Because of the Benue's more southerly location, this normally occurs from May to October—earlier than on the middle Niger. The lower Niger below its confluence with the Benue consequently has a high-water period that begins in May or June—about a month earlier than on the middle Niger—and a low-water period that is at least a month shorter, as the rains in the south start earlier. In January a slight rise occurs because of the arrival of floodwaters from the upper Niger. The difference between high and low water often measures as much as 10 metres (35 feet).

STUDY AND EXPLORATION

It was not until the late 18th century that Europeans made systematic attempts to find the source, direction, and outlet of the Niger. In 1795 Mungo Park, a Scottish explorer, traveled overland from the Gambia region and reached the Niger near Ségou, where in July 1796 he established that the river flowed eastward. In 1805 Park sailed more than 2,400 km (1,500 miles) down the river, seeking to reach its mouth, but he and his party were drowned in the rapids at Bussa (now covered by Lake Kainji). Another Scottish explorer, Alexander G. Laing, determined but did not visit the source of the river in 1822. Two English explorers, John and Richard Lander, established the lower course of the Niger in 1830 by canoeing down the river from Yauri (now also covered by Lake Kainji), to the Atlantic Ocean, via the Nun River passage. In the second half of the 19th century two German explorers, Heinrich Barth and Eduard

R. Flegel, in separate travels established the course of the Benue from its source to its confluence with the Niger.

THE NILE RIVER

The Nile River (Arabic: Baḥr al-Nīl or Nahr al-Nīl) is the father of African rivers and the longest river in the world. It rises south of the equator and flows northward through northeastern Africa to drain into the Mediterranean Sea. It has a length of about 6,650 km (4,132 miles) and drains an area estimated at 3,349,000 square km (1,293,000 square miles). Its basin includes parts of Tanzania, Burundi, Rwanda, Congo (Kinshasa), Kenya, Uganda, and Ethiopia, most of the Sudan, and the cultivated part of Egypt. Its most distant source is the Kagera River in Burundi.

The Nile is formed by three principal streams, the Blue Nile (Arabic: Al-Baḥr al-Azraq; Amharic: Abay) and the Atbara (Arabic: Nahr ʿAṭbarah), which flow from the highlands of Ethiopia, and the White Nile (Arabic: Al-Baḥr al-Abyaḍ), the headstreams of which flow into Lakes Victoria and Albert.

The name Nile is derived from the Greek Neilos (Latin: Nilus), which probably originated from the Semitic root *nahal*, meaning a valley or river valley, and hence, by an extension of the meaning, a river. The fact that the Nile—unlike other great rivers known to them—flowed from the south northward and was in flood at the warmest time of the year was an unsolved mystery to the ancient Egyptians and Greeks. The ancient Egyptians called the river Ar or Aur (Coptic: Iaro), or "Black," in allusion to the colour of the sediments carried by the river when it is in flood. Nile mud is black enough to have given the land itself its oldest name, Kem or Kemi, which also means

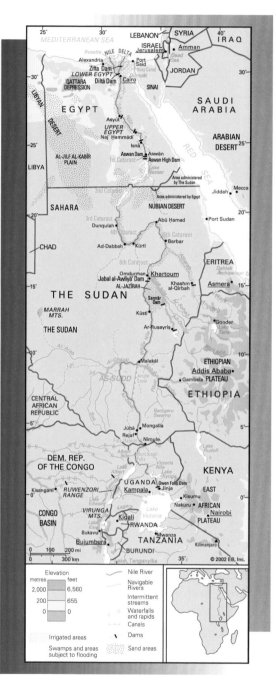

The Nile River basin and its drainage network.

"Black" and signifies darkness. In *The Odyssey*, the epic poem written by the Greek poet Homer (7th century BCE), Aigyptos is the name of the Nile (masculine) as well as the country of Egypt (feminine) through which it flows. The Nile in Egypt and the northern Sudan is now called Al-Nīl, Al-Baḥr, and Baḥr al-Nīl or Nahr al-Nīl.

The Nile River basin, which covers about one-tenth of the area of the continent, served as the stage for the evolution and decay of advanced civilizations in the ancient world. On the banks of the river dwelled people who were among the first to cultivate the arts of agriculture and to use the plow. The basin is bordered on the north by the Mediterranean; on the east by the Red Sea Hills and the Ethiopian Plateau; on the south by the East African Highlands, which include Lake Victoria, a Nile source; and on the west by the less well-defined watershed between the Nile, Chad, and Congo basins, extending northwest to include the Marrah Mountains of the Sudan, the Al-Jilf al-Kabīr Plateau of Egypt, and the Libyan Desert (part of the Sahara).

The availability of water from the Nile throughout the year, combined with the area's high temperatures, makes possible intensive cultivation along its banks. Even in some of the regions in which the average rainfall is sufficient for cultivation, such as in the Sudan, marked annual variations in precipitation often make cultivation without irrigation risky. The Nile River is also a vital waterway for transport, especially at times when motor transport is not feasible (e.g., during the flood season). Improvements in air, rail, and highway facilities in the 20th century, however, greatly reduced dependency on the waterway.

PHYSIOGRAPHY

It is thought that approximately 30 million years ago the early Nile, then a much shorter stream, had its sources about latitude 18° to 20° N. Its main headstream may then have been the present Atbara River. To the south lay the vast enclosed drainage system containing the large Lake Sudd. According to one theory on the evolution of the Nile system, about 25,000 years ago the East African drainage to Lake Victoria developed an outlet to the north, which sent its water into Lake Sudd. With the accumulation of sediments over a long period, the water level of this lake rose gradually. As a result of the overflow, the lake was drained, spilling over to the north. The overflow waters of Lake Sudd, rapidly forming a riverbed, linked the two major parts of the Nile system, thus unifying the drainage from Lake Victoria to the Mediterranean Sea.

The basin of the present-day Nile falls naturally into seven major regions: the Lake Plateau of East Africa, the Al-Jabal (El-Jebel), the White Nile, the Blue Nile, the Atbara, the Nile north of Khartoum in the Sudan and Egypt, and the Nile delta.

The Lake Plateau region of East Africa produces a number of headstreams and lakes that feed the White Nile. It is generally agreed that the Nile has several sources rather than one. The furthest headstream may be regarded as the Kagera River, which rises in the highlands of Burundi near the northern tip of Lake Tanganyika and then flows into Lake Victoria. The Nile proper, however, rises from Lake Victoria, the second largest freshwater lake in the world, which has an area of more than 69,400 square km (26,800 square miles) and forms a huge but shallow lake. The Nile begins near Jinja, Uganda, on the north shore of the lake, flowing northward over Ripon Falls, which has been submerged since the completion of the Owen Falls Dam (now the Nalubaale Dam) in 1954. The northward stretch of the river, known as the Victoria Nile, enters the shallow Lake Kyoga (Kioga) and, passing through its swamp vegetation, flows out in a westerly direction, descending into the East African Rift System over Murchison (Kabalega) Falls before entering the northern end of Lake Albert. Unlike Lake Victoria, Lake Albert is a deep, narrow lake with mountainous sides. There the waters of the Victoria Nile unite with the lake waters, passing northward as the Albert Nile—a portion of the river, somewhat wider and slower, that is fringed with swampy growth and is navigable for steamers.

The Nile enters the Sudan at Nimule, and from there to Jūbā—a distance of some 193 km (120 miles)—it is called the Al-Jabal River (Mountain Nile). This section of the river descends through narrow gorges and over a series of rapids, including the Fula (Fola) Rapids, and receives additional water from short tributaries on both banks. It is not commercially navigable. Below Jūbā the river flows over a large and extremely level clay plain, which extends through a narrow valley with hill country on either side, lying some 370 to 460 metres (1,200 to 1,500 feet) above sea level, and through the centre of which flows the mainstream. Because the gradient of the Nile there is only 1:13,000, the great volume of additional water that arrives during the rainy season cannot be accommodated by the river. And as a result, during those months almost the entire plain becomes inundated. This circumstance promotes the growth of enormous quantities of aquatic vegetation—including tall grasses and sedges (notably papyrus)—that collectively is called *sudd*, literally meaning "barrier." The region is known as Al-Sudd (or also As-Sudd). These great masses of vegetation, the growth of which is exacerbated by the gentle flow of the water, break off and float downstream, effectively choking the mainstream and blocking the navigable channels. Channels have become further choked since the 1950s by the rapid spread of the South American water hyacinth.

This basin receives drainage from numerous other streams. The Al-Ghazāl (Gazelle) River flows in from the southwestern Sudan, joining the Al-Jabal at Lake No, a large lagoon where the mainstream takes an easterly direction. The waters of the Al-Ghazāl undergo extensive loss through evaporation, and only a small proportion of them ever reach the Nile. A short distance above Malakāl the mainstream is joined by the Sobat (Baro in Ethiopia), and downstream from there the river is called the White Nile. The regime of the Sobat is quite different from the steady flowing Al-Jabal, with a maximum flow occurring between July and December. The annual flow of the Sobat is about equal to the water lost through evaporation in Al-Sudd marshes.

The White Nile, about 800 km (500 miles) in length, supplies some 15 percent of the total volume entering Lake Nasser (called Lake Nubia in the Sudan) downstream. It begins at Malakāl and joins the Blue Nile at Khartoum, receiving no tributaries of importance. Throughout this stretch the White Nile is a wide, placid stream, often having a narrow fringe of swamps. The valley is wide and shallow, however, thus causing a considerable loss of water by both evaporation and seepage.

The Blue Nile drains from the lofty Ethiopian Plateau, where it descends in a north–northwesterly direction from a height of about 1,830 metres (6,000 feet) above sea level. Its reputed source is a spring, considered holy by the Ethiopian Orthodox Church, from which a small stream, the Abay, flows down to Lake Tana (T'ana), a fairly shallow lake with an area of about 3,625 km (1,400 square miles). The Abay leaves Lake Tana in a southeasterly direction, flowing through a series of rapids and plunging through a deep gorge. It is estimated that the lake supplies the river with only about 7 percent of its total flow, but this water is important because it is silt-free. The river then flows west and northwest through the Sudan to join the White Nile at Khartoum. In the greater part of its course from Lake Tana down to the Sudanese plains, it runs in a canyon that in places is 1,220 metres (4,000 feet) below the general level of the plateau. All of its tributaries also run in deep ravines. While the White Nile at Khartoum is a river of almost constant volume, the Blue Nile has a pronounced flood season (late July to October) caused by the summer monsoon rains over the Ethiopian Plateau and the rapid runoff from its numerous tributaries; historically, it was this surge that contributed most to the annual Nile floods in Egypt.

The Atbara River, the last tributary of the Nile, flows into the mainstream nearly 320 km (200 miles) north of Khartoum. It rises in Ethiopia at heights of 1,830 to 3,050 metres (6,000 to 10,000 feet) above sea level, not far from Gonder, to the north of Lake Tana. The two principal tributaries that feed the Atbara are the Angereb (Arabic: Baḥr al-Salam) and the Tekezo (Amharic: "Terrible"; Arabic: Nahr Satīt). The Tekezo is the most important of these, having a basin more than double the area of the Atbara itself. It rises among the high peaks of the Ethiopian highlands and flows north through a spectacular gorge to join the Atbara in the Sudan. For most of its course in the Sudan, the Atbara is well below the general level of the plains. Between the plains and the river, the ground is eroded and cut into by gullies formed by water running off the plains after rainfall. The Atbara rises and falls rapidly, like the Blue Nile. In flood it becomes a large, muddy river, and in the dry season it is a string of pools. The Atbara contributes more than 10 percent of the total annual flow of the Nile, but almost all of this comes in the period of July to October.

Along the stretch of the Nile north of Khartoum, which is sometimes called the United Nile, two parts can be distinguished. The first part, which stretches from Khartoum to Lake Nasser, is about 1,340 km (830 miles) in length. There the river flows through a desert region where rainfall is negligible, although some irrigation takes place along its banks. The second part includes Lake Nasser—which contains the water held back by the Aswan High Dam in Egypt—and below the dam the irrigated Nile valley and delta region.

Below Khartoum, the Nile flows 80 km (50 miles) northward until it reaches Sablūkah (Sababka), the site of the sixth and highest cataract. There the river cuts through hills for a distance of 12.9 km (8 miles). Flowing northward at Barbar, the river takes an S-bend, in the middle of which, from Abū Ḥamad to Kūrtī and Al-Dabbah (Debba), the river flows southwestward for about 275 km (170 miles); the fourth cataract is in the middle of this stretch. At the end of this bend, at Dunqulah, it again resumes a northerly direction, crossing the third cataract and flowing into Lake Nasser.

For the roughly 1,300 km (800 miles) from the sixth cataract to Lake Nasser, the riverbed alternates between gentle stretches and series of rapids. Outcropping crystalline rocks that cross the course of the Nile cause the five famous cataracts. Because of these cataracts, the river is not completely navigable, although sections between the cataracts are navigable by sailing vessels and by river steamers.

Lake Nasser, the second largest man-made lake in the world, has a potential maximum area of about 6,740 square km (2,600 square miles); it inundates more than 480 km (300 miles) of the Nile's course, including the second cataract near the border between Egypt and the Sudan. Immediately below the high dam is the first cataract, which was once an area of rock-strewn rapids that partially obstructed the flow of the river. From the first cataract to Cairo—a distance of about 800 km (500 miles)—the Nile flows northward in a relatively narrow, flat-bottomed groove, sinuous in outline and generally incised into the underlying limestone plateau, which averages 16 to 23 km (10 to 14 miles) in width and is enclosed by scarps that rise in places to heights of about 460 metres (1,500 feet) above the river level. For the last 320 km (200 miles) of its course before reaching Cairo, the Nile shows a strong tendency to hug the eastern edge of the valley floor, so that the greater part of the cultivated land is found on the left bank.

North of Cairo the Nile enters the delta region, a level, triangular-shaped lowland. In the 1st century CE, the Greek geographer Strabo recorded the Nile as fanning out into seven delta distributaries. The flow has since been controlled and redirected, so that the river now flows across the delta to the sea through two main distributaries, the Rosetta and the Dumyāṭ (Damietta) branches.

The Nile delta, the prototype of all deltas, comprises a gulf of the prehistoric Mediterranean Sea that has been filled in. It is composed of silt brought mainly from the Ethiopian Plateau. The silt varies in its thickness from 15 to 23 metres (50 to 75 feet) and comprises the most fertile soil in Africa. It forms a monotonous plain that extends 160 km (100 miles) from north to south, its greatest east–west extent being 250 km (155 miles) between Alexandria and Port Said. Altogether it covers an area twice that of the Nile valley in Upper Egypt. The land surface slopes gently to the sea, falling some 16 metres (52 feet) from Cairo in a gentle gradient. In the north, on the seaward border, are a number of shallow brackish lagoons and salt marshes: Lake Marout (Buḥayrat Maryūṭ), Lake Edku (Buḥayrat Idkū), Lake Burullus (Buḥayrat al-Burullus), and Lake Manzala (Buḥayrat al-Manzilah).

Climate and Hydrology

Almost no area within the Nile basin experiences a true equatorial or a true Mediterranean type of climate. While the Nile basin in the Sudan and Egypt is rainless during the northern winter, its southern parts and the highlands of Ethiopia experience heavy rain—more than 152 cm (60 inches)—during the northern summer. Most of the region falls under the influence of the northeast trade winds between October and May, which causes the prevailing aridity of most of the basin.

Tropical climates with well-distributed rainfall are found in parts of the East African lakes region and southwestern Ethiopia. In the lake region there is little variation throughout the year in the mean temperature, which ranges from 16 to 27 °C (60 to 80 °F) depending on locality and altitude. Relative humidity, which varies similarly, is about 80 percent on the average. Similar climatic conditions prevail over the extreme southern parts of the Sudan, which receive as much as 127 cm (50 inches) of rain spread over a nine-month period (March to November), with the maximum occurring in August. The humidity reaches its highest at the peak of the rainy season and reaches its low level between January and March. Maximum temperatures are recorded during the dry season (December to February), with the minimums occurring in July and August.

To the north, the rainy season gets shorter, and the amount of rainfall decreases. The rainy season, which occurs in the south from April to October, is confined to July and August in the northern part of the central Sudan, where three seasons may be distinguished. The first of these is the pleasant, cool, dry winter, which occurs from December to February. This is followed by hot and exceptionally dry weather from March to June; and this is followed, in turn, by a hot rainy period from July to October. The minimum temperature occurs in January and the maximum in May or June, when it rises to a daily average of 41 °C (105 °F) in Khartoum. Only about 25 cm (10 inches) of rainfall occurs annually in the Al-Jazīrah area (between the White and Blue Nile rivers), as compared with more than 53 cm (21 inches) at Dakar, Senegal, which is at the same latitude. North of Khartoum less than 13 cm (5 inches) of rain falls annually, an amount insufficient for permanent settlement. In June and July the central parts of the Sudan are frequently visited by squalls during which strong winds carry large quantities of sand and dust.

These storms, which are of three to four hours duration, are called haboobs.

A desert-type climate exists over most of the remainder of the area north to the Mediterranean. The principal characteristics of the northern Sudan and the desert of Egypt are aridity, a dry atmosphere, and a considerable seasonal, as well as diurnal, temperature range in Upper Egypt. Temperatures often surpass 38 °C (100 °F); in Aswān, for example, the average daily maximum in June is 47 °C (117 °F). While no low temperatures are recorded anywhere in the Sudan or Egypt, winter temperatures decrease to the north. Thus, only Egypt has what could be called a winter season, which occurs from November to March, when the daily maximum temperature in Cairo is 20 to 24 °C (68 to 75 °F) and the night minimum is about 10 °C (50 °F). The rainfall in Egypt is of Mediterranean origin and falls mostly in the winter, with the amount decreasing toward the south. From 20 cm (8 inches) on the coast, it falls gradually to a little over 2.54 cm (1 inch) in Cairo and to less than 2.54 cm (1 inch) in Upper Egypt. During the spring, from March to June, depressions from the Sahara or along the coast travel east, causing dry southerly winds, which sometimes results in a condition called khamsin. These are sandstorms or dust storms during which the atmosphere becomes hazy; on occasion they may persist for three or four days, at the end of which the phenomenon of a "blue" sun may be observed.

The periodic rise of the Nile remained an unsolved mystery until the discovery of the role of the tropical regions in its regime. In effect, there was little detailed knowledge about the hydrology of the Nile before the 20th century, except for early records of the river level that the ancient Egyptians made with the aid of nilometers (gauges formed by graduated scales cut in natural rocks or in stone walls), some of which still remain. Today, however, no other river of comparable size has a regime that is so well known. The discharge of the main stream, as well as the tributaries, is regularly measured.

The Nile swells in the summer, the floods rising as a result of the heavy tropical rains in Ethiopia. In the southern Sudan the flood begins in April, but the effect is not felt at Aswān, Egypt, until July. The water then starts to rise and continues to do so throughout August and September, with the maximum occurring in mid-September. At Cairo the maximum is delayed until October. The level of the river then falls rapidly through November and December. From March to May the level of the river is at its lowest. Although the flood is a fairly regular phenomenon, it occasionally varies in volume and date. Before it was possible to regulate the river, years of high or low flood—particularly a sequence of such years—resulted in crop failure, famine, and disease. Following the river from its sources, an estimate can be made of the contribution of the various lakes and tributaries in the Nile flood.

Lake Victoria forms the first great natural reservoir of the Nile system. The heavy rainfall over the lake is nearly balanced by surface evaporation, and the outflow from the lake—some 23 billion cubic metres (812 billion cubic feet)—comes mostly from the rivers draining into it, particularly the Kagera. This water then flows via the Victoria Nile into Lake Kyoga, where there is little net loss of water, and then into Lake Albert. Water lost by evaporation is more than balanced by the rainfall over the lake and the inflow from other smaller streams, notably the Semliki. Thus the annual outflow from Lake Albert to the Al-Jabal River is about 26 billion cubic metres (918 billion cubic feet).

In addition to the water it receives from the great lakes, the torrential tributaries of the Al-Jabal supply it with nearly 20 percent of its water. The discharge of the Al-Jabal varies little throughout the year because of the regulatory effect of the large swamps and lagoons of the Al-Sudd region. About half of its water is lost in this stage by seepage and evaporation, but the flow of the Sobat River into the main stream just upstream of Malakāl nearly makes up for the loss.

The White Nile provides a regular supply of water throughout the year. During April and May, when the main stream is at its lowest level, more than 80 percent of its water comes from the White Nile. The White Nile obtains its water in roughly equal amounts from two main sources. The first source is the rainfall on the East African Plateau of the previous summer. The second source is the drainage of southwestern Ethiopia through the Sobat (contributed mainly by its two headstreams, the Baro and the Pibor) that enters the main stream below Al-Sudd. The annual flood of the Sobat, a consequence of the Ethiopian summer rains, is to a great extent responsible for the variations in the level of the White Nile. The rains that swell its upper valley begin in April and cause widespread inundation over the 320 km (200 miles) of plains through which the river passes, thus delaying the arrival of the rainwater in its lower reaches until November–December. Relatively small amounts of the mud carried by the Sobat's flood reach the White Nile.

The Blue Nile, the most important of the three great Ethiopian affluents, plays an overwhelming part in bringing the Nile flood to Egypt. It receives two tributaries in the Sudan—the Ar-Rahad and the Ad-Dindar—both of which also originate in Ethiopia. The regime of the Blue Nile is distinguished from that of the White Nile by the more rapid passage of its floodwater into the main stream. The river level begins to rise in June, reaching a maximum level at Khartoum in about the first week in September.

The Atbara River draws its floodwater from the rains on the northern part of the Ethiopian Plateau, as does the Blue Nile. While the floods of the two streams occur at the same time, the Blue Nile is a perennial stream, while the Atbara, as mentioned, shrinks to a series of pools in the dry season.

The swelling of the Blue Nile causes the first flood-waters to reach the central Sudan in May. The maximum is reached in August, after which the level falls again. The rise at Khartoum averages more than 6 metres (20 feet). When the Blue Nile is in flood it holds back the White Nile water, turning it into an extensive lake and delaying its flow. The Jabal al-Awliyā' Dam south of Khartoum increases this ponding effect.

The peak of the flood does not enter Lake Nasser until late July or August, when the average daily inflow from the Nile rises to some 710.8 million cubic metres (25.1 billion cubic feet). Out of this amount the Blue Nile accounts for almost 70 percent, the Atbara more than 20 percent, and the White Nile 10 percent. In early May the inflow drops to its minimum. The total discharge of 45.3 million cubic metres (1.6 billion cubic feet) per day comes mainly from the White Nile and the remainder from the Blue Nile. On the average, about 85 percent of the water in Lake Nasser comes from the Ethiopian Plateau, and the rest is contributed by the East African Lake Plateau system. Lake Nasser has an enormous storage capacity—more than 168 cubic km (40 cubic miles)—although the content of the reservoir varies with the extent of the annual flood upstream. Because it is situated in a very hot and dry region, however, Lake Nasser can lose up to 10 percent of its volume to evaporation annually when it is full, decreasing to about one-third that amount when it is at minimum capacity.

STUDY AND EXPLORATION

The ancient Egyptians were probably familiar with the Nile as far as Khartoum, the Sudan, and with the Blue Nile as far as its source in Lake Tana, Ethiopia, but they showed little or no interest in exploring the White Nile. The source of the Nile was unknown to them. The Greek historian Herodotus, who visited Egypt in 457 BCE, traveled up the Nile as far as the first cataract (Aswān). About the second century BCE the Greek scientific writer Eratosthenes sketched a nearly correct route of the Nile to Khartoum, showing the two Ethiopian affluents, and suggested lakes as the source of the river.

In 25 BCE the Greek geographer Strabo and a Roman governor of Egypt, Aelius Gallus, also explored the Nile as far as the first cataract. A Roman expedition to find the source of the Nile that took place in 66 CE, during the reign of the emperor Nero, was impeded by the Al-Sudd, and the attempt was therefore abandoned. Ptolemy, the Greek astronomer and geographer who lived in Alexandria, wrote in 150 CE that the White Nile originated in the high snow-covered Mountains of the Moon (since identified with the Ruwenzori Range).

From the 17th century onward several attempts were made to explore the Nile. In 1618 Pedro Páez, a Spanish Jesuit priest, located the source of the Blue Nile. In 1770 the Scottish explorer James Bruce visited Lake Tana as well as the source of the Blue Nile.

Modern exploration of the Nile basin began with the conquest of the northern and central Sudan by the Ottoman viceroy of Egypt, Muḥammad ʿAlī, and his sons from 1821 onward. As a result of this the Blue Nile was known as far as its exit from the Ethiopian foothills, and the White Nile as far as the mouth of the Sobat

River. Three expeditions under a Turkish officer, Selim Bimbashi, were made between 1839 and 1842, and two got to the point about 32 km (20 miles) beyond the present port of Jūbā, where the country rises and rapids make navigation very difficult. After these expeditions, traders and missionaries penetrated the country and established stations in the southern Sudan. From an Austrian missionary, Ignaz Knoblecher, in 1850 came reports of lakes farther south. In the 1840s the missionaries Johann Ludwig Krapf, Johannes Rebmann, and Jacob Erhardt, traveling in East Africa, saw the snow-topped mountains Kilimanjaro and Kenya and heard from traders of a great inland sea that might be a lake or lakes.

These reports led to fresh interest in the Nile source and to an expedition by the English explorers Sir Richard Burton and John Hanning Speke, who followed a trade route of the Arabs from the east coast and reached Lake Tanganyika. On the return journey Speke went north and reached the southern end of Lake Victoria, which he thought might be the origin of the Nile. This was followed in 1860 by another expedition by Speke and James A. Grant under the auspices of the Royal Geographical Society. They followed the previous route to Tabora and then turned toward Karagwe, the country west of Lake Victoria. There they saw the Virunga Mountains 160 km (100 miles) to the west (they thought that these might be the Mountains of the Moon) and discovered the Kagera River. Continuing around the lake, Speke finally reached the Ripon Falls (1862), at which point he wrote, "I saw that old Father Nile without any doubt rises in Victoria Nyanza." Speke then made his way northward with Grant, for part of the way traveling along the Nile, until the two reached Gondokoro, which lies nearly opposite the present Jūbā. They heard rumours on the way of another large lake to the west but were unable to visit it and passed the information on to Sir Samuel White Baker, who met them at Gondokoro, having come up from Cairo. Baker then continued his journey south and discovered Lake Albert. Neither Speke nor Baker had followed the Nile completely from the Ripon Falls to Gondokoro. And Baker, who saw the northern half of Lake Albert, was told that it extended a particularly long way to the south.

The question of the source of the Nile was finally settled when, between 1874 and 1877, General Charles George Gordon and his officers followed the river and mapped part of it. In particular Lake Albert was mapped, and Charles Chaillé-Long, an American, discovered Lake Kyoga. In 1875 Henry Morton Stanley traveled up from the east coast and circumnavigated Lake Victoria. His attempt to get to Lake Albert was unsuccessful, but he marched to Lake Tanganyika and traveled down the Congo River to the sea. In another memorable journey in 1889, taken to relieve the German traveler Mehmed Emin Paşa (Pasha), Stanley traveled up the Congo and across to Lake Albert, where he met Emin and persuaded him to evacuate his Equatorial Province, which had been invaded by the Mahdist forces. They returned to the east coast by way of the Semliki valley and Lake Edward, and Stanley saw the snowy peaks of the Ruwenzori Range for the first time.

Exploration and mapping has continued over the years: it was not until the 1960s, for example, that a detailed study of the upper gorges of the Blue Nile was completed.

The Amazon River and Mississippi River are the two most important rivers in the Americas. The Amazon basin is best known for draining the world's largest and most biologically diverse rainforest regions, whereas the Mississippi is an important commercial artery for the United States. In addition, both rivers are navigable by large vessels deep into their continental interiors.

THE AMAZON RIVER

The Amazon River (Portuguese: Rio Amazonas, Spanish: Río Amazonas), which is also called Río Marañón and Rio Solimões, is the greatest river of South America. It possesses the largest drainage system in the world in terms of the volume of its flow and the area of its basin. The total length of the river—as measured from the headwaters of the Ucayali-Apurímac river system in southern Peru—is at least 6,400 km (4,000 miles), which makes it slightly shorter than the Nile River but still the equivalent of the distance from New York City to Rome. Its westernmost source is high in the Andes Mountains, within 160 km (100 miles) of the Pacific Ocean, and its mouth is in the Atlantic Ocean, on the northeastern coast of Brazil. However, both the length of the Amazon and its ultimate source have been subjects of debate since the mid-20th century, and there are those who claim that the Amazon is actually longer than the Nile.

The vast Amazon basin (Amazonia), the largest lowland in Latin America, has an area of about 7 million square km (2.7 million square miles) and is nearly twice as large as that of the Congo River, the Earth's other great equatorial drainage system. Stretching some 2,780 km

(1,725 miles) from north to south at its widest point, the basin includes the greater part of Brazil and Peru, significant parts of Colombia, Ecuador, and Bolivia, and a small area of Venezuela; roughly two-thirds of the Amazon's main stream and by far the largest portion of its basin are within Brazil. The Tocantins-Araguaia catchment area in Pará state covers another 777,000 square km (300,000 square miles). Although considered a part of Amazonia by the Brazilian government and in popular usage, it is technically a separate system. It is estimated that about one-fifth of all the water that runs off the Earth's surface is carried by the Amazon. The flood-stage discharge at the river's mouth is four times that of the Congo and more than 10 times the amount carried by the Mississippi River. This immense volume of fresh water dilutes the ocean's saltiness for more than 160 km (100 miles) from shore.

The extensive lowland areas bordering the main river and its tributaries, called *várzeas* ("floodplains"), are subject to annual flooding, with consequent soil enrichment; however, most of the vast basin consists of upland, well above the inundations and known as *terra firme*. More than two-thirds of the basin is covered by an immense rainforest, which grades into dry forest and savanna on the higher northern and southern margins and into montane forest in the Andes to the west. The Amazon Rainforest, which represents about half of the Earth's remaining rainforest, also constitutes its single largest reserve of biological resources.

Since the later decades of the 20th century, the Amazon basin has attracted international attention because human activities have increasingly threatened the equilibrium of the forest's highly complex ecology. Deforestation has accelerated, especially south of the Amazon River and on the piedmont outwash of the Andes, as new highways and air transport facilities have opened the basin to a tidal wave of settlers, corporations, and researchers. Significant mineral discoveries have brought further influxes of population. The ecological consequences of such developments, potentially reaching well beyond the basin and even gaining worldwide importance, have attracted considerable scientific attention.

The first European to explore the Amazon, in 1541, was the Spanish soldier Francisco de Orellana, who gave the river its name after reporting pitched battles with tribes of female warriors, whom he likened to the Amazons of Greek mythology. Although the name Amazon is conventionally employed for the entire river, in Peruvian and Brazilian nomenclature it properly is applied only to sections of it. In Peru the upper main stream (fed by numerous tributaries flowing from sources in the Andes) down to the confluence with the Ucayali River is called Marañón, and from there to the Brazilian border it is called Amazonas. In Brazil the name of the river that flows from Peru to its confluence with the Negro River is Solimões; from the Negro out to the Atlantic the river is called Amazonas.

THE LENGTH OF THE AMAZON

The debate over the location of the true source of the Amazon and over the river's precise length sharpened during the second half of the 20th century, as technological advances made it possible to explore deeper into the extremely remote locations of the Amazon's headstreams and to more accurately measure stream lengths. Beginning in the 1950s, explorers of the region cited various mountains in Peru as possible sources, but they did so without taking precise measurements or applying hydrological research. An expedition in 1971, sponsored by the National Geographic Society, pinpointed Carruhasanta Creek, which runs off the north slope of Mount Mismi in southern Peru, as the source of the river. This location became widely accepted in the scientific community and remained so until the mid-1990s—although a Polish expedition in 1983 contended that the source of the river was actually another stream, nearby Apacheta Creek. (The Carruhasanta and Apacheta streams form the Lloqueta River, an extension of the Apurímac.)

With the introduction of Global Positioning System (GPS) technology in the 1990s, researchers again attempted to navigate the entire length of the Amazon. The American geographer Andrew Johnston of the Smithsonian Institution's Air and Space Museum in Washington, D.C., employed GPS gear to explore the various Andean rivers that flow into the Amazon. Using the definition of the river's source as being the farthest point from which water could flow into the ocean and where that water flows year-round (thereby eliminating those rivers that freeze in winter), he concluded that the source was Carruhasanta Creek on Mount Mismi.

By the early 21st century, advanced satellite-imagery technology was allowing researchers to match the river's dimensions even more precisely. In 2007 an expedition that included members of Brazil's National Institute for Space Research and other organizations traveled to the region of Carruhasanta and Apacheta creeks in an attempt to determine which of the two was the "true" source of the Amazon. Their data revealed that Apacheta was 10 km (6 miles) longer than Carruhasanta and carries water year-round, and they concluded that Apacheta Creek was indeed the source of the Amazon River. The team then proceeded to measure the river's length. As part of this process, they had to determine from which of the Amazon's three main outlets to the sea to begin the measurement— the Northern or Southern channels, which flow north of Marajó Island, or Breves Channel, which flows southward around the western edge of the island to join the Pará River estuary along the southern coast of the island. They chose to use the southern channel and estuary, because that constituted the longest distance from the source of the river to the ocean (at Marajó Bay). According to their calculations, the southern outlet lengthened the river by 353 km (219 miles). Their final measurement for the length of the Amazon—from Apacheta Creek to the mouth of Marajó Bay—was about 6,992 km (4,345 miles).

This team of researchers, using the same technology and methodology, then measured the length of the Nile River, which they determined to be about 6,853 km (4,258 miles). That value was some 200 km (125 miles) longer than previous calculations for the Nile but nearly 145 km (90 miles) shorter than the length the group gave for the Amazon. These measurements infer that the Amazon may be recognized as the world's longest river, supplanting the Nile. However, a river like the Amazon has a highly complex and variable streambed—made more so by seasonal climatic factors—which complicates the process of obtaining an accurate measurement. Thus, the final length of the river remains open to interpretation and continued debate.

LANDFORMS AND DRAINAGE PATTERNS

The Amazon basin is a great structural depression, a subsidence trough that has been filling with immense quantities of sediment of Cenozoic age (i.e., dating from about the past 65.5 million years). This depression, which flares out to its greatest dimension in the Amazon's upper reaches, lies between two old and relatively low crystalline plateaus, the rugged Guiana Highlands to the north and the lower Brazilian Highlands (lying somewhat farther from the main river) to the south. The Amazon basin was occupied by a great freshwater sea during the Pliocene Epoch (5.3 million to 2.6 million years ago). Sometime during the Pleistocene

Epoch (about 2.6 million to 11,700 years ago) an outlet to the Atlantic was established, and the great river and its tributaries became deeply entrenched in the former Pliocene seafloor. The modern Amazon and its tributaries occupy a vast system of drowned valleys that have been filled with alluvium. With the rise in sea level that followed the melting of the Pleistocene glaciers, the steep-sided canyons that had been eroded into the Pliocene surface during the period of lower sea levels were gradually flooded. In the upper part of the basin—in eastern Colombia, Ecuador, Peru, and Bolivia—more-recent outwash from the Andes has covered many of the older surfaces.

THE PHYSIOGRAPHY OF THE RIVER COURSE

The Amazon River's main outlets are the two channels north of Marajó Island, a lowland somewhat larger in size than Denmark, through a cluster of half-submerged islets and shallow sandbanks. There the mouth of the river is 64 km (40 miles) wide. The port city of Belém, Braz., is on the deep water of the Pará River estuary south of Marajó. The Pará is fed chiefly by the Tocantins River, which enters the Pará southwest of Belém. The port city's link with the main Amazon channel is either north along the ocean frontage of Marajó or following the deep but narrow *furos* (channels) of Breves that bound the island on the west and southwest and link the Pará River with the Amazon. There are more than one thousand tributaries of the Amazon that flow into it from the Guiana Highlands, the Brazilian Highlands, and the Andes. Six of these tributaries—the Japurá (Caquetá in Colombia), Juruá, Madeira, Negro, Purus, and Xingu rivers—are each more than 1,600 km (1,000 miles) long. The Madeira River exceeds 3,200 km (2,000 miles) from source to mouth. The largest ocean-going ships can ascend the river 1,600 km (1,000 miles) to the city of Manaus, Braz., while lesser freight and passenger vessels can reach Iquitos, Peru, 2,090 km (1,300 miles) farther upstream, at any time of year.

The sedimentary axis of the Amazon basin comprises two distinct groups of landforms: the *várzea*, or floodplain of alluvium of Holocene age (i.e., up to about 11,700 years old), and the *terra firme*, or upland surfaces of Pliocene and Pleistocene materials (those from 11,700 to 5.3 million years old) that lie well above the highest flood level. The floodplain of the main river is characteristically 19 to 50 km (12 to 30 miles) wide. It is bounded irregularly by low bluffs 6 to 30 metres (20 to 100 feet) high, beyond which the older, undulating upland extends both north and south to the horizon. Occasionally these bluffs are undercut by the river as it swings to and fro across the alluvium, producing the *terra caída*, or "fallen land," so often described by Amazon travelers. At the city of Óbidos, Braz., where the river width is some 2 km (1.25 miles), a low range of relatively hard rock narrows the otherwise broad floodplain.

The streams that rise in the ancient crystalline highlands are classified as either blackwater (Jari, Negro, and Tocantins-Araguaia) or clearwater (Trombetas, Xingu, and Tapajós). The blackwater tributaries have higher levels of humic acids (which cause their dark colour) and originate in nutrient-poor, often sandy uplands, so they carry little or no silt or dissolved solids. Clearwater tributaries have a higher mineral content and lower levels of humic acids. Some rivers flow as clearwater during the rainy season and blackwater during the dry season. Where such blackwater tributaries enter the main river, they are sometimes blocked off to form funnel-shaped freshwater lakes or estuaries, as at the mouth of the Tapajós.

In contrast, the Madeira River, which joins the Amazon some 80 km (50 miles) downstream from Manaus, and its principal affluents—the Purus, Juruá,

Ucayali, and Huallaga on the right or southern bank and the Japurá, Putumayo (Içá in Brazil), and Napo from the northwest—have their source in the geologically youthful and tectonically active Andes. There they pick up the heavy sediment loads that account for their whitewater designation. Where the silt-laden waters of the Amazon (Solimões in Brazil), derived from these streams, meet those of the Negro at Manaus, the darker and hence warmer and sediment-free waters of the latter tend to be overrun by those of the Amazon, creating a striking colour boundary that is erased by turbulence downstream.

The mother river, the Marañón above Iquitos, rises in the central Peruvian Andes at an elevation of 4,840 metres (15,870 feet) in a small lake in the Cordillera Huayhuash above Cerro de Pasco. The Huallaga and Ucayali, major right-bank affluents of the Marañón, originate considerably farther south. The headwaters of the deeply entrenched Apurímac and Urubamba, tributaries at the confluence of the Ucayali, reach to within 160 km (100 miles) of Lake Titicaca, the farthest of any stream in the system from the great river's mouth.

The Negro River, the largest of all the Amazon tributaries, accounts for about one-fifth of the total discharge of the Amazon, and 40 percent of its aggregate volume is measured just below the confluence at Manaus. Its drainage area of about 756,000 square km (292,000 square miles) includes that of the Branco, its major left-bank tributary, with its source in the Guiana Highlands. Another of the Negro's affluents, the Casiquiare, is a bifurcation of the Orinoco River that forms a link between the Amazon and the Orinoco's drainage system. The Branco watershed, approximately coincident with the state of Roraima, includes extensive tracts of sandy, leached soils that support a grassy and stunted arboreal cover (*campos*). Other tributaries of the Negro, such as the Vaupés and Guainía,

Canoe on the Negro River in the Amazon Rainforest, Amazonas state, north-ern Braz. Union Press/Bruce Coleman, Inc., New York

drain eastward from the Colombian Oriente. The river traverses some of the least populous and least disturbed parts of the Amazon basin, including several national parks, national forests, and indigenous reserves. In its lower reaches the Negro becomes broad and island-filled, reaching widths of up to 32 km (20 miles) in certain locations.

The Madeira River, the second largest affluent of the Amazon, has a discharge of perhaps two-thirds that of the Negro. Silt from its turbid waters has choked its lower valley with sediments. Where it joins the Amazon below Manaus, it has contributed to the formation of the 320-km- (200-mile-) long island of Tupinambarana. Beyond its first cataract, 970 km (600 miles) up the river, its three major affluents—the Madre de Dios, the Beni, and the Mamoré—provide access to the rubber-rich forests of the Bolivian Oriente. The meandering Purus and Juruá rivers that flank the Madeira on the west are also important tributaries that lead into those forests. Mamoré's tributary, the Guaporé, opens up to the Mato Grosso Plateau.

HYDROLOGY

Most of the estimated 1.3 million tons of sediment that the Amazon pours daily into the sea is transported north-ward by coastal currents to be deposited along the coasts of northern Brazil and French Guiana. As a consequence, the river is not building a delta. Normally, the effect of the tide is felt as far upstream as Óbidos, Braz., 970 km (600 miles) from the river's mouth. A tidal bore called the *pororoca* occurs at times in the estuary, prior to spring tides. With an increasing roar, it advances upstream at speeds of 16 to 24 km (10 to 15 miles) per hour, forming a breaking wall of water from 1.5 to 4 metres (5 to 12 feet) high.

At the Óbidos narrows, the flow of the river has been measured at 216,000 cubic metres (7,628,000 cubic feet) per second, its width constricted to little more than a mile. Here the average depth of the channel below the mean water-mark is more than 60 metres (200 feet), well below sea level; in most of the Brazilian part of the river its depth exceeds 45 metres (150 feet). Its gradient is extraordinarily slight. At the Peruvian border, some 3,200 km (2,000 miles) from the Atlantic, the elevation above sea level is less than 90 metres (300 feet). The maximum free width (without islands) of the river's permanent bed is 14 km (8.5 miles), upstream from the mouth of the Xingu. During great floods, however, when the river completely fills the floodplain, it spreads out in a band some 55 km (35 miles) wide or more. The average velocity of the Amazon is about 2.4 km (1.5 miles) per hour, a speed that increases considerably at flood time.

The rise and fall of the water is controlled by events external to the floodplain. The floods of the Amazon are not disasters but rather distinctive, anticipated events. Their marked regularity and the gradualness of the change in water level are the result of the enormous size of the basin, the gentle gradient, and the great temporary storage capacity of both the floodplain and the estuaries of the river's tributaries. The upper course of the Amazon has two annual floods, and the river is subject to the alternate influence of the tributaries that descend from the Peruvian Andes (where rains fall from October to January) and from the Ecuadoran Andes (where rains fall from March to July). This pattern of alternation disappears farther downstream, as the two seasons of high flow gradually merge into a single one. Thus, the rise of the river progresses slowly downstream in a gigantic wave from November to June, and then the waters recede until the end of October. The flood levels can reach from 12 to 15 metres (40 to 50 feet) above low river.

CLIMATE

The climate of Amazonia is warm, rainy, and humid. The lengths of day and night are equal on the Equator (which runs only slightly north of the river), and the usually clear nights favour relatively rapid radiation of the heat received from the sun during the 12-hour day. There is a greater difference between daytime and midnight temperatures than between the warmest and coolest months. Hence, night can be considered the winter of the Amazon. At Manaus the average daily temperature is about 32 °C (90 °F) in September and

24 °C (75 °F) in April, but the humidity is consistently high and often oppressive. During the winter months of the Southern Hemisphere, a powerful south-polar air mass occasionally drifts northward into the Amazon region, causing a sharp drop in temperature, known locally as a *friagem*, when the mercury may drop to about 14 °C (57 °F). At any time of the year, several days of heavy rain can be succeeded by clear, sunny days and fresh, cool nights with relatively low humidity. In the lower reaches of the river basin, cooling trade winds blow most of the year.

The main influx of atmospheric water vapour into the basin comes from the east. About half of the precipitation that falls originates from the Atlantic Ocean, and the other half comes from evapotranspiration from the tropical forest and associated convectional storms. Rainfall in the lowlands typically ranges from 150 to 300 cm (60 to 120 inches) annually in the central Amazon basin (e.g., Manaus). On the eastern and northwestern margins of the basin, rainfall occurs year-round, whereas in the central part there is a definite drier period, usually from June to November. Manaus has experienced as many as 60 consecutive days without rain. Moreover, in 2005 the Manaus region experienced a devastating drought, which caused parts of the river to dry up, making transportation difficult, depleting drinking supplies, and leaving millions of rotting fish in the riverbed. Such extreme periods of drought are uncommon to the Manaus region, but fluctuations in the river's level—thought to be related to climatic events and continued deforestation in the area—have continued to be of concern. The dry season is not sufficiently intense to arrest plant growth, but it may facilitate the onset and spread of fires, whether arsonous or natural. To the west the Andes form a natural barrier that prevents most of the water vapour from leaving the basin. The influence of mountains on rainfall is indicated by the high levels of precipitation in the upper piedmont and by the cloud-steeped Andean flanks, which feed the rivers that form a large part of the Amazon system. The highest amounts of precipitation, up to 350 cm (140 inches), are recorded in the upper Putumayo along the Colombian border.

Along the southern margin of the Amazon basin, the climate grades into that of west-central Brazil, with a distinct dry season during the Southern Hemispheric winter. As elevations increase in the Andes, temperatures fall significantly.

THE PARANÁ RIVER

After the Amazon, the Paraná River (Portuguese: Rio Paraná, Spanish: Río Paraná) is South America's longest river. It begins on the plateau of southeast-central Brazil and flows generally south to the point where, after a course of 4,880 km (3,032 miles), it joins the Uruguay River to form the extensive Río de la Plata estuary of the Atlantic Ocean.

The Paraná River's drainage basin, with an area of about 2.8 million square km (1,081,000 square miles), includes the greater part of southeastern Brazil, Paraguay, southeastern Bolivia, and northern Argentina. From its origin at the confluence of the Grande and Paranaíba rivers to its junction with the Paraguay River, the river is known as the Alto (Upper) Paraná. This upper course has three important tributaries, namely the Tietê, the Paranapanema, and the Iguaçu, all three having their sources near the Atlantic coast in southeastern Brazil. The Alto Paraná's passage through the mountains was formerly marked by the Guaíra Falls. This series of massive waterfalls was completely submerged in the early 1980s by the reservoir of the newly built Itaipú dam complex, which spans the Alto Paraná.

From its confluence with the Iguaçu River to its junction with the Paraguay River, the Alto Paraná continues as the frontier between Paraguay and Argentina. When it is joined by the Paraguay, it becomes the lower Paraná and commences to flow only through Argentine territory. Near Santa Fé, the lower Paraná receives its last considerable tributary, the Salado River. Between Santa Fé and Rosario the delta of the Paraná begins to form, being 18 km (11 miles) wide at its upper end and roughly 65 km (40 miles) wide at its lower end. Within the delta the river divides again and again into distributary branches, the most

Itaipú Dam on the Upper Paraná River, north of Ciudad del Este, Para.
Vieira de Queiroz—TYBA/Agencia Fotografica

important being the last two channels formed, the Paraná Guazú and the Paraná de las Palmas.

The volume of the lower Paraná River is dependent on the amount of water that it receives from the Paraguay River, which provides about 25 percent of the total; the Paraná's annual average discharge is 17,293 cubic metres per second (610,700 cubic feet per second). The basin of the Alto Paraná has a hot and humid climate year round, with dry winters and rainy summers. The climate of the middle and lower basins ranges from subtropical in the north to temperate humid in the south, with less plentiful rainfall. The Alto Paraná has two zones of vegetation, forests to the east and savanna to the west. Forests continue along the Paraná downstream to Corrientes, where the savanna begins to dominate both banks. The Paraná River has a rich and varied animal life that includes many species of edible fish. Much of the Paraná basin is economically unexploited. The main dam of the huge Itaipú project on the Paraná River was completed in 1982 and had a power generating capacity of 12,600 megawatts. The Yacyretá Dam on the lower Paraná River began operation in 1994. The lower river is a transport route for agricultural products, manufactured goods, and petroleum products, and its waters are used for irrigation of the adjacent farmlands.

SOILS

The vast Amazonian forest vegetation appears extremely lush, leading to the erroneous conclusion that the under-lying soil must be extremely fertile. In fact, the nutrients in the system are locked up in the vegetation, including roots and surface litter, and are continuously recycled through leaf fall and decay. Generally, the soils above flood level are well-drained, porous, and of variable structure. Often they are sandy and of low natural fertility because of their lack of phosphate, nitrogen, and potash and their high acidity. Small areas are underlain with basaltic and diabasic rocks, with reddish soils (*terra roxa*) of considerable natural fertil-ity. The *terra preta dos Indios* ("black earth of the Indians") is another localized and superior soil type, created by past settlement activity.

The agricultural potential of the annually flooded *várzea* areas is great. Their soils do not lack nutrients, because they are rejuvenated each year by the deposit of fertile silt left as the waters recede, but their usage for agricultural purposes is limited by the periodic inunda-tions. It is estimated that these valuable soils occupy some 65,000 square km (25,000 square miles).

STUDY AND EXPLORATION

In the early days the Amazon River was the only means of access into the forest. Francisco de Orellana descended the main course of the Amazon from the Ecuadoran and Peruvian Andes to the Atlantic in 1541–42. Nearly a century later, Pedro Teixeira went from Belém, Braz., to Quito, Ecua., and the region increasingly became known through the explorations of the Portuguese. In 1743 the French naturalist Charles-Marie de La Condamine made a raft trip down the Amazon, during which he made geographic and ethnographic observations of the basin.

At the outset of the 19th century, the German explorer Alexander von Humboldt confirmed the connection between the Amazon and Orinoco systems through the Casiquiare River. The English naturalist H.W. Bates spent time along the Amazon in 1848–59, collecting thousands of species of animals. His book *The Naturalist on the River Amazons*, originally published in two volumes in 1863, is still regarded as one of the great classics on the Amazon River. An official expedition was sent from the United States to Amazonia in the mid-19th century. In 1854 in Washington, D.C., William Lewis Herndon published the report that he and Lardner Gibbon—both lieutenants in the U.S. Navy—had made to Congress under the title of *Exploration of the Valley of the Amazon.*

The period since 1900 has been one of numerous exploratory and scientific expeditions. In 1913–14 U.S. Pres. Theodore Roosevelt and Brazilian Col. Cândido Rondon headed an expedition that explored a tributary of the Madeira and made natural history collections and observations. A party sponsored by Harvard University's Institute of Geographical Exploration did important scientific work in the years 1910–24. The American Geographical Society compiled data and published detailed maps of this vast region.

Since World War II the international scientific community has been increasingly attracted to Amazonia. British, French, German, Japanese, and North American groups have carried out detailed biophysical and cultural surveys; a large number of international workshops, conferences, and symposia on Amazonian problems have been held. The Amazon Cooperation Treaty, signed in Brasília in 1978 by representatives of all the basin's countries, pledged the signatories to a coordinated development of the region on sound ecological principles. (In 1995 those countries created the Amazon Cooperation Treaty Organization to strengthen and better implement the treaty goals.) Brazilian scientists have also contributed significant research on issues concerning the area. Particularly important has been the work of the National Institute of Amazonian Research (INPA) at Manaus, the Goeldi Museum in Belém, and the National Institute for Space Research in São José dos Campos.

THE MISSISSIPPI RIVER

The Mississippi River is the largest river of North America, draining with its major tributaries an area of approximately 3.1 million square km (1.2 million square miles), or about one-eighth of the entire continent. The Mississippi River lies entirely in the United States. Rising in Lake Itasca in Minnesota, it flows almost due south across the continental interior, collecting the waters of its major tributaries, the Missouri River (to the west) and the Ohio River (to the east), approximately halfway along its journey to the Gulf of Mexico through a vast delta southeast of New Orleans, a total distance of 3,780 km (2,350 miles) from its source. With its tributaries, the Mississippi drains all or part of 31 U.S. states and two Canadian provinces.

As the central river artery of a highly industrialized nation, the Mississippi River has become one of the busiest commercial waterways in the world, and, as the unruly neighbour of some of the continent's richest farmland, it has been subjected to a remarkable degree of human control and modification. Furthermore, the river's unique contribution to the history and literature of the United States has woven it like a bright thread through the folklore and national consciousness of North America, linking the names of two U.S. presidents—Abraham Lincoln and Ulysses S. Grant—with that of the celebrated author Mark Twain.

Although the Mississippi can be ranked as the fourth longest river in the world by adding the length of the Missouri-Jefferson (Red Rock) system to the Mississippi downstream of the Missouri-Mississippi confluence—for a combined length of 5,970 km (3,710 miles)—the 3,780-km (2,350-mile) length of the Mississippi proper is comfortably exceeded by 19 other rivers. In volume of discharge, however, the Mississippi's rate of roughly 17,000 cubic metres (600,000 cubic feet) per second is the eighth greatest in the world.

On the basis of physical characteristics, the Mississippi River can be divided into four distinct reaches, or sections. In its headwaters, from the source to the head of navigation at St. Paul, Minn., the Mississippi is a clear, fresh stream winding its unassuming way through low countryside dotted with lakes and marshes. The upper Mississippi reach extends from St. Paul to the mouth of the Missouri River near St. Louis, Mo. Flowing past steep limestone bluffs and receiving water from tributaries in Minnesota, Wisconsin, Illinois, and Iowa, the river in this segment assumes the character that led Algonquian-speaking Indians to name it the "Father of Waters" (literally *misi*, "big"; *sipi*, "water"). Below the Missouri River junction, the middle Mississippi follows a 320-km (200-mile) course to the mouth of the Ohio River. The turbulent, cloudy-to-muddy, and flotsam-laden Missouri, especially when in flood, adds impetus as well as enormous quantities of silt to the clearer Mississippi. Beyond the confluence with the Ohio at Cairo, Ill., the lower Mississippi attains its full grandeur. Where these two mighty rivers meet, the Ohio is actually the larger. Thus, below the Ohio confluence the Mississippi swells to more than twice the size it

Confluence of the Mississippi (left) *and Ohio rivers at Cairo, Ill.* © Alex S. MacLean/Landslides

is above. Often a mile and a half from bank to bank, the lower Mississippi becomes a brown, lazy river, descending with deceptive quiet toward the Gulf of Mexico.

To geographers, the lower Mississippi has long been a classic example of a meandering alluvial river. That is, the channel loops and curls extravagantly along its flood-plain, leaving behind meander scars, cutoffs, oxbow lakes, and swampy backwaters. More poetically, Mark Twain compared its shape to "a long, pliant apple-paring." Today the sunlight glittering on the twisted ribbon of water remains one of the most distinctive landmarks of a trans-continental flight. Now curbed largely by an elaborate system of embankments (levees), dams, and spillways, this lower section of the Mississippi was the golden, some-times treacherous, highway for the renowned Mississippi steamboats, those "palaces on paddle wheels" that so fired the public imagination. From the explosive master pilot Horace Bixby, portrayed by Mark Twain, to the nostalgic lyrics of Oscar Hammerstein's song "Ol' Man River," the creations of that era on the Mississippi have added colour to America's heritage.

PHYSIOGRAPHY

The geology and physical geography of the Mississippi drainage area are essentially those of the Interior Lowlands and Great Plains of North America. Fringes also touch upon the Rocky and Appalachian mountains and upon the rim of the Canadian (Laurentian) Shield to the north. The focus of the system, the floodplain of the lower Mississippi, is of particular interest in that the geology and physical geography of the region are of the river's own making. Like a huge funnel, the river has taken sediment and debris from contributory areas near the lip of the funnel and deposited much of the product in the alluvial plain of the funnel's spout, illustrating the interdependence of the entire Mississippi system.

The most significant contributory area in recent times has been to the west of the river. Rising in western uplands, notably in the foothills of the Rockies, rivers such as the Red, Arkansas, Kansas, Platte, and Missouri remove considerable silt loads from the rolling expanses of the Great Plains. These tributaries meander and braid across a wide, gently sloping mantle of unconsolidated materials, laid down over rock beds of the Cretaceous Period (i.e., about 100 million years old), toward the "Father of Waters." Precipitation in these western areas is light to moderate, usually less than 6.35 cm (25 inches) per year, but, because at least 70 percent of this precipitation falls as rain between April and September, the erosive capability of the rivers is enhanced (runoff from winter snowmelt is more gradual than from rainstorms). The sandy sediments, moreover, offer little resistance to erosion, so that many of these rivers are only braided in their courses.

The Mississippi's eastern contributory rivers drain the well-watered Appalachian Mountain system. Most of this group, including the Kentucky, Green, Cumberland, and Tennessee rivers, flows via well-defined valleys into the Ohio and thence into the Mississippi. The erosive capacity of these rivers varies in relation to the geologic structure of their basins. These consist of harder rocks in the higher elevations and a softer sill of limestone of the Late Carboniferous Period (i.e., about 300 million years of age), lying below the 305 metres (1,000-foot) elevation line between the Ohio and Tennessee rivers and in the glaciated area of the Ohio's right-bank tributaries.

The third contributory area of the Mississippi also differs from the other two. The upper Mississippi gathers its strength in a region marked by glacial action. After the great ice sheets of the Wisconsin Glaciation had put down layers of debris across much of Minnesota, Wisconsin, northern Illinois, and northern Iowa, huge quantities of meltwater flowed south, washing channels through this debris. Today the upper Mississippi and its tributaries, the Wisconsin, St. Croix, Rock, and Illinois rivers, all trace the lines of these former sluiceways.

Pouring southward, the glacial meltwaters were joined by the proto-Missouri and Ohio rivers. The combined waters then enlarged the great north-south trough along which the lower Mississippi now flows. Some 1,600 km (1,000 miles) long, this trough is 40 to 320 km (25 to 200 miles) wide and bounded by escarpments rising up to 61 metres (200 feet) above the valley floor. Geologic studies have revealed that the floor of the glacial trough was later buried by a deep layer of material washed out from an ice sheet and dumped to a thickness of about 30 to 90 metres (100 to 300 feet) in the central section.

The Mississippi's delta is an even more striking monument to the river's constructive work. There, at the tip of the drainage funnel, millions of years of sedimentation have spilled out across the floor of the Gulf of Mexico, forming cones of sediment that total 480 km (300 miles) in radius and 77,800 square km (30,000 square miles) in area. The surface expression of the many sub-deltas is the Mississippi delta, with an area exceeding 28,500 square km (11,000 square miles). Stretching its distributaries into the gulf, the Mississippi once delivered some 220 million tons of sediment there each year, most of it as silt. Today, however, much of this silt is captured behind upstream dams, causing the delta to erode and shrink in area. Compounding this problem are the many hundreds of miles of levees (walls that limit flooding) along the river's banks, which trap silt in the channel proper. This is especially damaging in the delta, where annual silt additions from flooding help to keep it from being eroded by waves.

CLIMATE

During winter, mean monthly temperatures in the Mississippi basin range from 13 °C (55 °F) in subtropical southern Louisiana to -12 °C (10 °F) in subarctic northern Minnesota. Mean monthly temperatures in summer range from 28 °C (82 °F) in Louisiana to 21 °C (70 °F) in Minnesota.

Precipitation sources are low-level moisture from the Gulf of Mexico and some low-level and high-level moisture from the Pacific Ocean. Winter and spring precipitation occurs in the vicinity of easterly and southerly fronts and storms. Average monthly precipitation in winter ranges from 13 cm (5 inches) or more in the south to more than 7.5 cm (3 inches) over much of the Ohio River basin to less than one inch over the western and northern Great Plains. Summer and early autumn rainfall occurs mostly as showers and isolated thunderstorms and weaker frontal storms. Average monthly rainfall ranges from 15 cm (6 inches) in southern Louisiana and over the mountains of Tennessee and North Carolina to only 5 to 7.5 cm (2 to 3 inches) over the Great Plains.

The climate is humid over the eastern half of the basin, with large quantities of winter and spring runoff generated over the Tennessee, Ohio, and southern Mississippi river basins. A north-south band of subhumid climates, neither fully humid nor semiarid, extends from central Texas northward to eastern North Dakota. To the west are the semiarid climates of the Great Plains, and along the Rocky Mountain crests an alpine climate prevails, in which winter snowfalls are released as spring and early summer meltwater runoff.

HYDROLOGY

It is not surprising that the hydrology of so powerful a river as the Mississippi has been the subject of intense study. In the 19th century Mark Twain described with considerable wit how the pilots of the Mississippi paddle wheelers banded together to run a common information service about changing conditions along the channel. Today the Mississippi River Commission is responsible for river work and considers it worthwhile to maintain a working scale model of the river so that its engineers can test new plans in miniature before embarking on expensive, full-scale projects. Indeed, by the 1920s it was generally believed that enough was known about the river's hydrology and enough control structures had been built to have tamed the river. Then in 1927 came the most disastrous flood in the recorded history of the lower Mississippi valley. More than 59,500 square km (23,000 square miles) of land flooded. Communications, including roads and rail and telephone services, were cut in many places. Farms, factories, and whole towns went temporarily underwater. An immense amount of property was damaged, and at least 250 people lost their lives. The river engineers took another look at the hydrology of the Mississippi.

Since the freak conditions of 1927, the mean discharge of water into the lower Mississippi by its major tributaries has been carefully monitored. The mean discharge of the main river at Vicksburg, Miss., is calculated at about 16,100 cubic metres (570,000 cubic feet) per second. About 220 km (135 miles) downriver from Vicksburg, approximately 25 percent of the sediment and water discharge of the river is diverted into the Atchafalaya River through the Old River Complex (Old River Control Structures). These statistics, however, conceal all-important variations in river flow linked with the fluctuating state of the Mississippi's larger tributaries.

Broadly speaking, the western tributaries have the most-irregular flow regimes. They reach a spring or early summer peak that is up to three or four times as great as their winter contribution. The upper Mississippi and its tributaries reach their maximum flow about the same time (March–June), when melting snows are followed by early summer rains. The winter runoff from this area, however, is also substantial. The crest of the Ohio's flow occurs slightly earlier. At Metropolis, Ill., just above the confluence with the Mississippi, the greatest monthly discharge is usually recorded in March, at which time the Ohio may be providing more than three-fifths of the water being monitored past Vicksburg in the lower river.

Thus, the Ohio is chiefly responsible for the lower Mississippi flood situations, which may be aggravated by such factors as early rains in the Great Plains, a sudden hot spell in early spring that melts the northern snows, and heavy downpours throughout the lower valley. Under such conditions the lower river will rise over its banks and put pressure against its man-made levees. Tributaries will back up and form lakes on the far side of these same levees. The current, which normally runs no more than 2 to 3.5 knots (2.5 to 4 miles per hour), may then double at constricted points along the main channel. Thus, for example, the monitoring station at Vicksburg, which at low water in 1936 recorded as little as 2,656 cubic metres (93,800 cubic feet) per second, measured 58,300 cubic metres (2.06 million cubic feet) per second at high-water stage the following year.

In late spring and early summer of 1993 another inevitable yet inconceivably large flood occurred on the Mississippi, this time confined to the parts of the river above its confluence with the Ohio (which was not in flood). Among the worst-hit rivers were the lower reaches of the Missouri, the Des Moines and Raccoon rivers in Iowa, and the Mississippi between the Wisconsin-Illinois border and Cape Girardeau, Mo. The floods were set off by persistent rains in this region. For the first time in recorded history, the Mississippi and the Missouri flooded at the same time—despite the 29 dams on the Mississippi and the 36 giant reservoirs on their tributaries. The Raccoon River in Des Moines crested at 2.1 metres (seven feet) above the previous high, which constituted a 500-year flood event (a flood so large that it occurs, statistically, only about once every five hundred years; or that it has a one in five hundred chance of happening in any year).

THE MISSOURI RIVER

The Missouri River in Montana. Travel Montana

The Missouri River is the longest tributary of the Mississippi River, formed by the confluence of the Jefferson, Madison, and Gallatin rivers in the Rocky Mountain area of southwestern Montana (Gallatin county), U.S., about 1,200 metres (4,000 feet) above sea level. The Missouri flows eastward to central North Dakota, where it turns southward across South Dakota to form a section of the South Dakota–Nebraska boundary, the Nebraska–Iowa boundary, the Nebraska–Missouri boundary, and the northern section of the Kansas–Missouri boundary. Then it meanders eastward across central Missouri to join the Mississippi River, about 16 km (10 miles) north of St. Louis, after traveling a course of 3,726 km (2,315 miles).

Its drainage basin occupies about 1,371,100 square km (529,400 square miles) of the Great Plains, of which 16,840 square km (2,550 square miles) are in Canada. Elevations within its basin are extreme: from 4,300 metres (14,000 feet) above sea level in the Rockies near the Continental Divide to 120 metres (400 feet) where it joins the Mississippi. The flow of the Missouri and of most of its tributaries is exceedingly varied—the minimum flow being 120 cubic metres (4,200 cubic feet) per second and the maximum 25,500 cubic metres (900,000 cubic feet) per second. With unprotected slopes and with such violent fluctuations in flow, erosion and silting are major problems.

Chief tributaries include the Cheyenne, Kansas, Niobrara, Osage, Platte, and Yellowstone rivers, flowing in on the south and west sides, and the James and Milk rivers, entering from the north. Other tributaries are the Bad, Blackwater, Cannonball, Gasconade, Grand, Heart, Judith, Knife, Little Missouri, Moreau, Musselshell, and White rivers, which enter from the south and west. The Big Sioux, the Chariton, Little Platte, Marias, Sun, and Teton rivers enter from the north and east.

The Missouri was named Peki-tan-oui on some early French maps and, later, Oumessourit. It has been nicknamed "Big Muddy" because of the amount of solid matter it carries in suspension. Its mouth was discovered in 1673 by the French explorers Jacques Marquette and Louis Jolliet while they were canoeing down the Mississippi River. In the early 1700s French fur traders began to navigate upstream. The first exploration of the river from its mouth to its headwaters was made in 1804–05 by Meriwether Lewis and William Clark. For many years commerce on the river was restricted to the fur trade, and the river was little used by the earliest American settlers moving west. The American Fur Company began to use steamers on the river in 1830. Steamboat traffic on the river reached its height in 1858 but began to decline in the following year with the completion of the Hannibal and St. Joseph Railway to St. Joseph, Mo.

For the first 150 years after settlement along the river, little was done to develop the Missouri as a useful waterway or as a source of irrigation and power. In 1944 the U.S. Congress authorized a comprehensive program for flood control and water-resource development in the Missouri River basin. It envisioned a system of more than one hundred dams and reservoirs on the Missouri and certain of its tributaries. Local flood protection, involving levees and bank stabilization, and a deeper river channel were provided on the Missouri itself from Sioux City, Iowa, to the Mississippi, a distance of 1,220 km (760 miles). By the time an even more ambitious plan, the Missouri River Basin program, or simply the Pick-Sloan program, was adopted in the 1950s, channel maintenance had enabled commercial barge lines to begin operating on the Missouri in 1953. The major dams built on the Missouri were Fort Peck (near Glasgow, Mont.), Garrison (N.D.), and Gavin's Point, Fort Randall, and Oahe (S.D.). The Fort Peck Dam is one of the largest earthfill dams in the world. The entire system of dams and reservoirs has greatly reduced flooding on the Missouri and provides water to irrigate millions of acres of cropland along the main river and its tributaries. Hydroelectric installations along the river generate electricity for many communities along the river's upper course.

The chief cities along the Missouri are Great Falls, Mont.; Williston and Bismarck, N.D.; Pierre, S.D.; Sioux City and Council Bluffs, Iowa; Omaha and Nebraska City, Neb.; Atchison, Leavenworth, and Kansas City, Kan.; and St. Joseph, Kansas City, Columbia, Jefferson City, and St. Charles, Mo.

In many parts of Iowa crops never got planted. In all, some 6 million hectares (15 million acres) flooded, and 40 federal levees and 1,043 nonfederal levees broke. This disastrous flood taught many that flood-control structures such as levees, floodwalls, and dams work for some events but fail to provide enough protection from the one-hundred-year (or larger) floods. The floods of 1993 taught many that tight and total control of rivers as large as the Mississippi is neither possible nor economically feasible. Since then, it has become clear that "living with the river" means moving homes, farmhouses, and even entire towns off the floodplains and allowing these lowland areas to flood naturally.

A variety of pollutants, derived from municipal, industrial, and agricultural sources, have been identified in the waters and sediments of the Mississippi River. Organic compounds and trace metals occur in relatively low concentrations. In addition to those naturally present in the water, they derive from industrial and municipal wastes and runoff from agricultural and urban areas. High concentrations of bacteria associated with human waste, however, have been found downstream from some cities and have been attributed to inadequately treated sewage flowing into the river. Concentrations downstream from New Orleans, for example, have been found to be many times greater than concentrations above the city. Pollutants have had little widespread effect on the composition of benthic invertebrate populations, which are indicative of changes in water quality. Water samples taken at New Orleans have shown a relatively high dissolved-oxygen content and low biochemical oxygen demand. Thus, by this index, river pollution may be said to be low.

CHAPTER 8
MAJOR RIVERS OF ASIA AND AUSTRALIA

Asia contains numerous large rivers. Some rivers such as the Ganges in India and the Yangtze in China are major cultural and economic conduits. Others, such as the Ob, Lena, and Yenisey rivers, drain large areas of lightly populated hinterlands. The most important river in Australia is the Murray River, but its length and basin characteristics often include the Darling River.

THE GANGES RIVER

The Ganges River is the great river of the plains of northern India. Although officially as well as popularly called the Ganga in Hindi and in other Indian languages, internationally it is known by its conventional name, the Ganges. From time immemorial it has been the holy river of Hinduism. For most of its course it is a wide and sluggish stream, flowing through one of the most fertile and densely populated regions in the world. Despite its importance, its length of 2,510 km (1,560 miles) is relatively short compared with the other great rivers of Asia or of the world.

Rising in the Himalayas and emptying into the Bay of Bengal, it drains a quarter of the territory of India, while its basin supports hundreds of millions of people. The Gangetic Plain, across which it flows, is the heartland of the region known as Hindustan and has been the cradle of successive civilizations from the Mauryan empire of Ashoka in the 3rd century BCE down to the Mughal Empire, founded in the 16th century.

For most of its course the Ganges flows through Indian territory, although its large delta in the Bengal area, which it shares with the Brahmaputra River, lies mostly in Bangladesh. The general direction of the river's flow is from northwest to southeast. At its delta the flow is generally southward.

PHYSIOGRAPHY

The Ganges rises in the southern Himalayas on the Indian side of the border with the Tibet Autonomous region of China. Its five headstreams—the Bhagirathi, Alaknanda, Mandakini, Dhauliganga, and Pindar—all rise in the northern mountainous region of Uttarakhand state. Of these, the two main headstreams are the Alaknanda (the longer of the two), which rises about 50 km (30 miles) north of the Himalayan peak of Nanda Devi, and the Bhagirathi, which originates about 3,000 metres (10,000 feet) above sea level in a subglacial meltwater cave at the base of the Himalayan glacier known as Gangotri. Gangotri itself is a sacred place for Hindu pilgrimage. The true source of the Ganges, however, is considered to be at Gaumukh, about 21 km (13 miles) southeast of Gangotri.

The Alaknanda and Bhagirathi unite at Devaprayag to form the main stream known as the Ganga, which cuts through the Outer (southern) Himalayas to emerge from the mountains at Rishikesh. It then flows onto the plain at Haridwar, another place held sacred by the Hindus.

The volume of the Ganges increases markedly as it receives more tributaries and enters a region of heavier rainfall, and it shows a marked seasonal variation in flow. From April to June the melting Himalayan snows feed the river, while in the rainy season from July to September the rain-bearing monsoons cause floods. During winter the river's flow declines. South of Haridwar, now within the state of Uttar Pradesh, the river receives the principal right-bank tributaries of the Yamuna River, which flows through the Delhi capital region to join the

Ganges near Allahabad, and the Tons, which flows north from the Vindhya Range in Madhya Pradesh state and joins the Ganges just below Allahabad. The main left-bank tributaries in Uttar Pradesh are the Ramganga, the Gomati, and the Ghaghara.

The Ganges next enters the state of Bihar, where its main tributaries from the Himalayan region to the north are the Gandak, the Burhi Gandak, the Ghugri, and the Kosi rivers and its most important southern tributary is the Son. The river then skirts the Rajmahal Hills to the south and flows southeast to Farakka, at the apex of the delta. In West Bengal, the last Indian state that the Ganges enters, the Mahananda River joins it from the north. In West Bengal in India, as well as in Bangladesh, the Ganges is locally called the Padma. The westernmost distributaries of the delta are the Bhagirathi and the Hugli (Hooghly) rivers, on the east bank of which stands the huge metropolis of Kolkata (Calcutta). The Hugli itself is joined by two tributaries flowing in from the west, the Damodar and the Rupnarayan. As the Ganges passes from West Bengal into Bangladesh, a number of distributaries branch off to the south into the river's vast delta. In Bangladesh the Ganges is joined by the mighty Brahmaputra (which is called the Jamuna in Bangladesh) near Goalundo Ghat. The combined stream, there called the Padma, joins with the Meghna River above Chandpur. The waters then flow through the delta region to the Bay of Bengal via innumerable channels, the largest of which is known as the Meghna estuary.

The Ganges-Brahmaputra system has the third greatest average discharge of the world's rivers, at roughly 30,770 cubic metres (1,086,500 cubic feet) per second. Approximately 11,000 cubic metres (390,000 cubic feet) per second is supplied by the Ganges alone. The rivers' combined suspended sediment load of about 1.84 billion tons per year is the world's highest.

Boat traffic on the Buriganga River, Dhaka, Bangl. Hubertus Kanus/ SuperStock

Dhaka (Dacca), the capital of Bangladesh, stands on the Buriganga ("Old Ganges"), a tributary of the Dhaleswari. Apart from the Hugli and the Meghna, the other distributary streams that form the Ganges delta are, in West Bengal, the Jalangi River and, in Bangladesh, the Matabhanga, Bhairab, Kabadak, Garai-Madhumati, and Arial Khan rivers.

The Ganges, as well as its tributaries and distributaries, is constantly vulnerable to changes in its course in the delta region. Such changes have occurred in comparatively recent times, especially since 1750. In 1785 the Brahmaputra flowed past the city of Mymensingh. It now flows more than 65 km (40 miles) west of it before joining the Ganges.

The delta, the seaward prolongation of sediment deposits from the Ganges and Brahmaputra river valleys, is about 355 km (220 miles) along the coast and covers an area of about 60,000 square km (23,000 square miles). It is composed of repeated alternations of clays, sands, and marls, with recurring layers of peat, lignite, and beds of what were once forests. The new deposits of the delta, known in Hindi and Urdu as the *khadar*, naturally occur in the vicinity of the present channels. The delta's growth is dominated by tidal processes.

The southern surface of the Ganges delta has been formed by the rapid and comparatively recent deposition of enormous loads of sediment. To the east the seaward side of the delta is being changed at a rapid rate by the formation of new lands, known as *char*s, and new islands. The western coastline of the delta, however, has remained practically unchanged since the 18th century.

The rivers in the West Bengal area are sluggish. Little water passes down them to the sea. In the Bangladeshi delta region, the rivers are broad and active, carrying plentiful water and connected by innumerable creeks. During the rains (June to October) the greater part of the region is flooded to a depth of 1 metre (about 3 feet) or more, leaving the villages and homesteads, which are built on artificially raised land, isolated above the floodwaters. Communication between settlements during this season can be accomplished only by boat.

To the seaward side of the delta as a whole, there is a vast stretch of tidal mangrove forests and swampland. The region, called the Sundarbans, is protected by India and Bangladesh for conservation purposes. Each country's portion of the Sundarbans has been designated a UNESCO World Heritage site, India's in 1987 and Bangladesh's in 1997.

In certain parts of the delta there occur layers of peat, composed of the remains of forest vegetation and rice plants. In many natural depressions, known as *bil*s, peat, still in the process of formation, has been used as a fertilizer by local farmers, and it also has been dried and used as a domestic and industrial fuel.

CLIMATE AND HYDROLOGY

The Ganges basin contains the largest river system on the subcontinent. The water supply depends partly on the rains brought by the southwesterly monsoon winds from July to October, as well as on the flow from melting Himalayan snows in the hot season from April to June. Precipitation in the river basin accompanies the southwest monsoon winds, but it also comes with tropical cyclones that originate in the Bay of Bengal between June and October. Only a small amount of rainfall occurs in December and January. The average annual rainfall varies from 76 cm (30 inches) at the western end of the basin to more than 2290 cm (90 inches) at the eastern end. (In the upper Gangetic Plain in Uttar Pradesh, rainfall averages about 76–102 cm [30–40 inches]; in the Middle Ganges Plain of Bihar, from 102 to 152 cm [40 to 60 inches]; and in the delta region, between 152 and 254 cm [60 and 100 inches].) The delta region experiences strong cyclonic storms both before the commencement of the monsoon season, from March to May, and at the end of it, from September to October. Some of these storms result in much loss of life and the destruction of homes, crops, and livestock. One such storm, which occurred in November 1970, was of catastrophic proportions, resulting in deaths of at least 200,000 and possibly as many as 500,000 people; another, in April 1991, killed some 140,000.

Because there is little variation in relief over the entire surface of the Gangetic Plain, the river's rate of flow is slow. Between the Yamuna River at Delhi and the Bay of Bengal, a distance of nearly 1,600 km (1,000 miles), the elevation drops only some 210 metres (700 feet). Altogether the Ganges-Brahmaputra plains extend over an area of 800,000 square km (300,000 square miles). The alluvial mantle of the plain, which in some places is more than 1,800 metres (6,000 feet) thick, is possibly not more than 10,000 years old.

THE LENA RIVER

The Lena River—Sakha (Yakut) Ulakhan Iuriakh ("Great River")—is a major river of Russia and the 10th longest river in the world. It flows 4,400 km (2,734 miles) from its sources in the mountains along the western shores of Lake Baikal, in southeastern Siberia, to the mouth of its delta on the Arctic Laptev Sea. The area of the river's drainage basin is about 2.49 million square km (961,000 square miles).

PHYSIOGRAPHY

The Lena has three main sections, each about 1,450 km (900 miles) long: the upper section from the source to the tributary Vitim River, the middle course from the Vitim to the mouth of the Aldan River, and the lower section from the Aldan to the Laptev Sea.

In the section from the headwaters to the Vitim River, the Lena flows in a deep-cut valley, the rocky and steep slopes of which rise up to 300 metres (1,000 feet) above the river. These slopes are formed on the right bank by the northern Baikal Mountains. The width of the river valley varies from 2 to 10 km (1 to 6 miles), but occasionally it narrows in ravines to only 200 metres (700 feet). The best-known ravine, named Pyany Byk (Russian: "Drunken Bull"), is situated 237 km (147 miles) below Kirensk.

In the first 177 km (110 miles) from its source, the Lena has a great number of rocky shoals, which occur as far as the tributary Kirenga River. Below the mouth of the Kirenga, water depth in the pools increases to 9 metres (30 feet), and the decreasing gradient reduces the rate of flow. In the middle course, from the mouth of the Vitim to the Aldan, the Lena becomes a large, deep river. The water supply increases, especially after the junction with the Olyokma River, and the width of the river reaches 1.6 km (1 mile). From the mouth of the Vitim to the Olyokma, the river skirts the Patom Plateau, on the right bank, forming an enormous bend. In places the width of the valley increases to 32 km (20 miles). Its slopes are gentle and green with forests, and along them run well-marked terraces formed by rivers. The floor of the valley in this section contains an extensive floodplain with scattered small lakes.

Below the Olyokma, the character of the valley changes sharply. For a stretch of about 640 km (400 miles), from Olyokminsk to Pokrovsk (100 km [60 miles] above Yakutsk), the Lena flows along the bottom of a narrow valley with sheer, broken slopes. The enormous limestone rock formations sometimes resemble the ruins of castles, or columns, or the figures of people and animals; and the area is a favourite place for tourists and rock-climbers. In the Lena's middle section, the river receives several of its largest tributaries: in addition to the Aldan and the Vitim, it receives the Great Chuya River on the right bank and the Nyuya River on the left.

Below the mouth of the Aldan, the Lena enters the Yakut Lowland. Its valley broadens to between 19 and 26 km (12 and 16 miles), and the width of the floodplain reaches 6 to 14 km (4 to 9 miles). In this section, the river receives one of its most important tributaries, the Vilyuy River. The Lena's course forms a great arc that trends to the northwest and then to the north around the Verkhoyansk Mountains, which lie to the east. The floodplain abounds with often marshy lakes, and the riverbed divides, forming many islands and branches. The depth is from 15 to 20 metres (50 to 70 feet), but there also are many shallow sections with sandbanks.

In the final section of the river—between the island of Zholdongo and the beginning of the delta—the Lena valley narrows to a width of about 1.6 km (1 mile) as the river flows through a gap between high hills on either side. The delta takes the shape of a rectangular peninsula that juts some 120 km (75 miles) into the Laptev Sea and is about 280 km (175 miles) wide. The islands of the delta, formed by numerous crisscrossing channels, are low-lying and covered with peat bogs.

CLIMATE

The climatic features of the Lena River basin are determined by its location, with its upper course well inside the continent and its lower course in the Arctic. In winter the powerful Siberian anticyclone (high-pressure system) forms and dominates all of eastern Siberia. Because of the anticyclone, the winter is notable for its clear skies and lack of wind. Temperatures fall as low as -60 to -70 °C (-76 to -94 °F), with average air temperature in January ranging from -30 to -40 °C (-22 to -40 °F). In July averages range between 10 and 20 °C (50 and 68 °F). Owing to the basin's remoteness from warm ocean water, precipitation is slight. Only in the southern mountains does the yearly total reach 60 to 70 cm (24 to

28 inches). In most of the basin it ranges between 20 to 40 cm (8 and 16 inches), and in the delta it drops to 10 cm (4 inches). Between 70 and 80 percent of the precipitation falls in the summer in the form of rain. Winters average not more than 5 cm (2 inches) of precipitation, resulting in a light snow cover.

The prolonged cold temperatures give rise to ice blisters and pingos. These are formed of groundwater that accumulates between the layers of permafrost (soil frozen permanently) over many years and layers of seasonally frozen soil. Sometimes the ice blisters disintegrate with considerable force, scattering ice blocks. The riverbeds and floodlands also have permafrost in some places.

HYDROLOGY

More than 95 percent of the Lena's water derives from melting snow and from rain; most of the remainder of the yearly flow comes from groundwater. Typical of the Lena basin are high floods (especially flash floods) in summer and very little flow in winter. Complete cessation of flow may occur with the freezing of the river to the bottom. The average annual flow of the Lena at the mouth is 16,400 cubic metres (579,200 cubic feet) per second. Maximum discharge has exceeded 120,000 cubic metres (4.2 million cubic feet) per second, and the minimum has fallen to 1,100 cubic metres (39,300 cubic feet). The total yearly volume approaches 420 cubic km (100 cubic miles). During the high-water period the water level in the upper and middle courses rises by an average of 9 to 15 metres (30 to 50 feet) and in the lower course by 18 metres (60 feet).

The highest temperature of the water in the upper course of the river is 19 °C (66 °F) and in the lower course about 14 °C (57 °F). The river is free of ice in the south for five to six months and in the north for four to five months. The breakup of ice in the spring causes significant damage to the shores: the ice floes grind the rocks, pull trees out by their roots, and carry away large sections of the banks.

The Lena discharges about 12 million tons of suspended sediment and 41 million tons of dissolved matter into the sea each year. The proportion of suspended alluvium in the water is small: even in floodwaters it does not exceed 50 to 60 grams per cubic metre (0.05 to 0.06 ounce per cubic foot). The mineralization of the water in the lower Lena during low water is 80 to 100 grams per cubic metre (0.08 to 0.1 ounce per cubic foot) and in floodwaters 160 to 500 grams per cubic metre (0.16 to 0.5 ounce per cubic foot).

STUDY AND EXPLORATION

The first European exploration of the Lena was conducted by Russians at the beginning of the 17th century. In 1631 a fortress and a settlement were founded at Ust-Kut. The first scientific research was conducted by the Great Northern Expedition in 1733–42. Cartography was begun in 1910, and in 1912 the icebreakers *Taymyr* and *Vaygach* surveyed and mapped the delta. Further surveying was conducted between World Wars I and II, when a complete and detailed description was compiled. During the postwar Soviet period, research on the Lena was conducted by the Yakut branch of the Academy of Science of the U.S.S.R. and by other government bodies. More recently, there has been a concentrated effort to understand environmental changes that have taken place in this region over thousands of years.

THE MURRAY RIVER

The Murray River is the principal river of Australia and the main stream of the Murray-Darling Basin. It flows some 2,530 km (1,572 miles) across southeastern Australia from the Snowy Mountains to the Great Australian Bight of the Indian Ocean. The main towns in the Murray River valley are Albury, Wodonga, Echuca, Swan Hill, Mildura, Renmark, and Murray Bridge. The river is named after Colonial Secretary Sir George Murray.

PHYSICAL FEATURES

Although the Murray-Darling Basin has a total catchment area of some 1,061,469 square km (409,835 square miles), the Murray's average annual discharge is only 0.89 cubic metre (31 cubic feet) per second, and in places it has dried up on at least three occasions. The river rises on The Pilot (a mountain), near Mount Kosciuszko in southeastern New South Wales. It flows west and northwest, passes through Hume Reservoir above Albury, and forms most of the boundary between New South Wales and Victoria. At Morgan, S.Aus., it bends sharply southward to flow through Lake Alexandrina to Encounter Bay on the Great Australian Bight.

For most of its course through South Australia (400 km [250 miles]), the river is bordered by a narrow floodplain and flows between cliffs 30 metres (100 feet) high. Its upper 320 km (200 miles) cut through mountainous terrain. The central section, however, lies on a broad and mature floodplain, with the Riverina plains of New South Wales to the north and the plains of northern Victoria to the south. Its principal tributaries are the Darling, Murrumbidgee, Mitta Mitta, Ovens, Goulburn, Campaspe, and Loddon rivers.

Economy and Water Management

The Murray-Darling Basin, occupying about one-seventh of Australia's area, is of immense economic significance, lying across the great wheat-sheep belt in its climatically most reliable section. During the second half of the 19th century, river shipping was of great importance, but, with growing competition from railways and demand for irrigation water (first used at Mildura in 1886), navigation practically ceased. The basin has by far Australia's greatest area of irrigated crops and pastures, some 1.5 million hectares (3.6 million acres), more than 70 percent of the national total. It is the country's second largest wine-producing region; other major products include cattle, sheep, grains, and fruit.

In 1915 the River Murray Commission, comprising representatives from the three state governments and the commonwealth, was established to regulate utilization of the river's waters. The largest reservoirs are the Dartmouth on the Mitta Mitta River and the Hume on the Murray. The Dartmouth Dam, 180 metres (591 feet) high, is the highest dam of its kind in Australia. The multipurpose Snowy Mountains project (completed in 1974) increased the amount of water available for irrigation and generated large quantities of electrical power for peak load periods. Irrigation, however, led to serious salinity problems, so much so that Adelaide (which is almost completely dependent on the Murray for its water supply) on occasion received water that, by World Health Organization (WHO) criteria, was unfit for drinking. The problem of Murray salinity has been recognized as of national significance to Australia. Legislative arrangements were drawn up in 1987 and 1992 to introduce comprehensive basin-wide responses to environmental crises and the demand for sustainable development.

THE DARLING RIVER

The Darling River is the longest member of the Murray–Darling river system in Australia. It rises in several headstreams in the Great Dividing Range (Eastern Highlands), near the New South Wales–Queensland border, not far from the east coast, and flows generally southwest across New South Wales for 2,739 km (1,702 miles) to join the Murray at Wentworth (on the Victoria border), some 240 km (150 miles) from the Murray's mouth in South Australia.

The main source of the Darling is usually considered to be the Severn, which becomes successively the Dumaresq, Macintyre, Barwon, and, finally, the Darling. Discharge of the lower tributaries (Culgoa, Warrego, Paroo, Gwydir, Namoi, Macquarie, and Bogan) of the main stream fluctuates as a result of droughts and floods. Because much of the Darling's course runs through extensive saltbush pastures, receiving an average of less than 25 cm (10 inches) of rain annually, the river often loses more water by evaporation than is gained from its tributaries, many of which sometimes fail to reach the main stream. There are instances in which distributaries leave the main stream and disappear in inland basins. Several, however, flow into salt flats and in wet years emerge to rejoin the parent stream. The Great Anabranch (which leaves below the Menindee Lakes to join the Murray some 480 km [300 miles] later) and the Talyawalka Anabranch (which leaves the main stem near Wilcannia to rejoin the Darling roughly 130 km (80 miles) downstream near Menindee) are examples of these anastomosing distributaries (i.e., streams that leave and link up again with the main river). The entire Darling system drains a 650,000-square-km (250,000-square-mile) basin with an average annual discharge of 102 cubic metres (3,600 cubic feet) per second at Menindee. The river has an average gradient of 1.5 cm to the kilometre (1 inch to the mile).

Headwaters of the Darling were gradually colonized by pastoralists from 1815 onward. In 1828 the explorer Charles Sturt was dispatched by the governor of New South Wales, Sir Ralph Darling, to investigate the lower course of the Macquarie River. He chanced first upon the Bogan and then, early in 1829, the Darling main stream from the Barwon–Culgoa confluence. In the latter part of the 19th century, the river was of importance to navigation, but waterborne traffic has long been superseded by the railway.

The 25-cm (10-inch) winter rainfall line separates the Darling Basin into a western arid or semiarid (steppe) pastoral region and an eastern humid farming portion. The 324,000 square km (125,000 square miles) of the pastoral region are owned almost exclusively by wool growers with large holdings suited to grazing. Agriculture is possible only in small irrigated areas along the Darling; there is fodder cropping at Wilcannia, Bourke, and Brewarrina and grape and citrus farming further south in the Mallee region. Several engineering projects have given the drainage area great potential for development. The Darling River Weirs Act of 1945 authorized construction of a series of dams to impound water in reservoirs that provide town water and support irrigation. The Menindee Lakes Storage Scheme, completed in 1960, has created reservoirs with 1,794,000,000 cubic metres (1,454,000 acre-feet) of water for irrigation and domestic use; by regulating the flow in the Lower Murray, the system also provides a more dependable irrigation supply in South Australia. On the coastal tablelands and western slopes, a system of dams controls floods and allows for diversified agriculture and closer settlement than on the drier western plains.

THE OB RIVER

The Ob River is a large river of central Russia. One of the greatest rivers of Asia, the Ob flows north and west across western Siberia in a twisting diagonal from its sources in the Altai Mountains to its outlet through the Gulf of Ob into the Kara Sea of the Arctic Ocean. It is a major transportation artery, crossing territory at the heart of Russia that is extraordinarily varied in its physical environment and population. Even allowing for the barrenness of much of the region surrounding the lower course of the river and the ice-clogged waters into which it discharges, the Ob drains a region of great economic potential.

The Ob proper is formed by the junction of the Biya and Katun rivers, in the foothills of the Siberian sector of

Ships docked at the port of Salekhard on the lower Ob River, northwestern Sib. © Novosti Information Agency

the Altai, from which it has a course of 3,650 km (2,268 miles). If, however, the Irtysh River is regarded as part of the main course rather than as the Ob's major tributary, the maximum length, from the source of the Black (Chorny) Irtysh in China's sector of the Altai, is 5,410 km (3,362 miles), making the Ob the seventh longest river in the world. The catchment area is approximately 2,975,000 square km (1,150,000 square miles). Constituting about half of the drainage basin of the Kara Sea, the Ob's catchment area is the sixth largest in the world.

PHYSIOGRAPHY

The West Siberian Plain covers about 85 percent of the Ob basin. The rest of the basin comprises the terraced plains of Turgay (Kazakhstan) and the small hills of northernmost Kazakhstan in the south and the Kuznetsk Alatau range, the Salair Ridge, the Altai Mountains and their foothills and outliers in the southeast.

There are more than 1,900 rivers within the basin, with an aggregate length of about 180,000 km (112,000 miles). The Irtysh, a left-bank tributary 4,250 km (2,640 miles) long, itself drains about 1,593,000 square km (615,000 square miles; a somewhat larger area than that drained by the upper and middle Ob above the Irtysh confluence). Some 70 percent of the whole basin is drained by left-bank tributaries.

The huge basin of the Ob stretches across a number of natural zones. Semidesert prevails in the far south around Lake Zaysan (recipient of the Black Irtysh and source of the Irtysh proper), bordered on the north by steppe grassland. The central regions of the West Siberian Plain (i.e., more than half of the basin) consist of taiga (swampy coniferous forest), with great expanses of marshland. In the north there are vast stretches of tundra (low-lying, cold-tolerant vegetation).

The upper Ob runs from the junction of the Biya and Katun to the confluence of the Tom River, the middle Ob from the junction with the Tom to the Irtysh confluence, and the lower Ob from the junction with the Irtysh to the Gulf of Ob.

The Biya and the Katun both rise in the Altai Mountains: the former in Lake Telets, the latter to the south among the glaciers of Mount Belukha. From their junction near Biysk the upper Ob at first flows westward, receiving the Peschanaya, Anuy, and Charysh rivers from the left. In this reach, the river has low banks of alluvium, a bed studded with islands and shoals, and an average gradient of 20 cm per km (1 foot per mile). From the Charysh confluence the upper Ob flows northward on its way to Barnaul, receiving another left-bank tributary, the Aley

River, and widening its floodplain as the valley widens. Turning westward again at Barnaul, the river receives a right-bank tributary, the Chumysh River, from the Salair Ridge. The valley there is 5 to 10 km (3 to 6 miles) wide, with steeper ground on the left than on the right; the floodplain is extensive and characterized by diversionary branches of the river and by lakes; the bed is still full of shoals; and the gradient is reduced, but the depth increases markedly. At Kamen-na-Obi, however, where the river begins to bend northeastward, the width of the valley shrinks to 3 to 5 km (2 to 3 miles). Just above Novosibirsk another right-bank tributary, the Inya River, joins the upper Ob; and a dam at Novosibirsk forms the huge Novosibirsk Reservoir. Below Novosibirsk, where the river leaves the region of forest steppe to enter a zone of aspen and birch forest, both valley and floodplain broaden notably until, at the confluence with the Tom River, they are, respectively, 19 and 5 or more km (12 and 3 or more miles) wide. The depth of the upper Ob (at low water) varies between 2 and 6 metres (6.5 and 20 feet).

The middle Ob begins where the Tom flows into the main stream, from the right. Taking at first a northwesterly course, the river thereafter becomes much deeper and wider, especially after receiving its mightiest right-bank tributary, the Chulym, shortly below the confluence of the Shegarka River from the left. Successive tributaries along the northwesterly course, after the Chulym, include the Chaya and the Parabel (both left), the Ket (right), the Vasyugan (left), and the Tym and Vakh rivers (both right). Down to the Vasyugan confluence the river passes through the southern belt of the taiga, thereafter entering the middle belt. Below the Vakh confluence the middle Ob changes its course from northwesterly to westerly and receives more tributaries: the Tromyegan (right), the Great (Bolshoy) Yugan (left), the Lyamin (right), the Great Salym (left), the Nazym (right), and finally, at Khanty-Mansiysk, the Irtysh (left). In its course through the taiga, the middle Ob has a minimal gradient, a valley broadening to 29 to 48 km (18 to 30 miles) wide, and a correspondingly broadening floodplain—19 to 29 km (12 to 18 miles) wide. In this part of its course, the Ob flows in a complex network of channels, with the main bed widening from about 1 km (0.6 mile) on the higher reaches to nearly 3 km (2 miles) at the confluence with the Irtysh and becoming progressively free of shoals. Low-water depths vary between 4 and 8 metres (13 and 26 feet). At high water there are great floods every year, sometimes spreading 24 to 80 km (15 to 50 miles) across the valley and lasting from two to three months.

From its start at the confluence of the Irtysh, the lower Ob flows to the northwest as far as Peregrebnoye and thereafter to the north, crossing the northern belt of the taiga until it enters the zone of forest tundra in the vicinity of its delta. The valley is wide, with slopes steeper on the right than on the left, and the vast floodplain—19 to 29 km (12 to 18 miles) wide—is crisscrossed by the braided channels of the river and dotted with lakes. Below Peregrebnoye the river divides itself into two main channels: the Great (Bolshaya) Ob, which receives the Kazym and Kunovat rivers from the right, and the Little (Malaya) Ob, which receives the Northern (Severnaya) Sosva, the Vogulka, and the Synya rivers from the left. These main channels are reunited below Shuryshkary into a single stream that is up to 19 km (12 miles) wide and 40 metres (130 feet) deep. After the confluence of the Poluy (from the right) the river branches out again to form a delta, the two principal arms of which are the Khamanelsk Ob, which receives the Shchuchya from the left, and the Nadym Ob, which is the more considerable of the pair. At the base of the delta lies the Gulf of Ob, which is some 800 km (500 miles) long and has a width reaching 80 km (50 miles). The gulf's own catchment area (forest tundra and tundra proper) is more than 105,000 square km (40,000 square miles).

CLIMATE AND HYDROLOGY

The Ob basin has short, warm summers and long, cold winters. Average January temperatures range from -28 °C (-18 °F) on the shores of the Kara Sea to -16 °C (3 °F) in the upper reaches of the Irtysh. July temperatures for the same locations, respectively, range from 4 °C (40 °F) to above 20 °C (68 °F). The absolute maximum temperature, in the arid south, is 40 °C (104 °F), and the minimum, in the Altai Mountains, is -60 °C (-76 °F). Rainfall, which occurs mainly in the summer, averages less than 40 cm (16 inches) per year in the north, 50–60 cm (20 to 24 inches) in the taiga zone, and 30–40 cm (12 to 16 inches) on the steppes. The western slopes of the Altai receive as much as 157.5 cm (62 inches) per year. Snow cover lasts for 240 to 270 days in the north and for 160 to 170 days in the south. It is deepest in the forest zone, where it ranges from 60–90 cm (24 to 36 inches), and in the mountains, where it averages 200 cm (80 inches) per year. It is much shallower on the tundra, ranging from 30–50 cm (12 to 20 inches), and very thin on the steppe, where 20–40 cm (8 to 16 inches) fall.

On the upper Ob the spring floods begin early in April, when the snow on the plains is melting; and they have a second phase, ensuing from the melting of snow on the Altai Mountains. The middle Ob, scarcely affected by the upper Ob's phases, has one continuous spring-summer period of high water, which begins in mid April. For the lower Ob, high water begins in late April or early May.

Levels, in fact, begin to rise when the watercourse is still obstructed by ice; and maximum levels, which occur by May on the upper Ob, may not be reached until June, July, or even August on the lower reaches. For the upper Ob, the spring floods end by July, but autumn rains bring high water again in September and October. In the middle and lower Ob, the spring and summer floodwaters gradually recede until freezing sets in. On the lower reaches, flooding may last four months. Flooding of the Ob proper and of the Irtysh obstructs the minor tributaries' drainage.

Ice forms on the Ob from the end of October to the second week of November, after which the lower reaches begin to freeze solid. By the last week of November the entire river is frozen; the upper reaches remain frozen for some 150 days, the lower for 220. The thawing of the ice—which takes longer than the freezing—lasts from the end of April (upstream) to the end of May, and the spring drift (about five days in duration) produces considerable ice jams. The difference in level between high water and low is 8 metres (25 feet) at Novosibirsk on the upper Ob. It reaches 13 metres (43 feet) at Aleksandrovskoye on the middle Ob but decreases to no more than 6 metres (20 feet) at Salekhard near the mouth. The water is warmest in July, reaching a maximum of 28 °C (82 °F) in the vicinity of Barnaul.

The Ob has the third greatest discharge of Siberia's rivers, after the Yenisey and the Lena. On average, it pours some 400 cubic km (95 cubic miles) of water annually into the Arctic Ocean—about 12 percent of that ocean's total intake from drainage.

The volume of flow at Salekhard, just above the delta, is about 42,000 cubic metres (1.5 million cubic feet) per second at its maximum and 2,000 cubic metres (70,000 cubic feet) per second at its minimum, while for Barnaul, on the upper Ob, the corresponding figures are 9,600 and 200 cubic metres (340,000 and 5,700 cubic feet) per second. The average annual discharge rate at the river's mouth is about 12,700 cubic metres (448,500 cubic feet) per second. Most of the water comes from the melting of seasonal snow and from rainfall; much less of it comes from groundwater, mountain snow, and glaciers.

The waters of the Ob are only slightly mineralized: dissolved substances account for an annual outpouring of 30.2 million tons into the Kara Sea. The average amount of solid matter discharged annually by the Ob totals only about 50 million tons.

STUDY AND EXPLORATION

Although paleo-Asiatic peoples have inhabited the Ob basin for millennia, Russian explorers and adventurers first penetrated the area only toward the end of the 16th century. During the reign of Ivan IV (the Terrible), the Cossack folk hero Yermak led an expedition into the Ob basin (1581–84/85) that claimed vast expanses for the tsar. Settlements and forts were established at Tyumen (1586), Tobolsk (1587), Obdorsk (now Salekhard; 1595), and Tomsk (1604). The lower Ob was explored in the first half of the 17th century, and a navigation chart of that section was published in 1667. Russian scientists investigated the lower Ob during the Great Northern Expedition (1733–42). For the next 150 years the river system was explored chiefly to foster the development of transportation. Detailed hydrologic observations and studies were initiated by the end of the 19th century and were pursued intensively during the 20th. During the 20th century Soviet scientists studied long-term climate change and the landscape evolution of this region and the adjacent Kara Sea.

THE IRTYSH RIVER

The Irtysh River (Kazakh: Ertis, Chinese: (Pinyin) Ertix He or (Wade-Giles romanization) O-erh-ch'i-ssu Ho) is a major river of west-central and western Asia. With a length of 4,248 km (2,640 miles), it is one of the continent's longest rivers. The Irtysh and the Ob River, of which the Irtysh is the principal tributary, together constitute the world's seventh longest river system.

The Irtysh rises from the glaciers on the southwestern slopes of the Altai Mountains in the Uygur Autonomous Region of Xinjiang in far northwestern China. It flows west across the Chinese border through Lake Zaysan (Zhaysang) and then northwest across Kazakhstan (as the Ertis River). Northwest of the city of Semey the river flows onto the southern portion of the West Siberian Plain, entering Siberia (Russia) about 160 km (100 miles) southeast of Omsk, through which it flows. Downstream of Omsk the Irtysh enters a vast swampy region, making a large U-shaped bend to the northeast and north before resuming a northwestward course. It again turns to the north, passing through the western portion of the Vasyuganye Swamp before joining the Ob River near Khanty-Mansiysk in western Siberia.

The Irtysh is navigable for most of its course. The Narym, Bukhtarma Om, and Tara rivers are its chief right-bank tributaries, and the Osha, Ishim (Esil), Vagay, Tobol (Tobyl), and Konda rivers are its main left-bank ones. The Öskemen hydroelectric station was completed in 1952 and that at Buqtyrma (Bukhtarma) in 1960, both in Kazakhstan. The main river ports are Khanty-Mansiysk, Tobolsk, Tara, and Omsk in Russia and Pavlodar, Semey, and Öskemen in Kazakhstan.

THE YANGTZE RIVER

The Yangtze River—Chinese: (Pinyin) Chang Jiang or (Wade-Giles romanization) Ch'ang Chiang—is the longest river in both China and Asia and the third longest river in the world, with a length of 6,300 km (3,915 miles). Its basin, extending for some 3,200 km (2,000 miles) from west to east and for more than 1,000 km (600 miles) from north to south, drains an area of 1,808,500 square km (698,265 square miles). From its source on the Plateau of Tibet to its mouth on the East China Sea, the river traverses or serves as the border between 10 provinces or regions. More than three-fourths of the river's course runs through mountains. The Yangtze has eight principal tributaries. On its left bank, from source to mouth, these are the Yalung, Min, Jialing, and Han rivers; those on the right bank include the Wu, Yuan, Xiang, and Gan rivers.

The name Yangtze—derived from the name of the ancient fiefdom of Yang—has been applied to the river mainly by those in the West. Chang Jiang ("Long River") is the name used in China, although it also is called Da Jiang ("Great River") or, simply, Jiang ("[The] River"). The Yangtze is the most important river of China. It is the country's principal waterway, and its basin is China's great granary and contains nearly one-third of the national population.

The Upper Course

The upper course of the Yangtze flows across the Plateau of Tibet and descends through deep valleys in the mountains east of the plateau, emerging onto the Yunnan-Guizhou (Yungui) Plateau. Summers there are warm, and the winters are cold. The source of the Yangtze is the Ulan Moron (Wulanmulun) River, which originates in glacial meltwaters on the slopes of the Tanggula Mountains in southern Qinghai province on the border with the Tibet Autonomous Region. From the confluence of this stream with several others, the river flows generally easterly through a shallow, spacious valley, the bottom of which is studded with lakes and small reservoirs. This part of its course lies in the higher regions of the Tibetan highlands.

The river's character changes sharply upon reaching the eastern limits of the highlands. There the river—which in this stretch is called the Jinsha—descends from a high elevation, winding its way south of the high Bayan Har Mountains and forming a narrow valley up to 3 km (2 miles) in depth. Individual mountain peaks exceed elevations of 4,900 metres (16,000 feet) above sea level and are crowned with glaciers and perpetual snow. The steep, rocky slopes are cut with gorges and deep valleys. For several hundred miles the Yangtze flows in a south-easterly direction, before turning south to flow downward in rushing rapids. For a considerable distance the river flows through passes that are so steep that no room is left even for a narrow path. Villages, which are rarely found, are located high above the river. In this region the Yangtze runs close and parallel to both the Mekong and Salween rivers; all three rivers are within 25 to 50 km (15 to 30 miles) of one another and continue to flow in mutual proximity for a distance of more than 400 km (250 miles).

North of latitude 26° N these great rivers diverge, and the Yangtze turns east to pass through a winding valley with steep slopes. The river receives the waters of many tributaries, among which the Yalong River is the largest and contributes the most water. The Yangtze then widens to between 300 and 400 metres (1,000 and 1,300 feet), reaching depths often exceeding 9 metres (30 feet). In narrower gorges the water width decreases by almost half, but the depth increases sharply.

Near the end of the upstream part of its course, the Yangtze descends to an elevation of 305 metres (1,000 feet) above sea level. Thus, over the first 2,600 km (1,600 miles) of its length, the river has fallen more than 5,200 metres (17,000 feet), or an average of more than 2 metres per km (10 feet per mile) of its course. In the mountains, however, there is a substantial stretch where the fall of the river is considerably greater.

THE MIDDLE COURSE

The middle course of the Yangtze stretches for about 1,010 km (630 miles) between the cities of Yibin in Sichuan province and Yichang in Hubei province. The climate is characterized by hot summers and relatively mild winters, as the high mountains to the west protect the region from the cold north and west winds. Annual precipitation measures between 100 to 150 cm (40 and 60 inches), a large part of it occurring in summer; the growing season lasts for more than six months. In most of this segment, the river crosses hilly Sichuan province, where the lower

Xiling Gorge, in the Three Gorges section of the Yangtze River (Chang Jiang), as it appeared before completion of the Three Gorges Dam, Hubei province, China. © Wolfgang Kaehler

mountains and plateaus connect the highlands of southwestern China with the Qin (Tsinling) Mountains lying between the Yangtze and Huang He (Yellow River) basins. Located in this area is Chongqing, a major industrial centre and river port. The river's width there is from about 300 to 500 metres (1,000 to 1,600 feet), and the depth in places exceeds 9 metres (30 feet). The current is swift; the banks often are high and steep. The river falls some 250 metres (820 feet) in Sichuan, more than 0.2 metre per km (1 foot per mile) of flow.

As the Yangtze flows through eastern Sichuan and into western Hubei, it traverses for a distance of 200 km (125 miles) the famous Three Gorges region before debouching onto the plains to the east. The gorges have steep, sheer slopes composed mainly of thick limestone rocks. Prior to the completion of the Three Gorges Dam in 2006, they rose some 400 to 600 metres (1,300 to 2,000 feet) above the river, although with the creation of the reservoir behind the dam their height has been diminished fairly significantly. Nonetheless, they still present the appearance of fantastic towers, pillars, or spears. Qutang, the first gorge—about 8 km (5 miles) long—is the shortest. Prior to its inundation, the river there was considered the most dangerous for navigation, being extremely narrow with many rapids and eddies. Wu, the second gorge, stretches for about 50 km (30 miles). It is a narrow, steep corridor with almost vertical walls of heights up to 490 metres (1,600 feet) or even 610 metres (2,000 feet) above the river. The last gorge, Xilang, is located upstream of Yichang and extends for a distance of 34 km (21 miles); in places limestone cliffs rise directly out of the water, although with the rise of the reservoir to much lower heights than before. The gorges are rocky, and the walls are speckled with cracks, niches, and indentations. Even before the river was inundated, its depth in the gorges was considerable, increasing to between 150 and 180 metres (500 and 600 feet) and giving the Yangtze the greatest depths of any river in the world.

THE LOWER COURSE

The lower part of the Yangtze basin is centred on the extensive lowland plains of east-central China. The region experiences a temperate climate with warm springs, hot summers, cool autumns, and relatively cold winters for the latitude. Monsoons (seasonally changing winds) dominate the weather of the region, and in the summer and autumn typhoons occur periodically. As the Yangtze exits from the Three Gorges Dam, near Yichang, it enters a complex system of lakes, marshes, and multiple river channels developed on the plains of Hunan and Hubei provinces. This vast region, lying at elevations below 50 metres (165 feet), has served as a natural flood-regulation basin in recent geologic history. Three main tributaries (the Yuan, Xiang, and Han rivers) and many smaller ones join the Yangtze in this region, which also is where the current slows as the river reaches the plain. Water levels fluctuate considerably between the flood and low-flow seasons. In addition, the presence of a number of large lakes, including Dongting Lake and Lakes Hong and Liangzi, also causes considerable fluctuations in water volume. The total area of the lakes, at average water levels, is some 17,100 square km (6,600 square miles). The lakes are of national economic significance, mainly as fisheries.

At the edge of the Lake Liangzi plain the Yangtze widens markedly, the course of its stream wandering in the form of a large loop. The width of the river is up to 800 metres (2,600 feet), the depth is more than 30 metres (100 feet), and the water current flows at a rate of about 1 metre (3 feet) per second. The banks are built up for protection from floods. In the southern part of the plain lies Dongting Lake, which once was the largest freshwater lake in China but now has been reduced in area by silting and land reclamation; it shares four tributaries and two canals with the Yangtze, whose flow it serves to regulate. The surrounding area, agricultural and studded with lakes, is China's most important rice-producing region.

At the centre of the lakes region is the large metropolis of Wuhan. Situated on the Yangtze near the mouth of the Han River, it was formed in 1950 by the merger of the cities of Hanyang and Hankou on the left bank and Wuchang on the right bank and has become one of China's most important metallurgical-industry centres and river ports. Farther east the Yangtze flows into a narrowing, picturesque valley and then passes onto the plain of Jiangxi province, which contains Lake Poyang, China's largest natural freshwater lake. The lake, with an average area of about 3,585 square km (1,385 square miles), receives the Kan River tributary and, in turn, is linked to the Yangtze by a wide tributary. The river then turns to the northeast, passes through a widening valley, and flows out onto the southern North China Plain. The width of the river increases at this point to between 900 and 1,800 metres (3,000 and 6,000 feet), and the depth in places approaches 30 metres (100 feet). In this region there are a number of large cities, including Anqing, Wuhu, and Nanjing. The Grand Canal (Da Yunhe), which, with a length of nearly 1,800 km (1,100 miles), is one of the longest canals in the world; it crosses the Yangtze in the vicinity of the city of Zhenjiang.

THE YANGTZE DELTA

The Yangtze delta, which begins beyond Zhenjiang, consists of a large number of branches, tributaries, lakes, ancient riverbeds, and marshes that are connected with the main channel. During major floods the delta area is completely submerged. Lake Tai, with an area of about 2,410 square km (930 square miles), is notable as the largest of the many lakes in the delta. The width of the Yangtze in the delta, as far as the city of Jiangyin, ranges from 1.6 to 3.2 km (1 to 2 miles). Farther downstream the channel gradually widens and becomes a large estuary, the width of which exceeds 80 km (50 miles) near the mouth of the river. Major cities in the delta include Wuxi, Suzhou, and, at the river's mouth, Shanghai.

Before emptying into the sea, the Yangtze divides into two arms that drain independently into the East China Sea. The left branch has a width of about 5 to 10 km (3 to 6 miles), the right branch of 10 to 25 km (6 to 15 miles). Between the branches is situated Chongming Island, which was formed over the centuries by the deposit of alluvium at the mouth of the Yangtze. The depth of the river in places approaches 30 to 40 metres (100 to 130 feet) but decreases to only several feet near the sea at the mouth of the river because of the presence of sandbars.

The section of river from the mouth to 400 km (250 miles) upstream is subject to the influence of tides. The maximum range of the tides near the mouth is 4 to 5 metres (13 to 15 feet). The Yangtze delta is rich in mud and silt and is dominated by fluvial and tidal processes.

The present-day bed of the Yangtze in this area is somewhat above the elevation of the plain. Thus, to protect the surrounding region from floodwaters, the banks of the main and other rivers are built up. The total length of banks on the Yangtze on which levees have been constructed is about 2,740 km (1,700 miles). Dams also have been built for flood protection on the shores of several lakes. The Qingjiang Reservoir, for example, built for this purpose near Dongting Lake, has a design capacity of 5.5 million cubic metres (194 million cubic feet). The delta is protected from the sea by two gigantic parallel banks that are faced with stone in most parts.

GEOLOGY

In its upper reaches the Yangtze River drains across the Plateau of Tibet, which is still uplifting as the Indian and Eurasian tectonic plates collide. The bedrock comprises an assemblage of marine sedimentary, igneous, and metamorphic rocks. Within intermontane basins, thick deposits of sediments of Cenozoic age (i.e., less than about 65.5 million years old) overlie the bedrock. The Yangtze descends abruptly from the Tibetan Plateau to flow across deeply eroded mountain plateaus consisting of Paleozoic and Mesozoic rocks roughly 350 million to 150 million years old. In its lower reaches, the Yangtze River flows across basin fills of Cenozoic material that is about 65.5 million to 25 million years old. These are the result of fluvial sedimentation as the Yangtze has migrated across its lower basin throughout its Cenozoic history.

HYDROLOGY

The Yangtze basin is comparatively well irrigated with an average yearly rainfall amounting to about 110 cm (43 inches). Most of the precipitation is brought by the monsoon winds and falls primarily as rain in the summer months. In the mountainous part of the basin the precipitation is mainly snow. Floods, which result from the monsoon rains in the middle and lower parts of the basin, usually begin in March or April and can occur at any time during the next eight months. In May the water level decreases somewhat but then sharply increases again, continuing to rise until August, when it reaches its highest level. After that the water level gradually falls to the premonsoon levels, the decrease continuing through the autumn and most of the winter until February, when the lowest annual level is reached.

The annual range of water-level fluctuations is considerable—an average of about 20 metres (65 feet)—with 8 to 11 metres (26 to 35 feet) during years of low water. Downstream from the Three Gorges Dam the impact of the water-level variation is lessened by the dam itself and by the regulating effect of the lakes. In the delta tides exert the greatest influence on the water level. Near the city of Wusong the daily tidal range is 4.5 metres (15 feet), and the yearly range is 6 metres (20 feet).

A breakdown of the water volume delivered to the mouth of the Yangtze shows that the highland part of the basin contributes 10 percent of the flow, while the remainder of the water in the river is contributed by the middle and downstream parts of the basin, with runoff from the basins of Dongting Lake and Lake Poyang being responsible for about two-fifths of the volume.

The Yangtze carries a tremendous volume of water. In the upstream areas the average flow exceeds 1,980 cubic metres (70,000 cubic feet) per second, which is more than the discharge rate of the second longest river in China, the Huang He, at its mouth. After the inflow from the first large tributary—the Yalong River—the volume in the Yangtze increases sharply, approaching an average of 5,500 cubic metres (194,000 cubic feet) per second. Farther downstream the Yangtze admits many tributaries, and the volume gradually increases. Prior to the completion of the Three Gorges Dam, it reached 15,000 cubic metres (529,000 cubic feet) per second at the end of the Three Gorges area, 24,000 cubic metres (847,000 cubic feet) per second at Wuhan, and some 31,100 cubic metres (1.1 million cubic feet) per second at its mouth; the total volume entering the sea annually was roughly 979 cubic km (235 cubic miles), ranking it third in volume of flow behind the Amazon and Congo rivers. Those numbers have decreased somewhat since the completion of the dam in 2006. The suspended sediment load at the mouth of the Yangtze is some 478 million tons per year, one of the highest sediment loads of any river in the world.

During the seasonal rains the Yangtze widely floods the lower areas, and the maximum volume of water entering the sea can be more than double the average flow. Likewise, the flow decreases during the dry season, sometimes to about one-fourth the average flow. In spite of the fact that the discharge volume of the Yangtze vastly exceeds that of the Huang He, the Yangtze is significantly less silty than the Huang He. This is because much of the Huang He's course is over the Loess Plateau with its easily erodible loess (wind-deposited soil), whereas the Yangtze flows over little loess, and its floodplains are more vegetated and less erodible. In the mountainous part of the basin, particularly in the Plateau of Tibet, the waters of the Yangtze contain little silt.

Downstream, however, the waters become muddy and acquire a coffee colour. It is estimated that the Yangtze annually carries between 280 million and 300 million tons of alluvium to its mouth, depositing an estimated 150 million to 200 million tons on the river bottom in addition. Thus, the total amount of suspended material carried or deposited is between 430 million and 500 million tons per year, one of the highest sediment loads of any river in the world. As a result of the depositing of alluvium at the river's mouth, the delta extends into the sea an average of 1.6 km (1 mile) every hundred years.

During the period of monsoon rains, the Yangtze and its tributaries formerly spilled over, creating extensive floods. If the floods in the main channel coincided with flooding in one or more of the major tributaries, powerful, destructive flood waves could result, an occurrence that happened repeatedly in the history of China. One of the major objectives of the Three Gorges project is to control such flooding by the river.

When flooding occurs, it frequently results from the deposit of silt in the bed of the Yangtze. Upon leaving the mountains and entering the plain, the current in the Yangtze sharply decreases, and thus the flow cannot continue to carry the entire amount of silt. As a result, a significant portion is deposited in the bed, causing the bottom to rise. A similar situation occurs in many of the Yangtze's tributaries. Flooding thus presents a great danger to the inhabitants of the adjacent plains.

Human adaptation to and utilization of the plains of the Yangtze valley have evolved in the context of such floods. Among the legends and myths handed down from the earliest historical times are accounts of floods that submerged vast areas. These are said to have turned the plains into inland seas, with water remaining in the lowest places for many years at a time. Catastrophic floods have occurred throughout recorded history. During the period from 206 BCE to 1960 CE, China experienced more than 1,030 major floods. Especially extensive flooding has occurred on the Yangtze more than 50 times and on the tributary Han River more than 30 times. On the average, the Yangtze basin has been the scene of catastrophic flooding every 50 to 55 years.

Widespread flooding also may take place at shorter intervals. This has been the case since the mid-19th century, as the Yangtze basin has flooded in 1870, 1896, 1931, 1949, and 1954. Of these, the 1931 and 1954 floods were national disasters. The 1931 flood resulted from heavy, continuous monsoon rains that covered most of the middle and lower parts of the basin. During May and June, six huge flood waves swept down the river, destroying the protecting dams and levees in two dozen places and flooding more than 90,000 square km (35,000 square miles) of land; 40 million people were rendered homeless or otherwise suffered. Many population centres, including Nanjing and the Wuhan conurbation, were underwater. In Wuhan the water remained for more than four months, the depth exceeding 1.8 metres (6 feet) and in places more than 6 metres (20 feet). In the summer of 1954 another powerful flood occurred, again the result of continued monsoon rains. The water level sharply increased and at times exceeded the 1931 flood levels by almost 1.5 metres (5 feet). Effective flood-control measures developed since the 1930s, however, averted many of the potential consequences of the flood.

THE YENISEY RIVER

The Yenisey River (Evenk: Ioanesi), or "Great River," of central Russia is one of the longest rivers in Asia. The world's sixth largest river in terms of discharge, the Yenisey runs from south to north across the great expanse of central Siberia. It traverses a vast region of strikingly varied landscapes where ancient peoples and customs as well as an enormous economic infrastructure are found.

PHYSICAL FEATURES

The river begins at the city of Kyzyl in the republic of Tyva (Tuva), Russia, at the confluence of its headstreams—the Great (Bolshoy) Yenisey, or By-Khem, which rises on the Eastern Sayan Mountains of Tyva, and the Little (Maly) Yenisey, or Ka-Khem, which rises in the Darhadïn Bowl of Mongolia. From the confluence the Yenisey River runs for 3,487 km (2,167 miles), mainly along the border between eastern and western Siberia, before emptying into the icy Kara Sea. If the Great Yenisey is considered the source, then the river is 4,090 km (2,540 miles) long. The headwaters of the Selenga (Selenge) River, which rise in western Mongolia and flow through Lake Baikal (the world's deepest freshwater lake) into the Angara tributary of the Yenisey, may, however, be considered the river's ultimate source. With the inclusion of the Selenga, the Yenisey is 5,539 km (3,442 miles) long and drains a basin that, at 2,580,000 square km (996,000 square miles), is the seventh largest in the world. The system within Siberia's boundaries comprises some 20,000 tributary or subtributary streams, with an aggregate length of approximately 885,000 km (550,000 miles). All of the major tributaries of the Yenisey flow from the Central Siberian Plateau to its east, a region constituting 80 percent of the basin area.

PHYSIOGRAPHY

Extending for some 3,500 km (2,200 miles) from north to south and for 1,700 km (1,100 miles) from east to west, the Yenisey basin exhibits a considerable diversity of features. Lowlands constitute only 6 to 7 percent of the total area: a narrow strip on the edge of the West Siberian Plain and part of the North Siberian Lowland. In the south the Western and Eastern Sayan, the Tyva, the Baikal, the Hangayn, and the Hentiyn mountains constitute a larger proportion of the basin's area, with elevations mostly between 700 and 2,200 metres (2,300 and 7,200 feet), steep valleys, and vast bowls between ranges. In southern Tyva and in the Sayans, there are some magnificent higher peaks, culminating in Mount Munku-Sardyk (Mönh Sarïdag), which reaches an elevation of 3,491 metres (11,453 feet). Most of the basin stretches over the western sector of the Central Siberian Plateau—with elevations between 500 and 700 metres (1,640 and 2,300 feet). The basin is bordered in the northeast by the Putorana

The Yenisey River near its confluence with the Angara River, south-central Sib. Masahiro Iijima/Ardea London

Mountains, which rise to 1,701 metres (5,580 feet); in the west by the Yenisey Ridge, with an elevation of 1,104 metres (3,622 feet); and in the southeast by the Angara Ridge, with an elevation of 1,022 metres (3,353 feet).

The Yenisey River proper is divisible into three principal sections: the 475 km (295 miles) from Kyzyl to Oznachennoye on the southern edge of the Minusinsk Basin, the 875 km (544 miles) from Oznachennoye to the Angara confluence, and the 2,137 km (1,328 miles) from the Angara confluence to the sea.

Flowing west through the Tyva Basin for the first 185 km (115 miles) from Kyzyl, the Yenisey varies in width from 90 to 640 metres (300 to 2,100 feet) and often splits into braided channels around gravelly shoals. At the western end of the basin, the river flows into the Sayano-Shushen Reservoir, which receives the Khemchik River. The Yenisey flows north through the reservoir, occupying a now-submerged canyon that cuts across the Western Sayan.

After leaving the reservoir and flowing out of the mountains at Oznachennoye, the Yenisey broadens its valley in the Minusinsk Basin: just below the Abakan confluence, the valley is more than 5 km (3 miles) wide; the bed, about 460 metres (1,500 feet) from bank to bank, is studded with islands; the flow velocity is reduced to about 2 metres (6 feet) per second; and the long and narrow Krasnoyarsk Reservoir, contained on the east by northwestern spurs of the Eastern Sayan, begins. The reservoir stretches some 390 km (240 miles) downstream to Divnogorsk. Downstream from the reservoir and slightly above Krasnoyarsk, the river valley broadens, as does the bed. Rapids are common there, the best-known being those at Kazachinskiy.

Below the Angara confluence, the right bank of the Yenisey remains an upland and is often precipitous, but the left bank becomes a floodplain. The bed, only 795 metres (2,610 feet) wide above the confluence, broadens to 2,743 metres (9,000 feet) wide below it. Depth increases to between 10 and 17 metres (32 and 56 feet), and the flow velocity drops by 50 percent or more. Farther downstream, however, just above the confluence of the Stony (Podkamennaya) Tunguska River, the Yenisey cuts through spurs of the Yenisey Ridge. Rapids occur at Osinovo, and below them the river plunges down a scenic gorge in which its bed narrows to a width of about 730 metres (2,400 feet). Below the confluence with the Lower (Nizhnyaya) Tunguska River, the valley widens to 37 km (23 miles), expanding to about 150 km (93 miles) wide around Dudinka and Ust-Port. The bed's width increases to 2,470 metres (8,100 feet) and then to some 5,030 metres (16,500 feet). Depths over the Yenisey's lower course range from 5 metres (16 feet) to more than 24 metres (80 feet).

The estuary of the Yenisey begins as far upstream as the confluence of the Kureyka (the next considerable tributary north of the Lower Tunguska). Below Dudinka the bed is in places divided by islands, some of them 16 or 19 km (10 or 12 miles) long, and a true delta begins north of Ust-Port, where the numerous Brekhov Islands divide the river into channels, with the westernmost bank about 76 km (47 miles) from the easternmost. The several channels empty into a long, wide bay leading into the Yenisey Gulf of the Kara Sea.

The largest tributaries of the upper and middle Yenisey are the Khemchik and Abakan rivers from the left and the Tuba River from the right. Fed chiefly by rainwater and melting snow, they begin their spring high water in late April and are swollen by summer rain floods. Conversely, the Angara is highly regulated by its source—the huge Lake Baikal—and rarely experiences low water. With a length of 1,778 km (1,105 miles), its own basin of more than 1,056,000 square km (407,700 square miles)—twice the size of the Yenisey's above their confluence—and a greater volume at its mouth than that of the Yenisey above the confluence, the Angara might better be recognized as the upper course of the main river than as a tributary. The Stony Tunguska and the Lower Tunguska rivers, with an aggregate volume of about 4,980 cubic metres (176,000 cubic feet) per second, also make a substantial contribution to the Yenisey's runoff.

HYDROLOGY

About half of the Yenisey's water comes from snow, a little more than one-third from rainwater, and the remainder from groundwater. For the greater part of the system, the eastern Siberian hydrologic regime prevails: violent spring floods are followed first by a rapid fall of levels, then by a slower fall, with summer and autumn rain floods punctuating the sequence; in winter the run-off is reduced sharply, but levels remain high as ice jams are formed. In terms of runoff, the Yenisey is the largest river in Russia, with about 620 cubic km (150 cubic miles) annually. It carries about 10.5 million tons of alluvium into the Kara Sea every year, in addition to nearly 30 million tons of dissolved mineral substances. In midsummer the water temperature varies from 14 °C (57 °F) to 19 °C (66 °F), but freezing begins on the lower Yenisey early in October and affects the entire river by mid-November. Ice jams and underwater ice are characteristic. Thawing occurs toward the end of April on the upper reaches, in May on the middle, and from May to mid-June on the lower. The water of the middle Yenisey is highly turbid in spring and summer and contrasts sharply with the limpid water of the Angara. And in summer the two streams flow in the same bed without mingling for 14 km (9 miles) or so from their confluence.

CLIMATE

The Yenisey basin has a subarctic climate in its northern part and markedly continental conditions in the middle and southern portions. The cold season prevails from late September to mid-June in the north and from mid-October to late April in the south. Even summer is cool in the northern basin, with average temperatures of 8 to 12 °C (46 to 54 °F) in July, when frosts may still occur; but summer is warm in the south, with July averages between 18 and 20 °C (64 and 68 °F). The average temperature for January in the north ranges from -32 to -28 °C (-25 to -18 °F) and in the south warms to about -20 °C (-4 °F). Annual precipitation averages 40 to 50 cm (16 to 20 inches) in the north, 50 to more than 75 cm (20 to more than 30 inches) in the central portion, and up to 119 cm (47 inches) in the mountains south of the basin. The closed depressions in the upper basin receive from less than 20 to about 30 cm (8 to about 12 inches) annually. Most of the rain (80 to 90 percent) falls in the warmer months, chiefly in late summer and early autumn. Snow cover is light in most of the basin, averaging 40 cm (16 inches) in the south, 60 cm (24 inches) in the north, and 90 cm (35 inches) on the Yenisey Ridge. Because the light snow offers little insulation, the soil and subsoil are frozen to a considerable depth for long periods over most of the basin. Permafrost is prevalent north of the Lower Tunguska.

STUDY AND EXPLORATION

Russians first settled on the Yenisey in 1607, when a winter station was established on the Turukhan River (a left-bank tributary joining the Yenisey just below the Lower Tunguska confluence). Novgorod merchants, however, may have been trading with peoples of the valley as early as the 11th century. In 1619 a fort was built at Yeniseysk. Nine years later Krasny Yar (now Krasnoyarsk) was founded, and Irkutsk was settled in 1652. From these places roads went eastward into the Buryat country and southward into the fertile Minusinsk Basin. The Russian hold on the line of the Yenisey was definitively secured early in the 18th century. Exploration of the rivers was then initiated, with a detachment of the Great Northern Expedition (1733–42) operating on the Yenisey. Later, the lower Yenisey was explored by an expedition of 1894–96; and from 1907 to 1912 a party made a more thorough investigation of the entire river. Studies for development plans or for scientific purposes continued throughout the 20th century.

CHAPTER 9
MAJOR RIVERS OF EUROPE

The great rivers of Europe—the Danube, the Rhine, and the Rhône—are better known for the roles they played in the evolution of European cultures than for their length. All three are vital economic waterways that facilitate European trade.

THE DANUBE RIVER

The Danube River (German: Donau, Slovak: Dunaj, Hungarian: Duna, Serbo-Croatian and Bulgarian: Dunav, Romanian: Dunărea, Ukrainian: Dunay) is the second longest river in Europe after the Volga. It rises in the Black Forest mountains of western Germany and flows for some 2,850 km (1,770 miles) to its mouth on the Black Sea. Along its course, it passes through nine countries: Germany, Austria, Slovakia, Hungary, Croatia, Serbia, Bulgaria, Romania, and Ukraine.

The Danube played a vital role in the settlement and political evolution of central and southeastern Europe. Its banks, lined with castles and fortresses, formed the boundary between great empires, and its waters served as a vital commercial highway between nations. The river's majesty has long been celebrated in music. The famous waltz *An der schönen, blauen Donau* (1867; *The Blue Danube*), by Johann Strauss the Younger, became the symbol of imperial Vienna. In the 21st century the river has continued its role as an important trade artery. It has been harnessed for hydroelectric power, particularly along the upper courses, and the cities along its banks—including the national capitals of Vienna (Austria), Budapest

The Danube River basin and its drainage network.

(Hungary), and Belgrade (Serbia)—have depended upon it for their economic growth.

PHYSIOGRAPHY

The Danube's vast drainage of some 817,000 square km (315,000 square miles) includes a variety of natural conditions that affect the origins and the regimes of its watercourses. They favour the formation of a branching, dense, deepwater river network that includes some three hundred tributaries, more than 30 of which are navigable. The river basin expands unevenly along its length. It covers about 47,000 square km (18,000 square miles) at the Inn confluence, 210,000 square km (81,000 square miles) after joining with the Drava, and 590,000 square km

Central Budapest, looking north along the Danube River, with the Parliament Building on the east bank. Jean S. Buldain/Berg & Assoc.

(228,000 square miles) below the confluences of its most affluent tributaries, the Sava and the Tisza. In the lower course the basin's rate of growth decreases. More than half of the entire Danube basin is drained by its right-bank tributaries, which collect their waters from the Alps and other mountain areas and contribute up to two-thirds of the total river runoff or outfall.

Three sections are discernible in the river's basin. The upper course stretches from its source to the gorge, called the Hungarian Gates, in the Austrian Alps and the Western Carpathian Mountains. The middle course runs from the Hungarian Gates to the Iron Gate Gorge in the Southern Romanian Carpathians. The lower course flows from the Iron Gate to the deltalike estuary at the Black Sea.

The confluence of the Sava (foreground) and Danube rivers from the Kalemegdan fortress, Belgrade, Serbia. Jean S. Buldain/Berg & Assoc.

The upper Danube springs as two small streams—the Breg and Brigach—from the eastern slopes of the Black Forest mountains of Germany, which partially consist of limestone. From Donaueschingen, where the headstreams unite, the Danube flows northeastward in a narrow, rocky bed. To the north rise the wooded slopes of the Swabian and the Franconian mountains, and between Ingolstadt and Regensburg the river forms a scenic canyon-like valley. To the south of the river course stretches the large Bavarian Plateau, covered with thick layers of river deposits from the numerous Alpine tributaries. The bank is low and uniform, composed mainly of fields, peat, and marshland.

At Regensburg the Danube reaches its northernmost point, from which it veers south and crosses wide, fertile, and level country. Shortly before it reaches Passau on the Austrian border, the river narrows and its bottom abounds with reefs and shoals. The Danube then flows through Austrian territory, where it cuts into the slopes of the Bohemian Forest and forms a narrow valley. To improve navigation, dams and protecting dikes have been built near Passau, Linz, and Ardagger. The upper Danube, some 965 km (600 miles) long, has a considerable average inclination of the riverbed (0.93 percent) and a rapid current of 3.2 to 8 km (2 to 5 miles) per hour. Depths vary from 1 to 8 metres (3 to 26 feet). The Danube swells substantially at Passau where the Inn River, its largest upstream tributary, carries more water than the main river. Other major tributaries in the upper Danube course include the Iller, Lech, Isar, Traun, Enns, and Morava rivers.

In its middle course the Danube looks more like a flatland river, with low banks and a bed that reaches a width of more than one mile. Only in two sectors—at Visegrád (Hungary) and the Iron Gate—does the river flow through narrow, canyonlike gorges. The basin of the middle Danube exhibits two main features—the flatland of the Little Alfold and the Great Alfold plains, and the low peaks of the Western Carpathians and the Transdanubian Mountains.

The Danube enters the Little Alfold plain immediately after emerging from the Hungarian Gates Gorge near Bratislava, Slovakia. There the river stream slows down abruptly and loses its transporting capacity, so that enormous quantities of gravel and sand settle on the bottom. A principal result of this deposition has been the formation of two islands, one on the Slovak side of the river and the other on the Hungarian side, which combined have an area of about 1,900 square km (730 square miles) that support some 190,000 inhabitants in more than one hundred settlements. The silting hampers navigation and occasionally divides the river into two or more channels. East of Komárno the Danube enters the Visegrád Gorge, squeezed between the foothills of the Western Carpathian and the Hungarian Transdanubian Mountains. The steep right bank is crowned with fortresses, castles, and cathedrals of the Hungarian Árpád dynasty of the 10th to 15th century.

The Danube then flows past Budapest and across the vast Great Alfold plain until it reaches the Iron Gate gorge. The riverbed is shallow and marshy, and low terraces stretch along both banks. River accumulation has built a large number of islands, including Csepel Island near Budapest. In this long stretch the river takes on the waters of its major tributaries—the Drava, the Tisza, and the Sava—which create substantial changes in the river's regime. The average runoff increases from about 2,400 cubic metres (83,000 cubic feet) per second north of Budapest to 5,600 cubic metres (200,000 cubic feet) at the Iron Gate. The river valley looks most imposing there, and the river's depth and current velocity fluctuate widely. The rapids and reefs of the Iron Gate once made the river unnavigable until a lateral navigation channel and a parallel railway allowed rivercraft to be towed upstream against the strong current.

Beyond the Iron Gate the lower Danube flows across a wide plain. The river becomes shallower and broader, and its current slows down. To the right, above steep banks, stretches the tableland of the Danubian Plain of Bulgaria. To the left lies the low Romanian Plain, which is separated from the main stream by a strip of lakes and swamps. The tributaries in this section are comparatively small and account for only a modest increase in the total runoff. They include the Olt, the Siret, and the Prut. The river is again obstructed by a number of islands. Just south of Cernavodă, the Danube heads northward until it reaches

Galați, where it veers abruptly eastward. Near Tulcea, some 80 km (50 miles) from the sea, the river begins to spread out into its delta.

The river splits into three channels: the Chilia, which carries 63 percent of the total runoff; the Sulina, which accounts for 16 percent; and the Sfântu Gheorghe (St. George), which carries the remainder. Navigation is possible only by way of the Sulina Channel, which has been straightened and dredged along its 63-km (39-mile) length. Between the channels, a maze of smaller creeks and lakes are separated by oblong strips of land called *grinduri*. Most *grinduri* are arable and cultivated, and some are overgrown with tall oak forests. A large quantity of reeds that grow in the shallow-water tracts are used in the manufacture of paper and textile fibres. The Danube delta covers an area of some 4,300 square km (1,660 square miles) and is a comparatively young formation. About 6,500 years ago the delta site was a shallow cove of the Black Sea coast, but it was gradually filled by river-borne silt; the delta continues to grow seaward at the rate of 24 to 30 metres (80 to 100 feet) annually.

HYDROLOGY

The different physical features of the river basin affect the amount of water runoff in its three sections. In the upper Danube the runoff corresponds to that of the Alpine tributaries, where the maximum occurs in June when melting of snow and ice in the Alps is the most intensive. Runoff drops to its lowest point during the winter months.

In the middle basin the phases last up to four months, with two runoff peaks in June and April. The June peak stems from that of the upper course, reaching its maximum 10 to 15 days later. The April peak is local. It is caused by the addition of waters from the melting snow in the plains and from the early spring rains of the lowland and the low mountains of the area. Rainfall is important. The period of low water begins in October and reflects the dry spells of summer and autumn that are characteristic of the low plains. In the lower basin all Alpine traits disappear completely from the river regime. The runoff maximum occurs in April, and the low point extends to September and October.

The river carries considerable quantities of solid particles, nearly all of which consist of quartz grains. The constant shift of deposits in different parts of the riverbed forms shoals. In the stretches between Bratislava and Komárno and in the Sulina Channel, draglines are constantly at work to maintain the depth needed for navigation. The damming of the river has also changed the way in which sediments are transported and deposited. Water impounded by reservoirs generally loses its silt load, and the water flowing out of the dam—which is relatively silt-free—erodes banks farther downstream.

The temperature of the river waters depends on the climate of the various parts of the basin. In the upper course, where the summer waters derive from the Alpine snow and glaciers, the water temperature is low. In the middle and lower reaches, summer temperatures vary between 22 and 24 °C (71 and 75 °F), while winter temperatures near the banks and on the surface drop below freezing. Upstream from Linz the Danube never freezes entirely, because the current is turbulent. The middle and lower courses, however, become icebound during severe winters. Between December and March, periods of ice drift combine with the spring thaw, causing floating ice blocks to accumulate at the river islands, jamming the river's course, and often creating major floods.

The natural regime of river runoff changes constantly as a result of the introduction of stream-regulating equipment, including dams and dikes. The mineral content of the river is greater during the winter than the summer. The content of organic matter is relatively low, but pollution increases as the waters flow past industrial areas. The river's chemistry also changes as city sewerage and agricultural runoff find their way into the river.

THE RHINE RIVER

The Rhine River (German: Rhein, French: Rhin, Dutch: Rijn, Celtic: Renos, Latin: Rhenus) is a river and waterway of western Europe, culturally and historically one of the great rivers of the continent and among the most important arteries of industrial transport in the world. It flows from two small headways in the Alps of east-central Switzerland north and west to the North Sea, into which it drains through the Netherlands. The length of the Rhine was long given as 1,320 km (820 miles), but in 2010 a shorter distance of about 1,230 km (765 miles) was proposed. An international waterway since the Treaty of Vienna in 1815, it is navigable overall for some 870 km (540 miles), as far as Rheinfelden on the Swiss-German border. Its catchment area, including the delta area, exceeds 220,000 square km (85,000 square miles).

The Rhine has been a classic example of the alternating roles of great rivers as arteries of political and cultural unification and as political and cultural boundary lines. The river also has been enshrined in the literature of its lands, especially of Germany, as in the famous epic *Nibelungenlied.* Since the time when the Rhine valley became incorporated into the Roman Empire, the river has been one of Europe's leading transport routes. Until the 19th century, the goods transported were of high value but relatively small in volume, but since the second half of the 19th century the volume of goods conveyed on

The Rhine River flowing through Germany. © Goodshoot/Jupiterimages

the river has increased greatly. The fact that cheap water transport on the Rhine helped to keep prices of raw materials down was the main reason the river became a major axis of industrial production: one-fifth of the world's chemical industries are now manufacturing along the Rhine. The river was long a source of political dissension in Europe, but this has given way to international concern for ecological safeguards as pollution levels have risen. Some six thousand toxic substances have been identified in Rhine waters.

No other river in the world has so many old and famous cities on its banks—Basel, Switz.; Strasbourg, France; and Worms, Mainz, and Cologne, Ger., to name a few—but there are also such industrial cities as Ludwigshafen and Leverkusen in Germany that pollute the waters and mar the scenic attraction of the riverbanks. Nonetheless, the middle Rhine (the section between the German cities

of Bingen and Bonn), with such steep rock precipices
as the Lorelei crag and numerous castles, still presents
breathtaking vistas and attracts tourists. This is the Rhine
of legend and myth, where the medieval Mouse Tower
(Mausturm) lies at water level near Bingen and the castle
of Kaub stands on an island in the river. The Alpine section of the Rhine lies in Switzerland, and below Basel
the river forms the boundary between western Germany
and France, as far downstream as the Lauter River. It
then flows through German territory as far as Emmerich,
below which its many-branched delta section epitomizes
the landscapes characteristic of the Netherlands.

PHYSIOGRAPHY

The Rhine rises in two headstreams high in the Swiss
Alps. The Vorderrhein emerges from Lake Toma at 2,344
metres (7,690 feet), near the Oberalp Pass in the Central
Alps, and then flows eastward past Disentis to be joined
by the Hinterrhein from the south at Reichenau above
Chur. (The Hinterrhein rises about 8 km (5 miles) west
of San Bernardino Pass, near the Swiss–Italian border,
and is joined by the Albula River below Thusis.) Below
Chur, the Rhine leaves the Alps to form the boundary first
between Switzerland and the principality of Liechtenstein
and then between Switzerland and Austria, before forming a delta as the current slackens at the entrance to Lake
Constance. In this flat-floored section the Rhine has been
straightened and the banks reinforced to prevent flooding. The Rhine leaves the lake via its Untersee arm. From
there to its bend at Basel, the river is called the Hochrhein
("High Rhine") and defines the Swiss-German frontier,
except for the area below Stein am Rhein, where the frontier deviates so that the Rhine Falls at Schaffhausen are

entirely within Switzerland. Downstream the Rhine flows swiftly between the Alpine foreland and the Black Forest region, its course interrupted by rapids, where—as at Laufenburg (Switzerland) and Säckingen and Schwörstadt (Germany)—barrages (dams) have been built. In this stretch the Rhine is joined by its Alpine tributaries, the Thur, Töss, Glatt, and Aare, and by the Wutach from the north. The Rhine has been navigable between Basel and Rheinfelden since 1934.

Below Basel the Rhine turns northward to flow across a broad, flat-floored valley, some 32 km (20 miles wide), held between, respectively, the ancient massifs of the Vosges Mountains and Black Forest uplands and the Haardt Mountains and Oden Forest upland. The main tributary from Alsace is the Ill, which joins the Rhine at Strasbourg, and various shorter rivers, such as the Dreisam and the Kinzig, drain from the Black Forest. Downstream, the regulated Neckar, after crossing the Oden uplands in a spectacular gorge as far as Heidelberg, enters the Rhine at Mannheim; and the Main leaves the plain of lower Franconian Switzerland for the Rhine opposite Mainz. Until the straightening of the upper Rhine, which began in the early 19th century, the river described a series of great loops, or meanders, over its floodplain, and today their remnants, the old backwaters and cutoffs near Breisach and Karlsruhe, mark the former course of the river.

The middle Rhine is the most spectacular and romantic reach of the river. In this 145-km (90-mile) stretch the Rhine has cut a deep and winding gorge between the steep, slate-covered slopes of the Hunsrück Mountains to the west and the Taunus Mountains to the east. Vineyards mantle the slopes as far as Koblenz, where the Moselle River joins the Rhine at the site the

Romans called Confluentes. On the right bank, the fortress of Ehrenbreitstein dominates the Rhine where the Lahn tributary enters. Downstream the hills recede, the foothills of the volcanic Eifel region lying to the west and those of the Wester Forest to the east. At Andernach, where the ancient Roman frontier left the Rhine, the basaltic Seven Hills rise steeply to the east of the river, where, as the English poet Lord Byron put it, "the castle crag of Dachenfels frowns o'er the wide and winding Rhine."

Below Bonn the valley opens out into a broad plain, where the old city of Cologne lies on the left bank of the Rhine. There the river is spanned by the modern Severin Bridge and by the rebuilt Hohenzollern railway bridge, which carries the line from Aachen to Düsseldorf and the Ruhr industrial region. Düsseldorf, on the right bank of the Rhine, is the dominant business centre of the North Rhine–Westphalia coalfield. Duisburg, which lies at the mouth of the Ruhr River, handles the bulk of the waterborne coal and coke from the Ruhr as well as imports of iron ore and oil.

The last section of the Rhine lies below the frontier town of Emmerich in the delta region of the Netherlands. There the Rhine breaks up into a number of wide branches, such as the Lek and Waal, farther downstream called the Merwede. With the completion of the huge Delta Project in 1986—constructed to prevent flooding in the southwestern coastal area of the Netherlands—all main branches of the Rhine were closed off. Sluices and lateral channels now allow river water to reach the sea. Since 1872, however, the New Waterway Canal, constructed to improve access from the North Sea to Rotterdam, has been the main navigation link between the Rhine and the sea; along this canal was built Europoort, one of the world's largest ports.

HYDROLOGY

The Alpine Rhine—with its steep gradient, high runoff coefficient (80 percent of the precipitation in its catchment area), pronounced winter minimum, high water in spring from snowmelt, and high early summer maximum resulting from heavy summer rains—has a characteristic Alpine regime. Although variations in flow are evened out by Lake Constance, which is fed by upland streams as well as by the Rhine (and which also acts as a filter), they are increased again by the confluence with the Aare, which on an average carries more water than the Rhine. Below Basel, however, the tributaries from the uplands, with their spring maximums at higher and winter maximums at lower elevations, increasingly moderate the unbalance. Thus, at Cologne the average deviations from mean flow are slight, and the regime is favourable to navigation. Winters in the navigable regions of the river, moreover, are generally mild, and the Rhine freezes only in exceptional winters.

THE RHÔNE RIVER

The Rhône River is a historic river of Switzerland and France and one of the most significant waterways of Europe. It is the only major river flowing directly to the Mediterranean Sea and is thoroughly Alpine in character. In this respect it differs markedly from its northern neighbour, the Rhine, which leaves all of its Alpine characteristics behind when it leaves Switzerland. The scenic and often wild course of the Rhône, the characteristics of the water flowing in it, and the way it has been used by humans have all been shaped by the influences of the mountains, right down to the river mouth, where sediments marking the Rhône's birth in an Alpine glacier are carried into the warmer waters of the Mediterranean.

The Rhône is 813 km (505 miles) long and has a drainage basin of some 97,775 square km (37,750 square miles). The course of the river can be divided into three sectors lying, respectively, in the Alps, between the Alps and the Jura Mountains and through the latter, and finally in the topographical furrow of Alpine origin running from the city of Lyon to the sea.

PHYSIOGRAPHY

The Rhône originates in the Swiss Alps, upstream from Lake Geneva. It comes into being at an altitude of about 1,830 metres (6,000 feet), emerging from the Rhône Glacier, which descends the south flank of the Dammastock, a nearly 3,660-metre (12,000-foot) peak. The river then traverses the Gletsch Basin, from which it escapes through a gorge, and flows along the floor of the Goms Valley at an altitude between 1,220 and 1,400 metres (4,000 and 4,600 feet). It next enters another gorge before reaching the plain of the Valais, which extends between the towns of Brig and Martigny, and descends in altitude 700 to 490 metres (2,300 to 1,600 feet). In crossing this high and rugged mountain area, the river makes successive use of two structural troughs. The first runs between the ancient crystalline rock massifs of the Aare and of the Gotthard; farther downstream the second runs between the arched rock mass of the Bernese Oberland and, on the south, the massive rock face of the Pennine Alps. From Brig onward, the landscape changes. During the last Ice Age a large glacier, fed by several small ones, plowed down the valley floor of the Valais, and, except for some harder rock obstacles found near the town of Sion, succeeded in widening and deepening the narrow valley floor. As it did so, it held back both the upper Rhône and those of its tributaries that come down from the Pennine Alps. When the ice sheets retreated, both the tributaries—the Vispa, Navigenze, Borgne, and Drance—and the Rhône cut new, deep gorges to connect their lower courses to the new valley floor. These gorges have created considerable difficulty for modern transportation, necessitating a series of hairpin-bend road links.

After Martigny, where the valley floor is wider, the youthful Rhône thrusts northward at a right angle, cutting across the Alps through a transverse valley. At first, near the town of Saint-Maurice, this is no more than a small gorge, but it soon becomes wider and flatter. There, too, the river route has been assisted by structural factors, specifically by a dip in the crystalline rock massifs running from Mont Blanc to the Aare and by the discontinuity between the limestone masses of the Dents du Midi and of the Dent de Morcles. Across the mountain barrier the muddy waters of the Rhône enter another wide plain surrounded by high mountains and then plunge into the clearer, stiller waters of Lake Geneva, forming an enlarging delta.

The second sector of the Rhône's course commences with Lake Geneva, large (580 square km [224 square miles]) and deep (305 metres [1,000 feet]) and lying between Switzerland and France in a basin hollowed out of the less resistant terrain by the former Rhône Glacier. Upon leaving Lake Geneva, which has turned the course of the river to the southwest and decanted the sediment from its waters, the Rhône very quickly regains in full the milky colour so characteristic of Alpine rivers. Just below the city of Geneva, it receives its powerful tributary the Arve, which rushes down from the glaciers of Mont Blanc.

From its juncture with the Arve to the French city of Lyon, the Rhône has to cross a difficult obstacle, the undulating series of ridges forming the Jura Mountains. It does this by cutting through deep longitudinal valleys called *vaux* and transverse valleys called *cluses,* which were formed when the Jura Mountains were uplifted during the Alpine orogeny. As a result, the river follows a complicated zigzag course. At the town of Bellegarde the river is joined from the north by the Valserine and, swinging south, plunges into a deep gorge now submerged in the 23-km- (14-mile-) long Génissiat Reservoir. In the wider sections of its course in this region, the Rhône runs through glacier-excavated basins that its own deposits have barely filled, causing intermittent marshy areas. It is also joined by the Ain, from the north, and, on the left bank, by the Fier and Guiers. The river next widens, and the terrain becomes less hilly and, at Le Parc (some 153 km [95 miles] above Lyon), becomes officially navigable, although the average depth is no more than three feet.

At Lyon the Rhône enters its third sector as it heads south toward the Mediterranean, which is characterized by the great north–south Alpine furrow that is also drained by its principal tributary, the Saône. The latter lies in the basins that the Ice Age glaciers hollowed out between the Jura Mountains to the east and, farther west, the eastern edge of the Paris Basin and the uplands of the Massif Central. It forms an important commercial link to the industrialized regions of northern France. From the city of Lyon onward, the river occupies the trough lying between the Massif Central and the Alps, a channel up which the sea of the Paleogene and Neogene periods (about 65.5 million to 2.6 million years ago) ascended covering the present Rhône valley. A body of water, Lake Bresse, spread over the Saône basin. Into this lake drained a river—the present Rhine—which then flowed south through the valley and into the Saône basin. Later tectonic movements caused the Rhine to reverse its flow, and the Doubs, a tributary of the Saône, now partly follows the former Rhine drainage pattern. About 5 million years ago the gulf of the sea was uplifted to expose the lower Rhône valley, and Lake Bresse drained out to the south through the Saône River. Though the Rhône–Saône corridor is underlain by sediments laid down during the Paleogene and Neogene periods, much of its present surface is formed by debris deposited by valley glaciers that extended from the Alps during the Pleistocene Epoch (about 2.6 million to 11,700 years ago). These sediments were instrumental in cutting deep channels through the edge of the crystalline Massif Central, as evidenced at Vienne and Tain. The valley consequently takes the form of a series of gorges and basins, the latter often having a series of terraces corresponding to variations in the levels of ice and of river. Although the tributaries—notably the Ardèche—rushing down into the Rhône from the Massif Central are formidable when in flood, the great Alpine rivers, the Isère, and the Durance, joining the left bank, are most important in their effect on riverbed deposits and on the volume of water. Below Mondragon the Rhône valley becomes wider, and what was once a marshy landscape open to flooding has been regulated by a series of dams and canals.

The river's delta begins near Arles and extends about 40 km (25 miles) to the sea. Twin channels of the river, the Grand and Petit Rhône, enclose the Camargue region. This region, formed by alluvium, is continuously extending into the Mediterranean. The finer materials are carried by onshore currents to form the barrier beaches of the coast and the sandbars closing off the Étang de Berre. One part of the delta has been set aside for a nature reserve, thereby protecting the feeding and nesting grounds of flamingos, egrets, ibis, and other rare species. Since 1962 the left bank of Fos has been transformed into a vast industrial complex consisting of port facilities, refineries, oil-storage tanks, and steel mills.

HYDROLOGY

The flow regime of the Rhône owes its remarkable mean volume to the influence of the Alps. At Lyon the flow amounts to 640 cubic metres (22,600 cubic feet) per second; there, the Saône alone contributes 400 cubic metres (14,100 cubic feet) per second. The Isère adds another 350 cubic metres (12,400 cubic feet) per second. The melting of the Alpine snows gives the highest mean flows in May, while the Saône attains its maximum in January. The flood volumes of spring and autumn are formidable, reaching 13,000 cubic metres (460,000 cubic feet) per second for the Rhône at Beaucaire, just above the delta. Thus, the Rhône has an abundant flow but maintains a strong gradient almost to its mouth. At Lyon, for example, its altitude is about 170 metres (560 feet) at 330 km (205 miles) from the sea. As the size of the delta region testifies, the river transports enormous amounts of alluvial deposits and is also powerful enough to cut through a variety of rock masses. As a result, the Rhône of today is well adapted to the production of electricity and, though difficult to navigate in the past, is now an important waterway from the Mediterranean to Lyon.

CONCLUSION

Rivers are among the most important features on Earth's surface. They are powerful ecological agents that move materials from high elevations to lower ones. Rivers that periodically flood deliver nutrients to low-lying lands, replenishing the soil with chemicals that are useful for plant growth. Rivers are also important agents of landscape change. Over long periods of time, the flow of water can wear away rock and carve new channels, modifying the geography of the landscape. Economically, rivers are important connections between the continental interior and the coast, and many have been dammed to produce electricity. Several of Earth's largest rivers also serve as reliable aquatic highways for trade.

As a result of intensive human exploitation, many rivers in the world face significant environmental challenges. The upper reaches of many rivers, which are characterized by higher flow rates, are often dammed to produce hydroelectric power. Damming inhibits the natural movement of the water downstream. For species dependent on upstream resources, damming can present significant threats to their survival. For example, hydroelectric dams on rivers in the Pacific Northwest of the United States prevent salmon from reaching their spawning grounds.

Physical changes to the lower reaches of rivers also threaten natural ecological processes. To facilitate navigation, streams are often dredged and channelized, a process that disrupts the plant and animal habitat of the river bottom. In addition to removing significant amounts of material, the extraction process stirs up the surrounding sediment in the water, reducing underwater visibility and access to sunlight.

One of the most significant threats to the world's rivers comes from chemical pollution. Because rivers often occur in the lowest parts of landscapes, chemical pesticides and fertilizers applied to agricultural fields can be washed into them after rainstorms or winter snowmelt. This pesticide runoff, along with chemicals that leak from boats and barges, contaminates human water supplies as well as fish and other organisms that come in contact with these chemicals. Chemical fertilizers, typically nitrates and phosphates, contribute to the growth of algae and riverine plants. When these photosynthetic organisms die at the end of the growing season, decomposition depletes the water of dissolved oxygen, threatening the survival of local fish and other organisms.

APPENDIX A
AVERAGE NET PRIMARY PRODUCTION OF THE EARTH'S MAJOR HABITATS

AVERAGE NET PRIMARY PRODUCTION OF THE EARTH'S MAJOR HABITATS	
HABITAT	NET PRIMARY PRODUCTION (GRAM PER SQUARE METRE PER YEAR)
Forests	
Tropical	1,800
Temperate	1,250
Boreal	800
Other Terrestrial Habitats	
Swamp and Marsh	2,500
Savanna	700
Cultivated Land	650
Shrubland	600
Desert Scrub	70
Temperate Grassland	500
Tundra and Alpine	140
Aquatic Habitats	
Algal Beds and Reefs	2,000
Estuaries	1,800
Lakes and Streams	500
Continental Shelf	360
Open Ocean	125

Source: Adapted from Robert E. Ricklefs, *Ecology*, 3rd edition (1990), by W.H. Freeman and Company, used with permission.

WORLD'S LONGEST RIVERS AND RIVER SYSTEMS

RANK	NAME	LENGTH (KM)*	LENGTH (MILES)
1	Nile	6,650	4,132
2	Amazon–Ucayali–Apurimac	6,400	4,000
3	Yangtze	6,300	3,915
4	Mississippi–Missouri–Red Rock	5,971	3,710
5	Yenisey–Baikal–Selenga	5,540	3,442
6	Huang He (Yellow)	5,464	3,395
7	Ob–Irtysh	5,410	3,362
8	Paraná	4,880	3,032
9	Congo	4,700	2,900
10	Amur–Argun	4,444	2,761
11	Lena	4,400	2,734
12	Mekong	4,350	2,700
13	Mackenzie–Slave–Peace	4,241	2,635
14	Niger	4,200	2,600
15	Volga	3,530	2,193

*Conversions of the rounded figures are again rounded to the nearest 10 or 100 miles or kilometres.

Figures based on official sources. In countries where the metric system is used, conversions are from kilometres to miles.

APPENDIX C
SELECTED WATERFALLS OF THE WORLD

SELECTED WATERFALLS OF THE WORLD (LISTED IN DECLINING ORDER BY HEIGHT AND VOLUME)						
NAME	RIVER	COUNTRY	TOTAL HEIGHT (M)	HEIGHT OF GREATEST UNINTERRUPTED LEAP (M)	AVERAGE DISCHARGE BY VOLUME (CU M/SEC)	NUMBER OF FALLS (C = CASCADE)
Angel (Churún Merú)	Churún	Venezuela	979	807	—	2
Tugela	Tugela	South Africa	948	411	—	5
Mtarazi	Inyangombe	Zimbabwe	762	479	—	2
Yosemite	Yosemite	United States	739	436	—	3
Cuquenán	Cuquenán	Venezuela	610	317	—	—
Sutherland	Arthur	New Zealand	580	248	—	3
Kile	—	Norway	561	—	—	C
Kahiwa	—	United States	533	—	—	C
Mardal (Eastern)	Eikesdal	Norway	517	297	—	—
Ribbon	Ribbon	United States	491	491	—	—
King George VI	Utshi	Guyana	488	488	—	—
Wollomombi	Wollomombi	Australia	482	335	—	—

Name	River	Country	Total Height (m)	Height of Greatest Uninter-rupted Leap (m)	Average discharge by Volume (cu m/sec)	Number of Falls (C = Cas-cade)
Mardal (Western)	Eikesdal	Norway	468	–	–	–
Kaliuwaa (Sacred)	Kalanui Stream	United States	463	80	–	C
Kalambo	Kalambo	Tanzania-Zambia	427	215	–	–
Gavarnie	Gave de Pau	France	422	–	–	C
Giessbach	Giessbach	Switzerland	391	–	–	–
Trümmel-bach	Trümmel-bach	Switzerland	391	–	–	–
Krimmler	Krimmler Ache	Austria	380	–	–	–
Vettis	Morkedola	Norway	371	–	–	–
Papalaua	Kawai Nui Stream	United States	366	–	–	–
Silver Strand	Merced	United States	357	–	–	C
Honoko-hau	Honokohau Stream	United States	341	–	–	C
Lofoi	Lofoi	Congo (Kinshasa)	340	340	–	–
Serio	Serio	Italy	315	–	–	–
Barron	Barron	Australia	300	–	–	–
Belmore	Barrengarry Creek	Australia	300	–	–	3
Canna-bullen	Cannabul-len Creek	Australia	300	300	–	–
Horse-shoe	Govetts Leap Creek	Australia	300	–	–	C

NAME	RIVER	COUNTRY	TOTAL HEIGHT (M)	HEIGHT OF GREATEST UNINTER-RUPTED LEAP (M)	AVERAGE DISCHARGE BY VOLUME (CU M/SEC)	NUMBER OF FALLS (C = CAS-CADE)
Wallaman	Stony Creek	Australia	300	—	—	—
Staubbach	Weisse Lutschine	Switzer-land	290	290	—	—
Pungwe	Pungwe	Zimbabwe	277	277	—	—
Helena	Helena	New Zealand	271	—	—	I
Mollijus	Reisenelva	Norway	269	269	—	—
Auster-krok	Torrfjordelva	Norway	257	257	—	I
King Edward VIII	Semang	Guyana	256	—	—	—
Takakkaw	Yoho	Canada	254	—	—	—
Jog (Gersoppa)	Sharavati	India	253	253	—	I
Kaieteur	Potaro	Guyana	251	226	—	2
Waipio	Kekee Stream	United States	244	—	—	2
Tully	Tully	Australia	240	—	—	—
Feigum	Feigumelvi	Norway	218	—	—	—
Fairy	Fairy	United States	213	—	—	—
Fossa	Ullo	Norway	210	210	—	—
Feather	Fall	United States	195	—	—	—
Aurstapet	Aura	Norway	193	193	—	—
Maletsun-yane (Semon Kong)	Maletsun-yane	Lesotho	192	192	—	—

NAME	RIVER	COUNTRY	TOTAL HEIGHT (M)	HEIGHT OF GREATEST UNINTER- RUPTED LEAP (M)	AVERAGE DISCHARGE BY VOLUME (CU M/SEC)	NUMBER OF FALLS (C = CAS- CADE)
Sakaika	—	Guyana	192	140	—	—
Reichen- bach	Reichen- bach	Switzer- land	190	91	—	—
Bridalveil	Bridalveil	United States	189	189	—	—
Khone	Mekong	Kampuchea- Laos	14	—	11,600	1
Niagara Horse- shoe)	Niagara	Canada– United States	49	—	5,525	—
Paulo Afonso	São Francisco	Brazil	84	—	2,800	3-C
Urubu- pungá	Paraná	Brazil	12	—	2,750	1
Iguaçu	Iguaçu- Paraná	Argentina- Brazil	82	—	1,750	C
Victoria	Zambezi	Zambia- Zimbabwe	108	108	1,080	1
Churchill (Grand)	Churchill (Hamilton)	Canada	75	—	990	—
Cauvery	Cauvery	India	98	—	935	—
Rhine	Rhine	Switzer- land	24	—	700	C
Kaieteur	Potaro	Guyana	251	226	660	1
Detti	Jokulsá	Iceland	44	—	200	—

GLOSSARY

alluvial Sedimentary material deposited by rivers, consisting of silt, sand, clay, gravel, and organic matter.

aquifer An underground geologic formation that acts as a natural catch basin for water; a water-bearing layer of earth.

arroyo Dry channel lying in a semiarid or desert area and subject to flash flooding during seasonal or irregular rainstorms.

cataract A waterfall, especially one containing great volumes of water rushing over a precipice.

clast A fragment of rock.

delta Low-lying plain composed of stream-borne sediments deposited by a river at its mouth.

ephemeral Short-lived.

estuary A section of coastal water that contains fresh and salt water, and is partly enclosed by land.

eutrophication The gradual accumulation of plant nutrients in a relatively sedentary body of water, such as a lake; the process by which a water body becomes enriched with nutrients that stimulate plant growth which leads to the depletion of dissolved oxygen.

evapotranspiration Loss of water from the soil both by evaporation from the soil surface and by transpiration from the leaves of the plants growing on it.

fjord A long narrow arm of the sea, commonly extending far inland, that results from marine inundation of a glaciated valley.

gully Trench cut into land by the erosion of an accelerated stream of water.

hydroelectric power Electricity produced from generators driven by water turbines that convert the energy in falling or fast-flowing water to mechanical energy.

hydrology Scientific discipline concerned with the waters of the Earth, including their occurrence, distribution, circulation via the hydrologic cycle, and interactions with living things.

karst Irregular limestone with sinks, underground streams, and caverns.

khamsin Hot, dry, dusty wind in North Africa and the Arabian Peninsula that blows from the south or southeast in late winter and early spring.

levee Any low ridge or earthen embankment built along the edges of a stream or river channel to prevent flooding of the adjacent land.

lobate Resembling a lobe.

loess Unstratified, geologically recent deposit of silty or loamy material that is usually buff or yellowish brown and is deposited chiefly by the wind.

moraine Accumulation of rock debris (till) carried or deposited by a glacier.

pluviometric equator Imaginary east-west line indicating the region of heaviest rainfall.

rift valley Elongated trough formed by the subsidence of a segment of the Earth's crust between dip-slip, or normal, faults.

rivulet A small stream.

silt Sediment particles 0.004–0.06 mm (0.00016– 0.0024 inch) in diameter, regardless of mineral type.

taiga Open coniferous forest (conifer) growing on swampy ground that is commonly covered with lichens.

viscous Having the quality of a fluid and a semifluid that enables it to develop and maintain an amount of shearing stress depending on the velocity of the flow and then to offer continued resistance to the flow.

watershed Region or area bounded peripherally by a water parting and draining ultimately to a particular watercourse or body of water.

BIBLIOGRAPHY

GENERAL WORKS

Discussions of all aspects of rivers are found in Stanley A. Schumm, and David E. Sugden, *Geomorphology* (1984); Dale F. Ritter, *Process Geomorphology*, 2nd ed. (1986); and Marie Morisawa, *Rivers: Form and Process* (1985); Trevor Day and Richard Garratt, *Lakes And Rivers* (2006); and Malcolm Newson, *Hydrology and the River Environment* (2008).

Environmental problems attendant on river use are discussed in *Cooling Water Discharges from Coal Fired Power Plants: Water Pollution Problems* (1983), proceedings of an international conference; R.G. Toms, "River Pollution-Control Since 1974," *Water Pollution Control*, 84(2):178–186 (1985); M. Chevreuil, A. Chesterikoff, and R. Letolle, "PCB Pollution Behavior in the River Seine," *Water Research*, 21(4): 427–434 (April 1987); and James R Penn, *Rivers of the World: A Social, Geographical, and Environmental Sourcebook* (2001).

RIVERS AS AGENTS OF LANDSCAPE EVOLUTION

Discussions and additional references about valley morphology in natural and experimental settings can be found in M. Paul Mosley, and William E. Weaver, *Experimental Fluvial Geomorphology* (1987). Detailed discussions of terrace formation can be found in Dale F. Ritter, "Complex River Terrace Development in the Nenana Valley near Healy, Alaska," 93(4):346–356 (April 1982). Important works treating processes and characteristics of alluvial fans in detail include R. Craig Kochel and Robert A. Johnson, "Geomorphology and Sedimentology of

Humid-Temperate Alluvial Fans, Central Virginia," in Emlyn H. Koster and Ron J. Steel (eds.), *Sedimentology of Gravels and Conglomerates* (1984), pp. 109–122; Neil A. Wells and John A. Dorr, Jr., "Shifting of the Kosi River, Northern India," *Geology*, 15(3):204–207 (March 1987); Richard H. Kesel, "Alluvial Fan Systems in a Wet-Tropical Environment, Costa Rica," *National Geographic Resources*, 1(4):450–469 (Autumn 1985); and Keith Richards, *Rivers: Form and Process of Alluvial Channels* (2004).

The characteristics and formative processes of estuaries are discussed in Maurice L. Schwartz (ed.), *The Encyclopedia of Beaches and Coastal Environments* (1982), with illustrated entries on estuaries and on estuarine coasts, deltas, habitats, and sedimentation; Russell Sackett, *Edge of the Sea*, rev. ed. (1985); Eric C.F. Bird, *Coasts: An Introduction to Coastal Geomorphology*, 3rd ed. (1984); Keith R. Dyer, *Estuaries: A Physical Introduction* (1998); and David Prandle, *Estuaries: Dynamics, Mixing, Sedimentation and Morphology* (2009).

Marianne Eelman, *Waterfalls and Rapids: Natural Phenomena of the World* (1998) is a general account describing the effects of waterfalls on the landscape. Technical works on the formation and change of river channels include Stephen Rice, Andre Roy, and Bruce Rhoads, *Confluences, Tributaries, and the Fluvial Network* (2008).

MAJOR RIVERS OF AFRICA

An introduction to the history and geography of the Congo River can be found in Peter Forbath, *The River Congo* (1977); and Peter Forbath, *The River Congo: The Discovery, Exploration, and Exploitation of the World's Most Dramatic River* (1991).

An overview of the Niger River basin is contained within Jean Claude Olivry, *Niger River Basin: A Vision for*

Sustainable Management (2005). Accounts of the Niger River environment include two essays in Bryan R. Davies and Keith F. Walker (eds.), *The Ecology of River Systems* (1986), both by R.L. Welcomme: "The Niger River System," pp. 9–23, and "Fish of the Niger System," pp. 25–48. Sanche De Gramont (pseud. for Ted Morgan), *The Strong Brown God: The Story of the Niger River* (1975), cover the history of the river's exploration.

General works on the Nile River include Rushdi Said, *The Geological Evolution of the River Nile* (1981); and Martin A.J. Williams and Hugues Faure (eds.), *The Sahara and the Nile* (1980), on landforms and human settlement in the region. Hydrology is discussed in A. Azim Abul-Atta, *Egypt and the Nile After the Construction of the High Aswan Dam* (1978); and John Waterbury, *Hydropolitics of the Nile Valley* (1979); Robert O. Collins, *The Nile* (2002); P.P. Howell and J.A. Allan (eds.), *The Nile: Sharing a Scarce Resource: A Historical and Technical Review of Water Management and of Economical and Legal Issues* (2008).

MAJOR RIVERS OF THE AMERICAS

Introductory overviews of the Amazon River basin include the treatment of the basin in N. Mark Collins (ed.), *The Last Rain Forests* (1990), pp. 110–129; and Catherine Caufield, *In the Rainforest* (1985).

Collections of essays on the basin include Harold Sioli (ed.), *The Amazon: Limnology and Landscape Ecology of a Mighty Tropical River and Its Basin* (1984); Robert E. Dickinson (ed.), *The Geophysiology of Amazonia* (1987); Marianne Schmink and Charles H. Wood (eds.), *Frontier Expansion in Amazonia* (1984); and John Hemming (ed.), *Change in the Amazon Basin*, 2 vol. (1985). Susanna Hecht and Alexander Cockburn, *The Fate of the Forest: Developers,*

Destroyers, and Defenders of the Amazon (1989), is an over-arching historical survey, richly documented, with a critical examination of the political, social, and economic background of the escalating degradation of the Amazon environment. D.A. Posey and Michael J. Balick (eds.), *Human Impacts on Amazonia: The Role of Traditional Ecological Knowledge in Conservation and Development* (2006), reflects on the history, development, conservation, and protection of the Amazon basin.

Works on resources and ecology include Eneas Salati et al., "Amazonia," in B.L. Turner II et al., *The Earth as Transformed by Human Action* (1990), pp. 479–493; David Cleary, *The Brazilian Rainforest: Politics, Finance, Mining, and the Environment* (1991); Kent H. Redford and Christine Padoch (eds.), *Conservation of Neotropical Forests* (1992); Michael Goulding, *Amazon: The Flooded Forest* (1989); William M. Denevan and Christine Padoch (eds.), *Swidden-Fallow Agroforestry in the Peruvian Amazon* (1988); Philip M. Fearnside, *Human Carrying Capacity of the Brazilian Rainforest* (1986); D.A. Posey and W. Balée (eds.), *Resource Management in Amazonia* (1989); and, on dwindling wildlife, Nigel J.H. Smith, *Man, Fishes, and the Amazon* (1981); and Kent H. Redford, "The Empty Forest," *BioScience*, 42(6):412–422 (June 1992).

John McPhee, "Atchafalaya," in his *The Control of Nature* (1989), pp. 3–92, a fascinating description of attempts to manage and control the lower Mississippi in Louisiana. Gerald M. Capers, *The Mississippi River Before and After Mark Twain* (1977), is a popular history. Technical accounts of the hydrology of the Mississippi River are found in Arthur C. Benke and Colbert E. Cushing (eds.), *Rivers of North America* (2005); and Ruth Patrick, *Rivers of the United States, Part A: The Mississippi: River and Tributaries North of St. Louis*, vol. 4 (1998).

MAJOR RIVERS OF ASIA
AND AUSTRALIA

Descriptions of the Ganges are found in surveys of the corresponding regions, such as R.L. Singh (ed.), *India: A Regional Geography* (1971, reprinted 2006); and S.D. Misra, *Rivers of India* (1970). More-focused subject studies are K.L. Rao, *India's Water Wealth*, rev. ed. (1979); and G.K. Dutt and A.K. Kundu (eds.), *Irrigation Atlas of India*, 2nd rev. ed., 2 vol. (1987–89). The Ganges itself is examined in Khurshida Begum, *Tension over the Farakka Barrage: A Techno-Political Tangle in South Asia* (1988), discussing the political repercussions in connection with the Farakka Dam; Eric Newby, *Slowly down the Ganges* (1966, reissued 1986) is an illustrated descriptive guide; and Steven G. Darian, *The Ganges in Myth and History* (1978, reissued 2001) is a photographic essay. More recent useful descriptive accounts include K.S. Bilgrami, *The Living Ganga* (1991); and Ted Lewin, *Sacred River* (1994). A useful discussion on environmental problems and their control is provided in P.K. Agrawal, *Environmental Protection and Pollution Control in the Ganga* (1994), a volume of edited papers.

The Lena River is described in broad geographic surveys of North Asia that provide information on physical features and on economic, social, and cultural conditions: Paul E. Lydolph, *Geography of the U.S.S.R.*, 5th ed. (1990); and *Great Rivers of the World* (1984), published by the National Geographic Society. Schemes for large-scale water transfer are described in two articles by Philip P. Micklin, "The Vast Diversion of Soviet Rivers," *Environment*, 27(2):12–20, 40–45 (March 1985), and "The Status of the Soviet Union's North-South Water Transfer Projects Before Their Abandonment in 1985–86," *Soviet Geography*, 27(5):287–329 (May 1986). A useful description of permafrost and long-term climate change in this region is V.V. Baulin and N.S. Danilova, "Dynamics of Late Quaternary Permafrost in Siberia," in A.A. Velichko, H.E. Wright, Jr., and C.W. Barnosky (eds.), *Late Quaternary Environments of the Soviet Union*, trans. from Russian (1984), pp. 69–86.

The Murray-Darling River system is described in Chris Hammer, *The River: A Journey Through the Murray-Darling* (2010); Murray-Darling Basin Commission, *Rivers as Ecological Systems: The Murray-Darling Basin* (2001); and Murray-Darling Basin Commission, *The Darling* (2005).

The Ob River is described in broad geographic surveys of North Asia that provide information on physical features and on economic, social, and cultural conditions: Paul E. Lydolph, *Geography of the U.S.S.R.*, 5th ed. (1990); and *Great Rivers of the World* (1984), published by the National Geographic Society. Useful discussions of landscape evolution, the extent of glaciation, and long-term climate change in this region include Mikhail G. Grosswald, "Late-Weichselian Ice Sheets in Arctic and Pacific Siberia," *Quaternary International*, 45-46(1):3–18 (1998), and Valery Astakhov "The Last Ice Sheet of the Kara Sea: Terrestrial Constraints on its Age," *Quaternary International*, 45-46(1):19–28 (1998).

Simon Winchester, *The River at the Center of the World: A Journey up the Yangtze River and Back in Chinese Times* (1996), provides useful descriptions of the Yangtze River from a historical perspective. Other descriptions in English include Jiang Liu, *China's Largest River* (1980); the pictographic account How Man Wong, *Exploring the Yangtze: China's Longest River* (1989); the valuable guidebook Judy Bonavia, *A Guide to the Yangzi River* (1985); and the comprehensive book Dai Qing (compiler), *The River Dragon Has Come!*, trans. from the Chinese by John G. Thibodeau and Philip B. Williams (1998). Physiography, culture, and history are imaginatively linked in Lyman P. Van Slyke, *Yangtze: Nature, History, and the River* (1988). A useful book on the Yangtze delta is Brian Hook (ed.), *Shanghai and the Yangtze Delta: A City Reborn* (1998). The issues surrounding the massive Three Gorges dam and reservoir project are presented from different points of view in Shiu-hung Luk and Joseph Whitney (eds.), *Megaproject: A Case Study of China's Three Gorges Project* (1993); and Margaret Barber and Gráinne Ryder (eds.), *Damming the Three Gorges*, 2nd ed. (1993). These arguments are updated in Catherine Caufield, *Rough Sailing at Three Gorges Dam* (1997).

The Yenisey River is described in broad terms in Maria Shahgedanova (ed.), *The Physical Geography of Northern Eurasia* (2003). Several useful papers on the role of glaciation in the landscape evolution and the recent geological history of the Yenisey River can be found in a special issue of *Quaternary International*, vol. 45–46, no. 1 (1998).

MAJOR RIVERS OF EUROPE

Josef Breu, *Atlas of the Danubian Countries*, 11 issues in 2 vol. (1970–89), is a comprehensive, multilingual source on the Danube region's geography. Much of the literature in English on the Danube itself consists of descriptive works based on travel experiences, such as Patrick Leigh Fermor, *Between the Woods and the Water: On Foot to Constantinople from the Hook of Holland: The Middle Danube to the Iron Gates* (1986); and Claudio Magris, *Danube* (1989; originally published in Italian, 1986).

Royal Institute of International Affairs, *Regional Management of the Rhine* (1975), is a collection of scholarly but readable papers on the effects of human activity on the ecology of the river, with analyses of transport, navigation, flood control, pollution, generation of electricity, regional planning, and recreational use. Roy E.H. Mellor, *The Rhine: A Study in the Geography of Water Transport* (1983), surveys the history of navigation on the river. A general treatment of attempts to control the Rhine River can be found in Marc Cioc, *The Rhine: An Eco-Biography: 1815-2000* (2002).

Much of what has been written on the Rhône is included in general and regional geographies of Switzerland, France, and western Europe, such as Aubrey Diem, *Western Europe, a Geographical Analysis* (1979). A short account focusing on economic conditions, from the series *Problem Regions of Europe*, is Ian B. Thompson, *The Lower Rhône and Marseille* (1975). A description of the environmental conditions of the Rhône River appears in F.B. Walle, M. Nikolopoulou-Tamvakli, and W.J. Heinen (eds.), *Environmental Condition of the Mediterranean Sea: European Community Countries* (1993).

INDEX